PROBLEMS AND
POSSIBILITIES

EXERCISES IN STATESMANSHIP 1814 - 1918

PROBLEMS AND POSSIBILITIES

EXERCISES IN STATESMANSHIP 1814 - 1918

KEITH WILSON

TEMPUS

First published 2003

PUBLISHED IN THE UNITED KINGDOM BY:
Tempus Publishing Ltd
The Mill, Brimscombe Port
Stroud, Gloucestershire GL5 2QG

PUBLISHED IN THE UNITED STATES OF AMERICA BY:
Tempus Publishing Inc.
2 Cumberland Street
Charleston, SC 29401

British Library Cataloguing in Publication Data.
A catalogue record for this book is available from the British Library.

ISBN 0 7524 2634 6

Typesetting and origination by Tempus Publishing.
Printed in Great Britain by Midway Colour Print, Wiltshire

CONTENTS

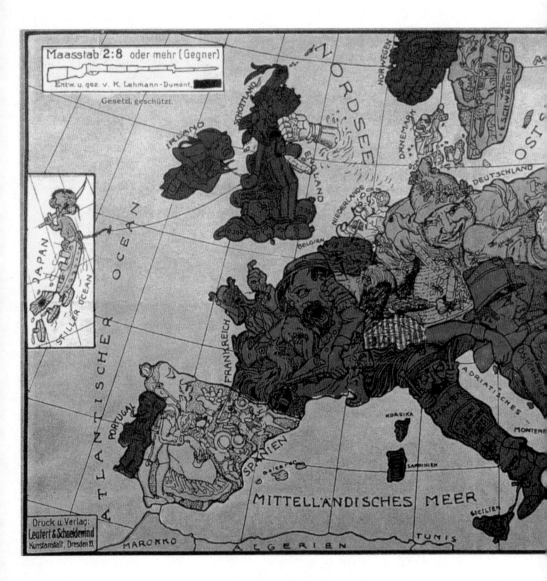

A satirical map produced early in the First World War by an unknown German cartoonist. (*British Library*)

PREFACE

Fewer than twenty individuals dominate the statesmanship of what might best be called 'the long nineteenth century', the decades between the end of the Napoleonic wars and the end of the First World War. They are all here. In chronological order, and including rulers of states as well as officials and elected politicians, we have Castlereagh (Great Britain), Alexander I (Russia), Metternich (Austria), Nicholas I (Russia), Nesselrode (Russia), Palmerston (Great Britain), Napoleon III (France), Gortchakov (Russia), Bismarck (Germany), Salisbury (Great Britain), Abdul Hamid II (Ottoman Empire), Giers (Russia), Delcassé (France), Wilhelm II (Germany) and Grey (Great Britain). All enjoyed successes and achievements. All experienced failure and setback. All had to deal, as best they could, with a succession of opposite numbers in the other states of which the international scene was composed. Hence one criterion against which 'statesmanship' is measured here is a neutral one – that of longevity: length of acquaintance with, exposure to, and of responsibility for, the conduct of the relations of their own country, state, or empire, with the other countries, states, or empires of their time.

Not every detail, or move, or element, or event, is covered in the chapters that follow. Rather, what I regard as the principal problems of the day or of the decade or of the era are singled out and focused upon, in such a way as to bring out the variety of solutions and responses considered, devised, attempted and implemented. In very broad terms, the questions facing all those involved up to and including the 1850s were: to what extent, and how, to maintain the Vienna settlement, to uphold and/or enforce the treaties made in the course of the peacemaking of 1814–1815; and what to do about the Ottoman Empire, which occupied physically so much of eastern Europe and of the Middle East, and whose relationship with western Europe had not been addressed at the Congress of Vienna except in the most fleeting of fashions. The turning point was the Crimean War, the beginning of which marked the end of the Quadruple Alliance of November 1815.

Henceforth, France was no longer constrained, and was able to foment and encourage changes to the Vienna settlement, starting with Italy in 1858–60, and to contemplate further changes in Poland and Germany. After the Franco-Prussian War of 1870–71, upon the events of which year the as yet unbloodied Lord Salisbury somewhat phlegmatically pronounced, 'We are looking into a future in which the equilibrium that governed Europe in past times has disappeared, and we have to reckon on new forces, new balances of power, possibly new enemies ...', the questions became: how the powers of Europe related to one another in a Europe of adjacent states (whether nation states such as France, Germany and Italy, or multinational empires such as Austria-Hungary and Russia) in a Europe without its former buffer zones or intermediary areas (with the possible exception of the Low Countries) over which local hegemonies could previously be pursued; what to do – still – about the Ottoman Empire; and in what perspective to view the issues raised by the disparity in power between the advanced economies of western Europe and the relatively undeveloped ones of Africa, Persia, Central Asia and China, and by the appearance on the world stage of non-European powers such as the United States and Japan. The 1870s marked the beginning of an era of defensive alliances. As Bismarck rationalised the situation, in a Europe composed of five Great Powers, security was most likely to be obtained by being a member of a unit of three. Some commentators regard this 'system' as being completed by the conclusion of the Franco-Russian Alliance in the early 1890s. Other commentators maintain that only with the improvement of British relations with France in 1904 and with Russia in 1907 was this 'system' complete.

Throughout this long nineteenth century there was a succession of scenarios and developments all of which presented challenges to statesmanship, all of which caused 'the interests of the state' to be kept constantly under review and debate, and ways of advancing or of protecting these interests to be devised and developed. The organisation of the chapters that follow is mainly, although not strictly, chronological. Where it is not strictly chronological this is because the positions in which certain Powers found themselves, and the problems that they faced, are sometimes best presented and illustrated over a period of several decades – all the more so when the individuals with the ultimate responsibility for dealing with the interests of their states against the changing face of the international scene retained that responsibility throughout, as in the cases, for instance, of Napoleon III, Abdul Hamid II and Bismarck.

1

PROBLEMS OF PEACEMAKING:
THE CONGRESS OF VIENNA, 1814–15

There were three phases to the peacemaking at the end of the 22-year-long period of French Revolutionary and Napoleonic wars. The first phase consisted of the armistice, of the replacment of the Emperor Napoleon by the Bourbon monarchy, in the person of Louis XVIII, the absolutist character of the monarchy having been diluted by some constitutional devices, and of the Peace of Paris of May 1814. This first Treaty of Paris gave France her frontiers as they were in 1792, plus some 600,000 extra citizens (or rather, so far as the Bourbons were concerned, subjects) as a result of minor modifications of those frontiers on every side except that of the Pyrenees. The second phase consisted of the Congress of Vienna, from October 1814 to June 1815, which addressed those parts of Europe until recently part of the Napoleonic Empire or occupied by French armies – in particular the Low Countries, Germany, Poland, and Italy. The third phase began with Napoleon's escape from prison on the island of Elba, contained his final defeat at Waterloo, and ended with the second Peace of Paris of November 1815. This treaty reduced the size of France to what it had been in 1790, imposed a large indemnity, and arranged for the occupation of parts of the country until this indemnity was paid off.

In what follows, the focus is upon the longest drawn-out phase of the peacemaking, namely the Congress of Vienna. As regards what took place at Vienna, diametrically opposed views exist. One view is that expressed by F.H. Hinsley in *Power and the Pursuit of Peace* (1967): 'The impressive thing about the behaviour of the Powers in 1815 is that they were prepared, as they had never previously been prepared, to waive their individual interests in the pursuit of an international system.' Contrast this view with that of the Secretary to the Congress of Vienna, Friedrich Gentz. Early in 1815, four months into the Congress, Gentz stated:

> The high-sounding phrases, 'reconstruction of the social order', 'reformation of the European political system', 'lasting peace based on a

just division of power', were at best produced to calm the people and to invest this solemn assembly with a dignified and sublime appearance. The true aim of the Congress consisted, however, in the division among the victors of the spoils.

At the end of the Congress Gentz wrote that although he had hoped for 'a general reform of the European political system, guarantees for an eternal peace – in short, for the return of the age of gold', the Congress had produced 'only some restitutions decided in advance by force of arms, some arrangements among the great Powers little propitious to future equilibrium and to the maintenance of peace in Europe, some transfers, arbitrary enough, in the possessions of the smaller states'. What the Congress had not produced was, in his opinion, rather more important. There was, he maintained, 'no act of a highly elevated character, no great measure of order or of public safety which would indemnify humanity for its long sufferings or reassure it as to the future'.

The above views are irreconcilable. They represent the extreme poles of two schools of thought, and to the first school of thought, that of Hinsley, must now be added the name of Paul Schroeder and his book *The Transformation of European Politics 1763–1848*, published in 1994. In attempting to determine which of the above schools of thought holds the more accurate views, it may help to note that, at the opening of the Congress, in fact on 12 October 1814, the British Foreign Secretary Lord Castlereagh had told Tsar Alexander I of Russia:

> it depends exclusively upon the temper in which your Imperial Majesty shall meet the questions which more immediately concern your own empire, whether the present Congress shall prove a blessing to mankind, or only exhibit a scene of discordant intrigue and a lawless scramble for power.

Castlereagh's statement suggests only slightly modified terms of reference, namely, was the Congress of Vienna 'a blessing to mankind' or was it 'a scene of discordant intrigue and a lawless scramble for power'?

❖

Castlereagh was right to say that much would depend upon the 'temper', or attitude, of the Tsar of Russia. In 1813, in treaties of 28 February, 27 June, and 9 September, Russia had agreed with Austria and Prussia to share the Duchy of Warsaw. At the beginning of the Congress of Vienna, Alexander I denounced those treaties, and announced that the whole of the Duchy of Warsaw would in future be the Kingdom of Poland, with

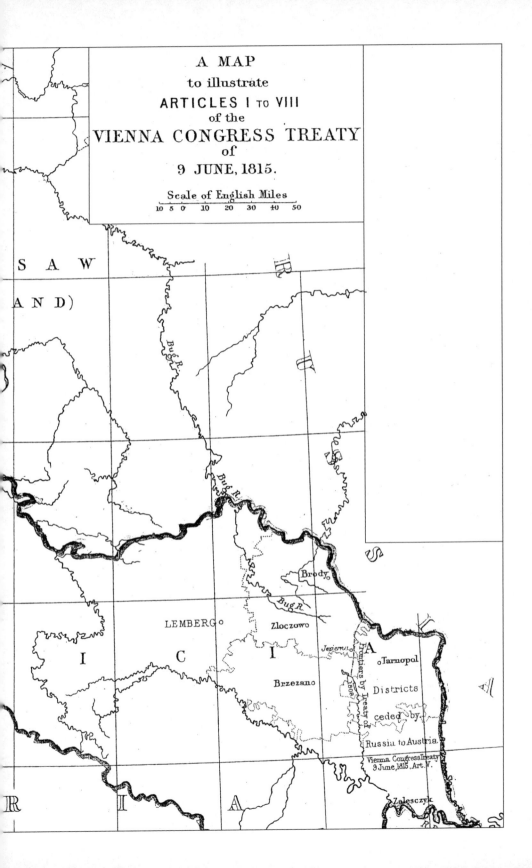

A MAP
to illustrate
ARTICLES I TO VIII
of the
VIENNA CONGRESS TREATY
of
9 JUNE, 1815.

Scale of English Miles
10 5 0   10   20   30   40   50

S A W

A N D)

Bug R.

Bug R.

Bug R.

Bug R.

Brody

LEMBERG

Zloczowo

Jezierna

Tarnopol

I   C   I   A

Brzezano

Districts

ceded by

Frontiers by Treaty of 1809

Russia to Austria

Vienna Congress Treaty
9 June, 1815, Art. V.

Zaleszczyk

R   I   A

himself as its ruler. The other powers argued in vain against this Russian decision, which they described as 'the forced annexation of so large a territory to Russia, already much increased by her recent conquests' and 'her advance into the heart of Germany'. Castlereagh deplored what he called 'so alarming an infraction of treaties'. Alexander I remained adamant. He would not settle, as it was suggested that he should, for only coming as far west as the river Vistula, which runs north–south through Warsaw itself. He insisted on the whole of the Duchy.

As a result, the gains which Prussia in particular had anticipated in Poland were no longer available. And as a result of that outcome, and with Russian encouragement, Prussia insisted on the whole of Saxony for herself. This in turn alienated Austria, and brought war between Prussia and Austria, and others, into sight on several occasions in the course of the Congress.

Castlereagh's complaints about Russia began immediately. On 25 October 1814 he wrote that, given the strong link between Russia and Prussia, it was necessary to think in terms of 'combinations'. He *had* hoped that, after so long a struggle against Napoleon, 'the several Powers might have enjoyed some repose, without forming calculations that always augment the risks of war'. But 'the tone and conduct of Russia have disappointed this hope, and forced upon us fresh considerations'. It was necessary, therefore, Castlereagh stated, 'to unite Germany for its own preservation against Russia'; a way had to be found of keeping Russia 'within due bounds', and of preventing 'further encroachments on the part of Russia'.

On 11 November Castlereagh inveighed against what he called Russia's 'intriguing spirit': the establishment of Russia in the heart of Germany constituted a great danger in itself; it was calculated to have 'a most pernicious influence' in the Austrian and Prussian cabinets; if Austro–Prussian rivalry developed, 'the supremacy of Russia would be established in all directions, and upon every question'. Castlereagh stated his 'perfect conviction, that unless the Emperor of Russia can be brought to a more moderate and sound course of public conduct, the peace, which we have so dearly purchased, will be but of short duration'.

By 25 November Castlereagh had concluded that only fear of the consequences of the Tsar's conduct would moderate Russian pretensions. Nothing could be expected from Alexander's generosity or from his sense of justice. On 5 December Castlereagh again deplored the 'misfortune' that 'Russia and Prussia are looked upon as one, pledged to support each other's objects, whatever may be their effect either upon Austrian or German interests'. War was not far away, whether between Austria and Prussia alone, or with Russian involvement also:

> if Russia and Prussia are determined to make common cause, it will not suit the exhausted finances of Prussia to remain long armed and inactive; nor can Russia expose herself indefinitely to the incumbrance of large armies remaining unemployed beyond or on the verge of her own frontier.

As Castlereagh concluded: 'the probability, therefore, is that one or both of these Powers, if they do not relax in their pretensions, will provoke rather than procrastinate the war.'

By Christmas Day 1814 Russia had secured all she wished as regards Poland, and there remained only Prussia to deal with. Castlereagh was inclined to be 'as liberal as we can to Prussia, notwithstanding her shabbiness'. On New Year's Eve Hardenberg, the Prussian delegate to the Congress, declared that should Prussia continue to consider the annexation of the whole of Saxony as necessary to her reconstruction, she could not submit to remain in a state of provisional occupation, and that Russia and Prussia would, in such a case, consider a refusal to acknowledge that annexation as tantamount to a declaration of war. Castlereagh protested against this as 'a most alarming and unheard of menace'. It appeared to him, as it did to Metternich, the Austrian Chancellor, and Talleyrand, the French Foreign Minister, 'to call for some precautionary corrective by which the other Powers may be induced to feel that ... they are not exposed individually and in detail to the destructive effects of such a domineering dictation'.

Accordingly, a Treaty of Defensive Alliance was concluded between Great Britain, Austria, and France. Without some such bond, said Castlereagh, 'I feel that our deliberations here are at an end'. This alliance was joined, in the course of January and February 1815, by Holland, Bavaria, and Hanover. Castlereagh justified it as appearing to him 'indispensable to check the intemperance of the two Northern Powers'. 'Such a combination', he said, meaning Russia and Prussia, 'could only be resisted by a counter-alliance.'

Given the making of the Treaty of Defensive Alliance, Castlereagh was obviously not alone in his interpretation of the conduct of Russia and Prussia. Gentz regarded the downfall of Napoleon as 'a pure and unqualified advantage for Russia'; for the rest of Europe, and especially for the states bordering on Russia, the downfall of Napoleon was largely cancelled out by the increased strength that Russia secured for herself 'at the expense of the general equilibrium'. Gentz was equally scathing about Prussia, of whom he said that she brought to the Congress 'only the one extravagant wish to extend her possessions at the expense of all, and without the slightest regard for justice or decency'. The Prussian interest in Saxony he described as 'monstrous', even though he admitted that it followed from Prussian unwillingness to enter into rivalry with Russia. Gentz saw it, moreover, as 'but the first step in a series of operations through which they [the Prussians] hoped sooner or later to acquire most of north Germany, put Austria out of action, and set themselves at the head of all Germany'. Talleyrand agreed with Gentz:

> In Germany, Prussia is the great danger; her situation necessitates a greed for territory, and to her any pretext is justifiable. She knows no scruples; everything advantageous to her is right.... At this very moment her agents and partisans are agitating in Germany, representing France as a power that is constantly planning new invasions and Prussia as the only one that can defend Germany, so that she must be delivered up to Prussia in order to be saved. Prussia would have liked to have Belgium; she wants everything that lies between France, the Moselle, and the Rhine; she wants Luxembourg; if she does not get Mainz all will be lost, she says; if she does not get Saxony she will enjoy no security.... If she has her own way there will be 20 million [Prussians] and all Germany will be subject to her. Bounds must be set to this urge.

❖

Nothing, thus far, suggests that the Congress of Vienna was anything other than 'a lawless scramble for power', certainly on the part of Russia and Prussia. Talleyrand was also inclined to view Austria in the same light, at least as regards one area: 'The pressure of Austria for expansion at the cost of Italy must be opposed.' So far as France was concerned, Castlereagh had expressed doubts about Talleyrand's motives as early as October 1814: 'Talleyrand is more intent upon particular points of influence than upon the general balance to be established, and his efforts upon the Neapolitan and Saxon questions are frequently at the expense of the more important question of Poland.' The Talleyrand who appears in Schroeder's publication of 1994 is even more devious:

> France's aims in joining Britain and Austria against Russia and Prussia were to destroy the wartime coalition, overthrow the settlement, shed responsibility for the Revolutionary Napoleonic era, and perhaps try again for the natural frontiers, certainly for greater influence in the Rhineland and Low Countries. The specific side-payments demanded by France were disturbing – an immediate overthrow of Murat [the King of Naples], changes in the Italian settlement, perhaps an altered Belgian frontier ... the United Provinces to assume debts to Dutch contractors for building French warships for Napoleon.

❖

Throughout this chapter the question has been that put to Alexander I by Castlereagh in October 1814: was the Congress of Vienna to be 'a blessing to mankind' or 'a scene of discordant intrigue and a lawless scramble for power'? Or, taking into account some of the secondary literature, was the period of the Congress a period during which the Great Powers of Europe were prepared, as never before, to waive their individual interests in the pursuit of an international system that would maintain the peace between them? On the basis of the material presented, the verdict must be resoundingly in favour of the view taken of the Congress by Gentz, against Hinsley's finding there of the deliberate pursuit of an international system, and against Schroeder's ascription to the Vienna settlement of a 'truly revolutionary character'. With the possible exception of Castlereagh, there are present only what the French representative in Naples described in 1823 as 'the politics of the interests ... the old politics' – only threats, only combinations, only compromises induced by force and the threats to use force. There is no new found, or invented, respect for 'rights and the rule of law'. It was much more a case of *plus ça change, plus c'est la même chose.*

❖

The Congress of Vienna, and the peacemaking as a whole, left much to pray for and much to play for. The newly constitutionalised monarchy in France had still to establish itself and prove itself. The union of Belgium and Holland was recognised as a distinct gamble. Fortresses along the French frontier to protect Belgium, Luxembourg and the German Confederation had still to be built. The organisation of the German Confederation remained to be settled. The affairs of eastern Europe, and relations between the Western Powers and the Ottoman Empire, had not been addressed at all. These and other issues will be taken up in the chapters that follow.

2

WESTERN QUESTIONS: DEFINITIONS AND INTERPRETATIONS, 1815–23

In the second week of February 1815 Lord Castlereagh, the British Foreign Secretary, wrote to Lord Liverpool, the Prime Minister, that it was obvious that Tsar Alexander I of Russia wished, before leaving Vienna, to renew the Quadruple Alliance of the powers that had defeated Napoleonic France. Castlereagh argued strongly against what he called 'any exclusive system of alliance':

> I thought it material to dissipate this notion by representing the objections to the formation of any Alliance at this moment to the exclusion of France. That on the contrary, after the proofs which we had received on the Saxon and other points of the desire fully felt by the Cabinet of the Tuilleries to pursue a conciliatory and moderate line of policy, our interest and duty equally required that we should encourage such a disposition, and thus strengthen the king's authority against the bad principles that must still abound in France.

Castlereagh suggested to the Tsar that, instead of renewing the Quadruple Alliance against France, 'the best Alliance that could be formed in the present state of Europe' was 'that the Powers who had made the peace should by a public declaration at the close of the Congress announce to Europe ... their determination to uphold and support the arrangement agreed upon; and further, their determination to unite their influence and, if necessary, their arms, against the Power that should attempt to disturb it'.

Castlereagh was so encouraged by the reception accorded to this suggestion of his that, on 13 February, he sent the following letter to all British ambassadors:

> It affords me great satisfaction to acquaint you that there is every prospect of the Congress terminating with *a general accord and Guarantee* between the Great Powers of Europe, with a determination to support the arrangement agreed upon, and to turn the general influence and if

necessary the general arms against the Power that shall first attempt to disturb the Continental peace.

No such general alliance, or guarantee of the work that it had done, was to emerge from the Congress of Vienna. On the contrary, what emerged towards the end of the year 1815 was precisely a renewal of the Quadruple Alliance against France. This took the form of the Treaty of Alliance and Friendship between Great Britain, Austria, Russia, and Prussia, and was signed at Paris on 20 November 1815. Exactly eight months after informing Lord Liverpool of his rebuttal of the Tsar's preference of February Castlereagh wrote again, spelling out the extent to which he had changed his mind:

> I feel a strong persuasion that nothing can keep France quiet and within bounds but the strong hand of European power, and that a Treaty of this nature signed by the four great Powers (which happily at present implies the military power of all Europe extra France) will be more operative to that purpose, even than the instrument which we shall sign with the French Government itself. It is the fear of our union that will keep France down, and the knowledge that the Duke of Wellington commands only the advanced guard of the force against which they will have to contend, if they again involve themselves in war.

In addition to Castlereagh's change of mind, but complementary to it, something else, and something new, also emerged from the Treaty of Alliance and Friendship. Article VI, introduced into the draft treaty by Castlereagh, announced that the sovereigns of Britain, Austria, Russia and Prussia had agreed to renew their meetings at 'fixed periods', 'for the purpose of consulting upon their common interests, and for the consideration of the measures which at each of those periods shall be considered the most salutary for the repose and prosperity of Nations, and for the maintenance of the Peace of Europe'. In Castlereagh's mind, the purpose of Article VI was to combat any institutional, or organisational, development of a treaty signed by the rulers of Russia, Austria and Prussia at Paris on 26 September, in which they solemnly declared 'their fixed resolution, both in the administration of their respective States, and in their political relations with every other Government, to take for their sole guide the precepts ... of Justice, Christian Charity, and Peace, which, so far from being applicable only to private concerns, must have an immediate influence on the councils of Princes, and guide all their steps, as being the only means of consolidating human institutions and remedying their imperfections'. No one knew quite what this meant, or into what it might develop. It was a product of the mind of Tsar Alexander I and this, according to Castlereagh, was 'not completely sound'. According to Alexander himself, it was an effort to revive and implement the project of a general guarantee which in February 1815 Castlereagh had preferred to Alexander's inclination of that month towards a renewal of the Quadruple Alliance. As Castlereagh wrote to Lord Liverpool on 28 September:

> You may remember my sending home a Project of Declaration with which I proposed the Congress should close, in which the Sovereigns were solemnly to pledge themselves in the face of the world to preserve to their people the peace they had conquered, and to treat as a common enemy whatever Power should violate it. The Emperor told me that this idea, with which he seemed much pleased at the time, had never passed from his mind, but that he thought it ought to assume a more formal shape, and one directly personal to the Sovereigns.

For Castlereagh in February 1815 it had been 'the Powers' who would declare their determination to uphold and support the arrangement agreed upon; for the Tsar in March it had been 'the Cabinets' who intended 'to establish the inviolability of the acts of the Congress by reciprocal guarantees'; by September, for the Tsar, it had become 'the Sovereigns' who would do this, and in his letter to Lord Liverpool of 28 September Castlereagh even credited himself as using 'Sovereigns' rather than 'Powers' in the previous February.

The year 1815 ended with the creation of two potentially competitive concepts of approaches to the conduct of international relations. The Holy Alliance, based on precepts of justice, charity and peace which remained to be defined in practice, was open to all Christian monarchs, including the King of France, who signed it immediately. The Quadruple Alliance excluded France and was directed against her; it was explicitly drawn up to maintain the exclusion from supreme power in France of Napoleon Bonaparte and his family, and to provide a forum for the victorious allies to concert together in the future, should as the text put it 'the same Revolutionary Principles which upheld the last criminal usurpation ... again, under other forms, convulse France, and thereby endanger the repose of other states'. It remained to be seen which grouping would dominate the international scene, and on the basis of the application of what principles. It remained to be seen whether efforts would be made to guarantee only the territorial status quo, or forms of government also. It remained to be seen whether the powers would restrict their interest in combatting 'Revolutionary Principles' to the manifestations of the latter in French politics and to their impact on the foreign policy of France, or treat any manifestation of 'the revolution' as cause for concern, concert, intervention and suppression.

❖

At the end of September 1818 representatives of all the Great Powers, including France, met at Aix-la-Chapelle (Aachen). This conference was called not under Article VI of the treaty of 20 November 1815, but under Article V, which governed the duration of the ocupation of France by allied troops. The conference of Aix-la-Chapelle saw efforts on the part of the French Government to secure the abolition of the Quadruple Alliance, efforts on the part of Prussia to secure a territorial guarantee of the whole of continental Europe, and efforts on the part of the Tsar and his advisers to establish a common league of all the powers of Europe, 'guaranteeing to each other the existing order of things in thrones as well as in territories, all being bound to march, if requisite, against the first Power that offended either by her ambitions or by her revolutionary transgressions'. It also saw a difference of opinion between Castlereagh and the Tsar as to what the obligations of the alliance of 20 November 1815 were; Castlereagh discovered that Alexander was under the impression that a revolution in France automatically entailed the intervention of the Quadruple Alliance powers to quash it.

At Aix-la-Chapelle the Quadruple Alliance was renewed, not abolished. It was also agreed that, in future, France should attend any meetings that were called under Article VI; and that such 'reunions' would not take place at 'fixed periods', as the original language of Article VI specified, but 'shall be special, namely that they shall arise out of the occasion and be agreed upon by the five Courts at the time'. Castlereagh hoped that the reunions would be strictly limited to the interests that grew out of the peace treaties mentioned in the treaty of alliance of 20 November 1815. What these interests were was still not clear; and whether certain events would be regarded in the same way by all the powers was much less likely at the end of this conference than at the beginning. For, in conversations with the Tsar in particular, Castlereagh had had to spell out certain differences between parliamentary regimes and autocratic ones. At the beginning of November, for instance, Castlereagh reported to London:

> The Emperor observed that great dangers often had small beginnings, and that if not taken in the bud they might baffle all our efforts. I admitted this truth, and that it was perhaps a misfortune in our [political]

system that we could not act upon precautionary principles so early or so easily as His Imperial Majesty, but that the only chance we had of making the nation feel the wisdom of such a course was to be free, at the moment, to urge the policy of so acting, not because we had no choice, but as having a choice ... the public mind must be managed; the nation must not be alarmed with the apprehension of war when the danger was not at hand.

Had Alexander I concluded, there and then, that the weaknesses of the British political system outweighed its strengths, this would have been quite understandable; and one wonders if Castlereagh's seminars on the British constitution were not more than a little counterproductive.

Certainly Prussian doubts about the ability of Great Britain to act to preserve the status quo were increased. This apprehension was behind their last-minute proposal, to which reference has already been made, for a territorial guarantee of the whole of continental Europe.

❖

Until 1820 it was on France that the eyes of those who feared a re-appearance of revolutionary principles were focused. In 1820, however, revolutions took place in Spain, Italy and Portugal. As instances of 'the revolution' multiplied, so did calls for intervention in the domestic and internal affairs of states. The increasingly emphatic way in which the British rejected these calls distanced them from the continental Great Powers.

A military insurrection at Cadiz on 1 January 1820 spread quickly to Madrid, where King Ferdinand was induced to accept the constitution of 1812. Alexander I immediately anticipated the necessity of intervention. This idea was supported by Prussia, anxious to curry favour with St Petersburg, and already under pressure from there to convert the Holy Alliance into a general guarantee. The French then called for another 'reunion' of the five Great Powers. Towards the end of April Castlereagh, under the supervision of the British Cabinet, produced a memorandum designed to refute most of the suggestions made thus far. The wish of the French for another conference was rejected as unsuitable to the circumstances of this particular case. Castlereagh maintained that, of all the powers in Europe, Spain was the least likely 'to menace other States with that direct and imminent danger which had always been regarded, at least in this country, as alone constituting the case which would justify external interference'. Castlereagh re-asserted that the Quadruple Alliance had been made only against France: 'It never was ... intended as a union for the government of the world or for the superintendence of the internal affairs of other States.' The distinction made at Aix-la-Chapelle between autocratic and constitutional regimes was made even more forcefully and pointedly, so far as the progress of democratic principles was concerned:

> The principle of one State interfering by force in the internal affairs of another in order to enforce obedience to the governing authority, is always a question of the greatest possible moral, as well as political, delicacy.... It is only important on the present occasion to observe that to generalise such a principle and to think of reducing it to a system, or to impose it as an obligation, is a scheme utterly impracticable and objectionable.... No country having a representative system of Government could act upon it, and the sooner such a doctrine shall be distinctly abjured as forming in any degree the basis of our Alliance the better.

Great Britain 'cannot and will not act upon abstract and speculative principles of precaution'; she could and would act only when 'the territorial Balance of Europe is disturbed'.

When this memorandum was communicated to the other powers, Russia found herself deserted, even by Prussia. Metternich showed his gratitude for British support of Austria in German affairs by adopting the British position as revealed here in relation to Spain. On this occasion the British bluff, to exclude herself from the European system, were that system to be defined and interpreted in a way contrary to her own views and requirements, was not called. The revolution which began in Naples, in July 1820, was to have a different outcome. It was to bring to a head the irreconcilibity between what Metternich described as 'the impossibilities of England' and 'the forms of Russia'.

❖

Immediately upon hearing of the revolt in Naples, Castlereagh told the Austrian ambassador that 'the British Government cannot take any part forcibly to counteract or control it'. These sentiments were repeated in September: the revolution in Naples, said Castlereagh, should be treated 'as a *special* rather than as a *general* question, as an *Italian* question rather than as an *European*, and consequently as in the sphere of action of *Austria* rather than of the *Alliance*'. By this time the Russians were suggesting that the five Great Powers meet at Troppau (now Opava, Czech Republic) to discuss how to respond not only to the Neapolitan revolution but also to the Spanish one and to another which had broken out in Portugal in August 1820. Castlereagh was unwilling to attend any such gathering .

He authorised his half-brother, Lord Stewart, the British ambassador to Vienna, merely to observe and report, telling him:

> All we ask of our Allies is not to annoy and cripple us when it can be avoided, by phrases and forms, which in fact lead to nothing more substantial than to indulge the Emperor of Russia and his Minister [Capo d'Istria], the latter in composing and the former in promulgating high sounding declarations which ... do not fall in with the sentiments which are to be found on either side of the House of Commons.

Stewart's instructions laid stress on the integrity of the territorial system established in 1815 and on the balance of power:

> His Majesty deeming it to be his undoubted right and bounden duty to satisfy himself that the particular measures which any independent State or States may in the present conjuncture think fit to adopt on principles, as they may feel, of self – defence against a danger which, in their judgement, menaces them, shall not be so pursued as to endanger or alter the general balance of power as established in Europe.

In London, both the Austrian and Russian ambassadors were warned that if at a conference at Laibach (now Ljubljana, Slovenia) public declarations on general principles were made, there would be no further British cooperation. This was a view shared by the French, whose government had problems of survival similar to those of the British government, and who decided to send only their amabassador at Vienna to represent them at the conference. In the last week of October, Castlereagh told the Russian ambassador in London that Britain could not follow the Tsar along the path which he had chosen:

> It is a vain hope, a beautiful phantom, which England above all cannot pursue. All speculative policy is outside her powers. It is proposed now to overcome the *revolution*; but so long as this revolution does not appear in more distinct shape, so long as this general principle is only translated into events like those in Spain, Naples, and Portugal – which, strictly speaking, are only reforms, or at the most domestic upsets, and do not attack materially any other State – England is not ready to combat it.

Stewart was reminded that 'it is not possible for the British Government ... to take the field in fruitlessly denouncing by a sweeping joint declaration the revolutionary dangers of the present day.... Nor can they venture to embody themselves *en corps* with the non-representative

Governments in what would seem to constitute a scheme of systematic interference in the internal affairs of other States'.

The condition Castlereagh laid down on 25 October to Austria for Britain not moving away from the Alliance, was that the other powers should 'take into account the considerations due to our position'. In asking not to be crippled by phrases and forms, Castlereagh was asking too much. As regards Italian affairs, in contrast to those of Spain, Austria needed the support of Russia rather than of Britain. As a result, at Troppau, Metternich accepted the terms Capo d'Istria embodied in a *Protocole préliminaire* of 19 November. The preamble to this document claimed that the action of Russia, Austria and Prussia was based on 'the principles of the Alliance', and also on 'the rights consecrated by Treaties'. The intention announced was 'to prevent the progress of the evil with which the body social is menaced, and to devise remedies where its ravages have begun or are anticipated'. Three principles were expounded:

1. States, forming part of the European Alliance, which have undergone a change, due to revolution, in the form of their constitution, and the results of which menace other States, *ipso facto* cease to be part of the Alliance and remain excluded from it, until their situation gives guarantees of legal order and stability.

2. The Allied Powers do not limit themselves to announcing this exclusion; but faithful to the principles which they have proclaimed and to the respect due to the authority of every legitimate government as to every act emanating from its own free will, agree to refuse recognition to changes brought about by illegal methods.

3. When States where such changes have been made, cause by their proximity other countries to fear immediate danger, and when the Allied Powers can exercise effective and beneficial action towards them, they will employ, in order to bring them back to the bosom of the Alliance, first friendly representations, secondly measures of coercion, if the employment of such coercion is indispensable.

On 4 December Castlereagh told the Russian ambassador that 'on viewing in an abstract manner the spectacle now presented by the Troppau reunion, it is impossible not to consider the right which the Monarchs claim to judge and to condemn the actions of other States as a precedent dangerous to the liberties of the world. There is a very great danger in allowing such a system to be established.' On the same day Stewart was sent a Cabinet memorandum in which the British government announced its refusal to participate in any inter-Allied action as regards Naples, Spain and Portugal, and, in the latter two cases, rejected the right of any other power to take action. The British position was made public through a despatch of 16 December, copies of which were given to the ambassadors in London. The extent to which the principles expressed by the *Protocole préliminaire* were at variance with the political and constitutional system of Great Britain was indicated by a reference to the Act of Settlement. It was asserted, moreover, that 'the extreme right of interference between nation and nation can never be properly made a matter of stipulation or be assumed as the attribute of any Alliance'. The British Government would not go to what it regarded as the extreme 'of becoming armed guardians of all thrones'; it would not 'charge itself as a member of the Alliance with the moral responsibility of administering a general European Police'. In a private letter to Stewart, also of 16 December, Castlereagh wrote:

> It is singular at this day that it should have occurred to the Ministers of the three Courts to reform an Alliance which has been found to acommodate itself with great facility to all the exigencies of affairs, upon the exploded doctrines of *divine right* and of passive obedience. They might have foreseen that the House of Hanover could not well maintain the principles upon which the House of Stuart forfeited the throne.

These explosions on the part of Castlereagh and of his colleagues marked an open and deliberately public breach with the Alliance as defined by Russia, Austria and Prussia. The Tsar was unmoved, however: Stewart reported Alexander's determination, not only to crush the revolution in Spain, which had served as such an example to others, but 'to secure to the other Great Powers of the Continent the same advantages that France enjoyed, viz. that in an especial case of military revolt or revolutions by illegitimate means, the European Alliance was to be united against such nation, and concert together as to the means of coping with it by conciliation or force of arms'.

Those attending the conference moved from Troppau to Laibach in the New Year, to settle arrangements for Austrian action against the Neapolitan revolution. They also decided to hold another 'reunion' in 1822. Another British circular, dated 19 January 1821, was sent out. This denied, once again, that existing treaties entitled the Alliance to act on general principles or in the particular case of Naples. It maintained that intervention was justified only when the immediate security, or essential interests, of a State were seriously endangered by the internal transactions of another State. The British Government could not admit that such a limited right to intervene (although here extended beyond the case of

France) 'can receive a general and indiscriminate application to all revolutionary movements, without reference to their immediate bearing upon some particular State or States, or be made prospectively the basis of an Alliance'.

Well might Metternich say 'les bienfaits de l'Alliance Européenne étaient suspendus'. Debates in the British Parliament on 19 and 21 February only confirmed him in this opinion. So did a British rejection of a suggestion from Paris that Britain and France intervene jointly in Naples and in Piedmont, where revolution broke out in Turin on 10 March. Writing from Laibach on 10 March, Metternich said: 'England is dead so far as the Continent is concerned.' The reason was obvious. Writing to Stewart on 13 March, Castlereagh described as 'immutable' the principles upon which the British political system was based, and criticised Russia, Austria and Prussia for persevering in 'the open promulgation of their Ultra doctrines'. In Parliament on 21 June 1821, in the knowledge that Alexander I now wanted France to do in Spain what Austria had done in Naples, Castlereagh repeated that:

> he could not recognise the principle that one State was entitled to interfere with another because changes might be effected in its Government in a way which the former state disapproved. For certain States to erect themselves into a tribunal to judge of the internal affairs of others was to arrogate to themselves a power which could only be assumed in defiance of the law of nations and the principles of common sense.

❖

On 12 August 1822 Lord Castlereagh committed suicide. Long before this, the Alliance which he had created, and whose sphere of competence he had tried to define and circumscribe, had been taken out of his hands. Over his loss of control of the Alliance he himself had little control. He in turn was increasingly circumscribed by the Cabinet, by Parliament, and by an increasingly isolationist British public opinion. Only in person might he have succeeded in getting the Tsar in particular to share his own appreciations and definitions of what it was appropriate and what it was not appropriate for the Alliance to address. Yet he attended, in person, only the first of the 'reunions' which he had written into the Treaty of Alliance and Friendship of 20 November 1815. On 24 August 1815 he had said that both England and Europe needed seven years of peace. These seven years, but no more, he lived to see. The prospect of further such years receded as he and the British allowed the view taken of revolutions by the continental autocracies to drive them away from the other members of the Quadruple Alliance, and failed to understand that, for the autocracies, manifestations of revolution did engage their 'essential interests' and did embody a 'material attack' upon them, embodying as these manifestations did a challenge to the nature of autocratic regimes and the authority upon which the whole *raison d'être* of these regimes rested.

At his last interview with the King, on 9 August 1822, Castlereagh stated, 'Sir, it is necessary to say goodbye to Europe; you and I alone know it and have saved it; no one after me understands the affairs of the Continent.' Castlereagh's death left the field to one George Canning, the most bitter of Castlereagh's domestic opponents, who neither understood nor wanted to understand the affairs of the Continent, and who since 1818 had been deploring, from within the Cabinet, 'that system of periodical meetings of the four Great Powers' as 'new, and of very questionable policy'. It was early in Canning's time as British Foreign Secretary, following yet another 'reunion', this time at Verona, which Britain did not attend, that a French government finally steeled itself to intervene in Spain, lest Russia do so, or lest a Russian-sponsored European army 'whose aim should be to crush out the centre of revolutions in Spain or anywhere else it could go' came into being and went there for that purpose.

3

EASTERN QUESTIONS, 1824–56

I. France and Austria, 1824–44

From the early 1820s French governments defined the various Eastern questions that arose in terms of the opportunities that they provided for France. The basin of the eastern Mediterranean was, to start with, a field for commercial opportunity. In the years 1787–1789, immediately before the outbreak of the French Revolution, the Levant had reached fourth place in imports by France and ninth place in exports from France. It was French policy to recover these rankings, on which the prosperity of much of southern France, and especially of Marseilles, depended. (In 1798 Marseilles was the base for eighty-one French commercial houses in the Levant and on the Barbary coast, and did 70 million francs' worth of trade exchanges annually; in 1816 there were only twenty-three such establishments.) The Levant was all the more important for French commerce because Great Britain, after the Napoleonic period, dominated the markets of the Baltic, which had not been the case in the time of Louis XIV and Colbert.

The Near East was also a field that presented political opportunities. It gave the French, if they played their cards well, chances to end their relative isolation, and to assume an equal role with the other Great Powers of Europe in international affairs. It offered them the chance, through developing friendly relations or ententes with at least one of the other Great Powers, to bring about a reconsideration of the Quadruple Alliance of November 1815, which in 1818 had been renewed and which was, of course, directed against France. Moreover the Eastern Question might, under what might be called a 'best-case scenario', develop in such a way as to enable the French to use it to revise the treaties of 1815, as part of a wholesale redrawing of the map of Europe.

This latest element, which might be called 'strategic', comes to the fore only once in the years under review in this chapter – in 1829 – although there are adumbrations of it at other moments, on the part of certain individuals, for example Thiers in 1840. Not until the Second

Empire of Napoleon III was it to be as conspicuous a feature of French foreign policy as it was towards the end of the Russo-Turkish war of 1828–29. In August 1829, as the Russian armies moved towards Adrianople, the French Minister for Foreign Affairs, Polignac, expressed to King Charles X the positive conviction that the fall of the Ottoman Empire might well be combined with a general re-organisation of Europe. Charles X agreed, the French Cabinet was summoned, and a memorandum was ordered to be drawn up.

Polignac's memorandum proposed major changes to the existing map of Europe: the Kingdom of the Netherlands, set up in 1814, would be entirely eliminated; France would acquire that kingdom's Belgian provinces up to the rivers Meuse and Rhine; France would also recover from Prussia the frontier in Alsace that she had lost with the defeat of Napoleon at Waterloo; in return for Saxony, Prussia would also give up her Rhineland provinces, those between the Rhine and the Meuse to be ruled by the former King of Saxony, and those in the east of Germany to be taken over by Bavaria; Prussia would also take Holland from the Rhine to the North Sea; the displaced King of Holland would be transferred to Constantinople, to rule there as a Christian monarch over a part of Turkey in Europe; Greece would be given the Asiatic banks of the Dardanelles and the Bosporus; Russia would acquire the Ottoman provinces of Moldavia and Wallachia, together with Ottoman territory in Asia; Austria would receive Serbia and Bosnia; Great Britain would be offered some Dutch colonies.

This was quite a well-balanced redistribution of territories. There was something in it for all of the Great Powers, with the conspicuous exception of Britain. But it was obviously France who would benefit most in western Europe, at the expense of the United Netherlands and the German Confederation. Polignac's plan was approved by the French government, and on 4 September 1829 the French ambassador in St Petersburg was given instructions as to how to present it to the Russians. He was told to emphasise that France asked for no territorial cessions on the Italian frontier, and simply to say that France could not feel secure so long as Belgium offered facilities for an invasion and so long as Prussian armies occupied the Rhineland. Prussia's compensation in Holland for vacating the Rhineland would make her a naval power, which both France and Russia should welcome. Should a congress be proposed, France and Russia should come to a secret preliminary agreement and secure the adhesion to the plan of Prussia and Bavaria. This would bring Austria on board, and isolate Great Britain. France was prepared to place 200,000 troops on a war footing to enforce the arrangements, and hoped the other powers in favour of the plan would do likewise.

Because peace was concluded as quickly as it was between Russia and the Ottoman Empire, the French government's plan was not formally presented to the Russians. Subsequent soundings by the French suggested that neither Tsar Nicholas I nor Metternich nor even the Prussians would have subscribed to it. Circumstances, and personnel, had changed since the summer of 1821 when Alexander I, contemplating war against the Ottoman Empire, had put out feelers to France for an alliance. The matter was not pressed. It remains one of the great 'might have beens' of the international history of the nineteenth century, one of the most spectacular (and speculative) of the attempts to connect developments in the east of Europe with changes in the west of Europe. It was not really representative of French policy throughout the years under review, for obviously everything depended upon a particular constellation of attitudes and dispositions coming into existence, and the particular constellation required was only close (and even then only in the wishful thinking of Polignac and his colleagues) on this one occasion.

What was more representative of the policy of France, and more consistently pursued, was the establishment of a relationship with Mehemet Ali of Egypt, and support for his plans for expansion and for independence of the Ottoman Empire. In October 1824 General Belliard, who had been involved in the French expedition to Egypt of 1798–1801, wrote:

> The great question of emancipation [of Egypt from the Ottoman Empire] can only be treated verbally and with the greatest circumspection. The enterprise can and must not take place without the certainty of success, and without the patent or secret support of a strong Power, France. I repeat, this is a question of highest interest and cannot be too fully matured.

At the same time, the French government began to pour money into an Egyptian navy, which they thought might be used by France in the future to redress the balance of naval power in the Near East against Great Britain. This fitted in neatly with the French realisation that, whilst their commerce in the Levant as a whole continued to be weak, it did show marked increases as far as Egypt was concerned, mainly because of cotton.

However, it was not only for commercial reasons that the Franco-Egyptian relationship prospered. The French recognised, as they stated in 1833, that Mehemet Ali had a dual ambition – 'of making Egypt the centre of a new empire' as well as 'the commercial entrepôt of a part of the world'. They knew that Mehemet Ali wanted to retain Crete and

Arabia, and to acquire Syria, and wanted all these areas to be independent of the Ottoman Empire. The French hoped not only to be the power behind, but the major beneficiary of, any such new state. They expected, with the help of Mehemet Ali's armies, to dominate the north African coast, and ultimately to acquire Algeria, Tunis and Tripoli for themselves. If this came about, the French would dominate the Mediterranean and control, or have controlled by a friend of theirs, the trade routes overland to the east through Suez and Syria. This would help them to endure the treaties of 1815, if these remained unamended and in force.

It should be noted that, although the French wanted Mehemet Ali to detach Egypt, Syria and Arabia from the Ottoman Empire, and themselves to detach its north African provinces, they wanted the rest of the Ottoman Empire, in Europe and Asia Minor, to be preserved. They would not support Mehemet Ali in bringing down the Sultan, or in the transfer of the Caliphate from Constantinople to a place under Mehemet's direct control. French mediation in the Ottoman–Egyptian war of 1832-33 helped secure Syria for Mehemet Ali. The Treaty of Kutiah, which ended the conflict, cut the Muslim world in half. From 1833 to 1840 the French encouraged the maintenance of the status quo established in 1833. As the French Foreign Minister de Broglie wrote in September 1833:

> It is important that Mehemet Ali remain with care within the limits of his duties towards the Porte; that in his attitudes and in his language he prudently avoid giving the Sultan any inquietude or wounding of pride.... Such must be constantly the conduct of Mehemet Ali and of his; and I insist more especially on this point because of reports from Syria that Ibrahim Pasha, less circumspect than his father, has not put aside the intention to utilise the first occasion for renewing the war with the Porte to reverse the empire and overthrow the Sultan.

In 1840 another French government, in which Thiers was Foreign Minister, rather overreached itself in suport of Mehemet Ali, with whom a new Sultan had lost patience towards the end of the 1830s. Thiers insisted that the Ottoman fleet, which had defected to Egypt, remain in Egyptian hands. As all the other Great Powers insisted on the return of the fleet, France found herself isolated in Europe as a result of her approach to this phase of the Eastern Question. Thiers' policy helped return her to the isolation of the years 1815–25, from which she had been at such pains to escape, and to which end she had successfully and instrumentally taken advantage of the possibilities afforded by successive Eastern Questions. For although by the mid-1820s the French had identified Mehemet Ali and Egypt as their best bet for a long-term ally and satellite in the Near East, they had not ignored the temporary advantages of acting with other powers against the immediate interests of Egypt. They had participated in the international efforts to deal with the Greek revolt; they had contributed to the Anglo-Russian fleet action at Navarino in 1827; they had made an input to the Treaty of London; they had sent an expeditionary force to the Greek mainland in 1828. As neither the French nor the British liked what they knew of the Russo-Turkish Treaty of Unkiar-Skelessi of 1833, an entente between them on this subject lasted until the débâcle of 1840.

❖

Gentz wrote, during the Congress of Vienna, that 'the end of the Turkish monarchy could be survived by the Austrian for but a short time'. Fourteen years later Metternich wrote:

> We look on the Ottoman Empire as the best of our neighbours.... We regard contact with her as equivalent to contact with a natural frontier which never claims our attentions or dissipates our energies. We look on Turkey as the last bastion standing in the way of the expansion of another Power.

By the later 1820s Metternich had carried his pro-Ottoman policy of the maintenance of the status quo in the Balkans to such an extreme that he had brought about the isolation of Austria over the question of the existence and independence of a Greek state. When asked to join the Anglo-Russian Protocol of 4 April 1826, which stipulated 'joint formulation, and joint *or* separate mediation, of a settlement between Turkey and the Greeks, on the basis of an autonomous and tributary Greek principality', Metternich refused. Gentz wrote of this Anglo-Russian project: 'it would simply dispose of the life of Turkey, which had not given occasion for it by any offence.' Austria was not a party to the Treaty of London of 6 July 1827, in which France joined Britain and Russia in stipulating that Greece was to be a dependency of Turkey and to pay tribute to the Sultan. Austria did not participate with Britain, Russia and France in discussions at Constantinople between August and December 1827 on Greek affairs. Nor did she join them in discussions on the boundaries of Greece in October 1828, or in their declaration of 22 March 1829 that Greece was to be under the sovereignty of the Porte, a state of affairs and a relationship which the Ottoman Empire accepted in Article X of the Treaty of Adrianople with Russia of 14 September 1829. Indeed, just a week before the signing of the Treaty of Adrianople,

Metternich, who had encouraged the Turks throughout to reject all proposals for change, had written:

> What do we mean by the *Greeks*? Do we mean a people, a country, or a religion? If either of the first two, where are the dynastic and geographical boundaries? If the third, then upwards of fifty million men are Greeks: the Austrian Empire alone embraces five million of them.... The Emperor, our august Master, will never consent that the Greeks, his subjects, should consider themselves at the same time to be citizens of the new Greece. In this respect he can only follow the rules of public justice which prevent him from considering his Milanese and Venetian subjects as members of an Italian body politic, or his Galician subjects as belonging to a kingdom of Poland. Long experience has taught us to realise that in racial denominations there may lie elements of trouble between empires and bones of contention between people and governments. And what a powerful and ever hostile weapon such denominations become in the hands of those who overthrow, or seek to overthrow, the existing order!

Austria remained aloof when Britain, Russia and France, at a conference in London on 3 February 1830, advanced matters by declaring that Greece was to be an independent, rather than a tributary state. Austria remained aloof as, on 7 May 1832, Britain, Russia and France agreed with Bavaria to offer the throne of the independent Greek state to Prince Otto of Bavaria, and to take that state under their guarantee. Nor was Austria involved in the final development, when the continental limits of Greece were definitively settled between Britain, Russia, France and the Ottoman Empire at Constantinople on 21 July 1832.

Not until 1833 did relations between Austria and Russia improve so far as eastern questions were concerned, by which time the Russians had repeated their demonstration of September 1829 that they were determined to maintain the Ottoman Empire, on the latest occasion by intervening against Mehemet Ali, whose armies Metternich had once hoped would quell the Greek revolt for the Sultan. Even so, just a few months before the Convention of Munchengrätz (near Turnov, now in the Czech Republic), Metternich had rejected certain ideas for the future of the Ottoman Empire in Europe which the Tsar had adumbrated. Noting that the Ottoman Empire had followed the Greek Empire by conquest and that there was still a largely Christian population in the relatively new Ottoman provinces of the former Greek Empire, Nicholas I went on:

Why should we not try to recreate a Greek empire if the Turkish empire destroys itself through its own incapacity? There is the beginning of a Greek state. I do not know King Otto; I do not know whether he is of the calibre for such a future. For my part I see nothing better to do.

Metternich objected to this idea of reviving a Greek empire: 'Austria could not be a party to this combination now a Bavarian prince has been placed on the Greek throne, for it would be unwise of her to have the same foe at her back as facing her.'

The Russians went on to make the Treaty of Unkiar-Skelessi with the Ottoman Empire. The adverse reaction to this on the part of Great Britain and France helped bring about a Russo–Austrian understanding at Munchengrätz in September 1833 which was to last until Metternich was displaced in 1848. Russia and Austria pledged themselves to maintain the existing Ottoman dynasty, and to prevent Mehemet Ali from acquiring either direct or indirect authority over any part of European Turkey. If the Ottoman Empire broke up, Austria and Russia would concert together in establishing a new order of things. What that new order might be was not specified. What it might have been was outlined ten years later, in September 1843, by the Russians. By this time Nicholas I had changed his mind about a Greek empire. He told the Austrians: 'I do not want the re-establishment of a Byzantine empire; I will never permit it. I do not want the French or English, either together or separately, to occupy Constantinople or give it material protection.' The Tsar wanted nothing beyond the Danube – it should all go to Austria. Moreover, as he put it, 'If you [Austria] occupy Constantinople, you will need a bridgehead in Asia – that goes without saying'. In November 1843 Metternich made it clear that Austria had no wish to assume responsibilities as successor state to the Ottoman Empire. He was convinced, he said, that what the Tsar envisaged would turn all Europe against Russia and Austria, and inevitably cause a tremendous political upheaval. Nicholas I tried again in March 1844, sending Count Orlov on a mission to Vienna, and receiving the same negative response. He then turned to Great Britain in June 1844, hoping that if the future of the Ottoman Empire could be settled with her, Austria might then be more forthcoming, less static, and less opposed as a matter of principle to any changes. The Russians raised the matter again in December 1845, saying that 'It is Austria which in the general interest ought to receive the heritage of European Turkey', and have Constantinople. Once again, Metternich would not be drawn; the real task facing the powers, he maintained, was to preserve the Ottoman Empire, rather than to define the shape of a new order if it collapsed.

What was, arguably, Metternich's finest hour in relation to the Eastern Question came in 1839. In the midst of the commotion of that year, Metternich proposed a conference or, as he preferred to call it, a concert, to be held at Vienna to settle matters. Metternich let it be known that he favoured the establishment of a European guarantee of the independence of the Ottoman Empire. Nicholas I, who had no wish to allow Metternich to control negotiations on the Eastern Question, refused to do more than send an envoy to a conference of ambassadors at Vienna. This conference of ambassadors produced a collective note to the Sultan, dated 27 July 1839, which was the basis of all future negotiations. The internationalisation of the Eastern Question had been promoted by Metternich, and was to have some positive results.

Aware that Metternich was disposed to act in concert with Great Britain and France, the Russians, foreseeing their own isolation, hastened to compromise. Baron Brunnow was sent to London with two propositions: that the idea of a general guarantee of the territories of the Sultan be abandoned, and that the closure of the Dardanelles to warships during peace and war become a principle of European public law. Metternich, to whom Brunnow's instructions had been communicated by the Russian government, for once showed some flexibility, as indeed did Brunnow. Metternich proved willing to drop the idea of a general guarantee of the territories of the Sultan. On the other hand, he insisted that not just the Dardanelles but also the Bosporus be closed to foreign warships if the Ottoman Empire was at peace. He also insisted that the Sultan be given the right to open the Straits, should the Ottoman Empire be at war with another power, in such a way as to utilise his resources in favour of his friends and against his enemies. Metternich thus influenced considerably, even without a full congress at Vienna, the four-power pact of 1840 and the content of the Straits Convention of 1841. In so doing, he contributed both to the development and extension of the concept of European public law and, through the internationally agreed closure of both Straits, to the maintenance of the Ottoman Empire in Europe, without which state as a neighbour he could not envisage any future for the Habsburg Monarchy itself.

II. Russia: Nesselrode *versus* Official Nationalism

The Russian Empire possessed a direct and permanent interest in the Near East, based on geography, history, culture and religion. The empire of the Tsars owed much to its Near Eastern cultural heritage, and religious ties bound it to populations within the Balkan provinces of the

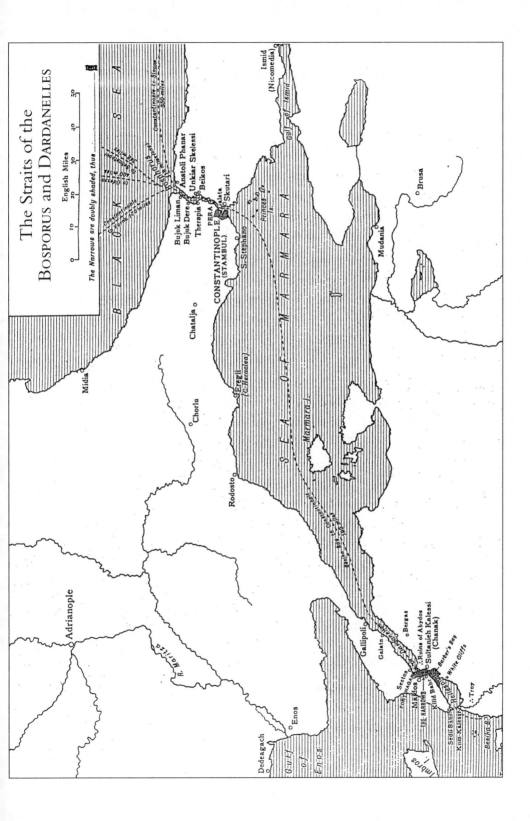

The Straits of the
Bosporus and Dardanelles

English Miles

0   10   20   30   40   50

The Narrows are doubly shaded, thus

BLACK SEA

Midia

Adrianople

Chatalja

Chorlu

CONSTANTINOPLE
(STAMBUL)

Bujuk Liman
Bujuk Dere
Therapia
Galata
PERA

Anatoli Phanar
Unkiar Skelessi
Beikos
Skutari

Ismid
(Nicomedia)

GULF OF ISMID

Brusa

Mudania

S. Stephano

Princes Is.

Eregli
(G. Heraclea)

SEA OF MARMARA

Marmara I.

Rodosto

Enos

GULF OF ENOS

Dedeagach

R. Maritza

Gallipoli

Galata

Sestos

MAIDOS
FORT NAGARA
THE NARROWS
Kilid Bahr
Sedd-ul-Bahr
Kum-Kalessi
Besika Bay

Bergas
Ruins of Abydos
Sultanieh Kalessi
(Chanak)
Nagara Pt.
HELLES Pt.
WHITE CLIFFS
Troy

Imbros

Ottoman Empire. The outlet for the commerce and produce of the fertile southern provinces of the Russian Empire was the Turkish Straits. The strategic keys for the defence of her southern shores, from the north-western corner of the Black Sea to its south-eastern corner, were the Dardanelles and the Bosporus.

To the Russian Empire the Eastern Question was: would the maintenance of the Ottoman Empire in Europe be more advantageous to Russian interests than its dissolution? Or, to put it slightly differently, striking a more defensive note: was the Ottoman Empire the best power to guard the Straits, the 'keys to the Russian house', or not? As the nineteenth century developed, so did two schools of thought in Russia in relation to these matters. Russian policy reflected the existence of these two schools of thought. It reflected the tension between them, and the struggle that went on between their representatives.

Representative of one school of thought was Capo d'Istria, at one point Russian Foreign minister before Greece gained her independence. On the eve of the Russo-Turkish war, on 30 March 1828, he proposed the creation of five independent states in the Balkans: kingdoms of Dacia (Romania), Servia (including Bulgaria and Bosnia), Macedonia, Epirus (including Albania) and Greece. Constantinople itself, with some adjacent territory, would be a free city and the centre of a confederation of these five states.

Capo d'Istria's proposal was considered at the end of the Russo-Turkish war, in September 1829, at which time representatives of another school of thought pointed out that the creation of Constantinople as a free city would not safeguard access to the Black Sea by itself – Russia would in addition have to obtain territories on both shores of the Bosporus and would have to fortify them. Capo d'Istria's opponents took the view that the destruction, or dismantling, of Turkey in Europe would result in a general European war. What was of importance was 'not at all new acquisitions, nor the expansion of Russian frontiers, but security and the development of Russia's action in the midst of neighbouring peoples'. The expulsion of the Turks to Asia Minor, where they would find a more thoroughly Muslim population, might lead to a Turkish revival and offer grave dangers to relatively recently acquired Russian possessions in the Caucasus and Trans-Caspian territories. Both the partition of Turkey in Europe by the Great Powers and the creation of independent states would create difficulties:

> There was a time when the partition of Turkey could enter into the secret calculations of Russian policy. But now that the confines of the Empire extend from the White Sea to the Danube and the Arax, from

Kamchatka to the Vistula, only certain acquisitions could be of real utility. The possession of the Bosporus and Dardanelles would not fail to encourage our commerce, but at the price of what sacrifices could we obtain it! Moreover, other Powers, thanks to their geographical position, could make more advantageous acquisitions at the expense of Turkey than could Russia. Austria could acquire Serbia, Hercegovina, Bosnia, Albania, and subjugate Montenegro; England and France could seize the islands of Greece, Candia and Egypt. In such circumstances the Russian flag would be called on to meet dangerous enemies in southern Europe instead of indifferent Turks.

Such were the views of Dashkov and Nesselrode, both members of a Special Committee on the Affairs of Turkey set up by Nicholas I. It unanimously concluded 'that the advantages of the maintenance of the Ottoman Empire in Europe are superior to the disadvantages it presents; that its fall would be contrary to the true interests of Russia'.

Nicholas I accepted these conclusions, which coincided with the assurance given to the Great Powers before the outbreak of the Russo–Turkish war that Russia had no desire to add to her territories, no intention 'of keeping Constantinople or any part of the Ottoman Empire, the acquisition of which would upset the equilibrium of Europe'. These conclusions were in line with Kochubey's opposition of 1802 to an expansionist policy and the division of the Ottoman Empire with France. Kochubey had argued that that traditional policy should be abandoned and that Russian interests could be secured by agreement to uphold the status quo. Nesselrode was a pupil and *protégé* of Kochubey.

What is just as interesting as the decision arrived at is that there was such a debate, such a review of the issues, at all, given the assurances delivered to the Great Powers before the outbreak of the Russo–Turkish war. It was as if those assurances could be cancelled. This possibility existed because the Russian nationalists, who had helped precipitate a war with Persia in 1827, and relished the annexation of Erivan (now Yerevan, Armenia) and Naklichivan (Naxçıvan) from Persia by the Treaty of Turkmenchai, wanted to see a victory over the Ottoman Empire that would be followed by further annexations. As it was, those nationalists, who included one Prince A.S. Menshikov, had to be satisfied only with gains in the southern Caucasus at the expense of the Ottoman Empire in the Treaty of Adrianople.

❖

In this debate between the expansionists and the adherents of the status quo, between Russian nationalists and those of a more cosmopolitan cast

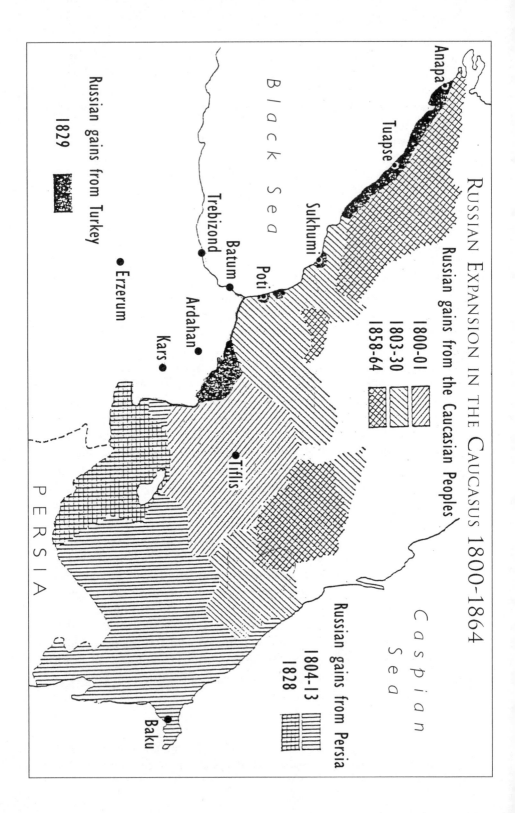

RUSSIAN EXPANSION IN THE CAUCASUS 1800–1864

Russian gains from the Caucasian Peoples

1800–01
1803–30
1858–64

Russian gains from Turkey

1829

Russian gains from Persia

1804–13
1828

Black Sea

Caspian Sea

PERSIA

Anapa
Tuapse
Sukhumi
Trebizond
Batum
Poti
Ardahan
Kars
Erzerum
Tiflis
Baku

of mind, between those who had no time for a concert with the other powers and those who preferred a collaborationist approach, in short between easterners and westerners, the position of the Tsar was absolutely critical. Nesselrode had accompanied Nicholas I into the field during the Russo-Turkish war, and perhaps that paid dividends in the relatively lenient Treaty of Adrianople. But the Tsar could change his mind.

Nicholas overruled Nesselrode who, afraid of a confrontation between Russia on the one hand and France and Great Britain on the other, advised against intervention against Mehemet Ali early in 1833. Nesselrode was able to retrieve the position, and re-assert his influence, but not without difficulty. There is no doubt that amongst the moves envisaged by the Tsar at that time was the occupation and fortification of a point on the Bosporus. The Treaty of Unkiar-Skelessi with the Ottoman Empire was, for the nationalists, a second-best alternative. They saw it as a temporary postponement of Russia's eventual possession of the Straits. As Count Orlov, who helped to negotiate it, wrote to Nesselrode in April 1833:

> There is no doubt but that in a year or two at the most, we shall be summoned back, but we shall have the great advantage of coming back, thanks to our antecedents, without arousing suspicion and of coming back in such a way as never to leave again.

From the point of view of the Russian nationalists, the real point of the Treaty of Unkiar-Skelessi was in preparing the way for a repetition of the expedition of 1833, and in accustoming the Porte to the position of vassal. If the dissolution of the Ottoman Empire could be announced as a fact, it entitled Russia to be first on the ground, in order to take what she desired, or at least make sure that no other power took what the Russian nationalists had it in mind to take.

❖

In 1833 Official Nationalism was adopted as the state ideology of the Russian Empire. Official Nationalists believed in 'a Russian policy, a policy of being isolated as far as possible from Western Europe, of avoiding its influence, and of retreating from contact with it'. So far as Official Nationalists were concerned, Russia was to be not a part of Europe, or of Asia, but 'a separate world isolated from all, internally harmonious, externally unapproachable'. In 1836 Nicholas I remarked that his predecessor Peter the Great might have been wrong to have moved the capital to St Petersburg.

Against this background of the development of Russian nationalism, Nesselrode's achievements between the mid-1830s and mid-1840s are truly staggering. Between 1836 and 1839 he extricated Russia from a series of crises of confrontation in Asia and the Near East, any one of which could easily have touched off war with Great Britain. Throughout, Nesselrode argued that common interests outweighed differences and that the reasons for rivalry were shallow and best put aside. In 1839–40, having brought about something of a *rapprochement*, he tried to build upon it. His thinking was that the Concert was inoperable as long as Europe was divided by opposed alignments; bipartisan co-operation was the best way to proceed. His overtures to Great Britain in the course of the second Mehemet Ali crisis brought the Concert back to life in 1840–41 and went far in the direction of substituting an international guarantee of the Ottoman Empire for the previously purely Russian one. He repeatedly asserted that economic interests united Great Britain and Russia – the *rapprochement* began with the lowering of restrictions on trade with Great Britain at the end of 1836. Taken together with economic initiatives as regards other countries, what appears is a grand design, a desire for a large community in which trade and commerce would unite Russia with Asia and with Europe.

Nesselrode was not entirely unaided in this task. His closest collaborator was Baron Brunnow, who in 1839 volunteered that Russia was prepared to see closed not only the Dardanelles (as provided for under the Treaty of Unkiar-Skelessi) but also the Bosporus, and that if Great Britain would accept this Russia would not seek to renew the treaty of 1833. Brunnow, like Nesselrode, believed that there was such a thing as 'the European family', and that it should enjoy peace and prosperity in a 'union of nations'. Like Nesselrode, Brunnow hated those Official Nationalists who wished to return to 'the ancient barbarity, to the times of the Grand Dukes of Muscovy', and who wished to move the capital of the Russian Empire from the Baltic to the Kremlin. When Brunnow went to London in 1839 Nesselrode had instructed him to tell Palmerston, the British Foreign Secretary, that Russia was prepared to negotiate a treaty to guarantee the territorial status quo in Asia as well as in the Near East. Here Nesselrode was taking up again an overture that he had made to the British government in October 1838. He had written to the Russian ambassador in London:

> Great Britain and Russia must have one and the same interest at least –
> that is to maintain peace in the centre of Asia and to see that a general
> conflagration does not begin in this vast part of the globe.
>
> Now, in order to prevent such a great tragedy, it is necessary to

conserve carefully the repose of the intermediate countries which separate the possessions of Russia from those of Great Britain; to consolidate the tranquillity of these countries; to refrain from exciting one against the other by feeding mutual animosities; to confine rivalry to trade, and not to engage in a contest for political influence; finally, above all else, to respect the independence of the intermediate countries.... In order to avoid the possibility of a conflict between the two Great Powers, in order to remain friends, they must not touch and must not collide in Central Asia.

This was Nesselrode's 'theory of buffers'.

Palmerston did not respond, either in 1838 or 1839. Nesselrode, however, took up the matter again in December 1840, urging that negotiations be opened for a treaty to fix the territorial limits of the Russian and British Empires in Central Asia and secure free trade in the buffer zone. He was inviting Palmerston to accept parity with Russia in the rights and privileges she would enjoy in the buffer zone, a zone which Nesselrode's opponents in Russia wished to see Russia conquer. One historian, Harold Ingle, has described Nesselrode's effort here as 'an offer to put an end to imperialism'.

Nicholas I, although he praised Nesselrode for the Near Eastern settlement of 1840, had strong reservations about it. He did not really believe that the status quo could be upheld. He leaned towards Orlov's opinion that a power vacuum could not be maintained in the Near East. Nicholas wrote to Nesselrode in August 1840:

> I will not now change my mind and eliminate the possibility of what may in the future prove to be a viable agreement, but ... if Turkey dies, what will take its place? One would hope it would be an independent Christian State, or one would hope for a partition à l'amicable, one would hope excluding France.

Nationalistic Russians would never accept Nesselrode's argument that the Treaty of Unkiar-Skelessi had been continued in another form, because to them there was a world of difference between independent action and the commitment to act in concert. To them, the new Convention constituted an immense setback for their goal of eventual control of the Straits. Official Nationalism rested on the conviction that Russia could not be reconciled with her western rivals, and at the end of 1841 Nesselrode said of Nicholas I that he continued to see the present relationship between the European Powers as 'one coalition against the other'. Nesselrode, on the other hand, wanted to see, and tried to create, what he called 'a compact community'; for him the days of opposed alliances had come to an end.

What Nesselrode was increasingly confronted with emerged very pointedly from a visit by Nicholas I and Orlov to England in June 1844. To Sir Robert Peel, the Prime Minister, to Lord Aberdeen, the Foreign Secretary, and to the Duke of Wellington, the Tsar stated: 'In Russia there are two views of Turkey. Turkey must fall to pieces.... Nesselrode denies this, but I for my part am fully convinced of it. We cannot preserve her existence no matter how hard we try.' The Russia of Nicholas I was determined to have her share of the pieces when the Ottoman Empire crumbled, and hoped for a partition à l'amicable with Great Britain to the exclusion of France.

Nicholas, through Orlov, had put a similar programme to Metternich in February and March 1844, as mentioned in the previous chapter, namely that Austria and Russia partition the European side of the Straits, Russia obtaining a cordon to the Bosporus and a common border with an enlarged Greece, Constantinople itself as a city to be neutralised and governed by all the powers. Metternich had stood up firmly against this, and done Nesselrode's work for him, in effect. But as regards the British, Nesselrode felt it necessary to come himself to England, to try to put his own interpretation on what the Tsar had said to British ministers. Nesselrode embodied what he himself said in a memorandum which he then sent to Lord Aberdeen as 'the most certain guide for the course we would follow in common accord', should the Ottoman Empire be in trouble. Bipartisan co-operation, he maintained, was vital – 'independent action by the two Powers could only result in misfortune', whereas, 'in concert ... it is to be hoped that the peace of Europe will be maintained even in the midst of trying conditions'. This was a delaying tactic on the part of Nesselrode, who felt the Tsar no longer shared his views. Had 'independent action' not been a real possibility, there would have been no need to compose the Nesselrode memorandum, and no reason for Nesselrode to fear that the treaty of 1841 and the European concert would be swept aside.

❖

Nesselrode continued his rearguard action, with the help of Metternich until 1848, and with the help of most British Foreign Secretaries (the confrontational Palmerston being the notable exception) who could only hope that Nesselrode's approach would prevail in Russian counsels and that he would remain in control of Russian foreign policy. For quite a time, Nesselrode's approach did prevail. In the end, however, Official Nationalism overcame both the mind of the Tsar and the content of Russian foreign policy. In 1853 the day of Menshikov came; the years of Nesselrode were over; the latter still walked, but no longer cast a shadow on the land.

III. The British Empire: Palmerston and the Great Game in Asia

For the British Empire, the Eastern Question was a question of the defence of India. Had the British Empire not existed, had the British not assumed huge responsibilities on the Indian subcontinent, there would have been for the British no Eastern Question at all. As it was, in the two decades preceding the Crimean War the questions with which the British had to concern themselves were: how to stop the emergence and development of an Arab state stretching from the eastern Mediterranean and the Levant to the Persian Gulf; and, how to attack the Russian Empire, with a good possibility of defeating it?

The Arab state in question was, of course, the one that Mehemet Ali of Egypt had every intention of setting up by liberating Egypt, the Sudan, Arabia, Syria and Mesopotamia from the Ottoman dominions. Two individuals in particular were responsible for the education of Lord Palmerston on this matter. They were Stratford Canning, the British ambassador in Constantinople, and Sir Henry Ellis, a member of the Board of Control of the East India Company in London. In a letter to Palmerston of 9 January 1833 Ellis wrote: 'I would lay it down as a principle that it is not the interest of the European Sovereign of India that a powerful Mahommedan state should be placed at the mouth of the Euphrates.' Ellis gave the following reasons for this:

> It is quite possible that such a government should unite with Russia in a partition of Persia. A Mahommedan Government so placed would undoubtedly soon spread its influence throughout Arabia and might at no long time become a maritime power of importance. The absence of such a power is at present a complete security against any attack upon our Indian possessions from the Southern parts of the Indus.

Moreover, such a state, placed at the Persian Gulf and 'wielded by an ambitious Sovereign', might form 'a Mahommedan League' of all the Muslim rulers of Central Asia 'for the purpose of driving out a Christian Government from India'.

By the end of January 1833 Palmerston had adopted these views as his own. He wrote to Lord Granville on 29 January: 'My ... opinion is that we ought to tell the Pasha [Mehemet Ali] forthwith to retire to Egypt.

That the possession of Syria must carry with it that of Baghdad, a glance at the map will serve to show, because it would enable Mehemet to cut off all communications between Caramania and Baghdad.' That such a new state should be created in Egypt, Syria, and Baghdad was not 'for the advantage of England'. For one thing, 'Russia would soon come to an understanding with the new Sovereign. Persia would probably be nibbled at by both, and their union might produce inconvenient consequences to our Eastern possessions'. On 5 February Palmerston wrote again that he had clearly discovered that Mehemet Ali 'wants to establish an Arabian Kingdom to include all the districts of the Turkish empire in which Arabic is the vernacular tongue'. He went on:

> If such a new power were created, it seems evident that whenever that power and Russia chose to come to an understanding the Sultan would be squeezed to death, unless the Powers of Europe made war to assist him; and there is no telling how far it might be convenient for them to do so, and how easy it might be for them to bring their assistance to bear upon the points assailed.

Although Palmerston was disposed, by this time, to accede to the Sultan's application for naval assistance against his rebellious Egyptian vassal, the British Cabinet was not. The Prime Minister, Lord Grey, had asked one colleague, Lord Holland, in January 1833: 'would either Parliament or the people support us in a war which would be generally felt to arise for the sake of a remote and problematic interest?' In other words, had the great British public, or the part of it that constituted 'the political nation', been sufficiently educated to appreciate what was at stake? On 23 April 1833 the Prime Minister told Palmerston that the matter was settled: 'At all events it was not in our power, already engaged in the affairs of Belgium and Portugal, to enter into a third business of the same nature. We had no force for such a passage and I am quite sure that Parliament would not have granted us one.' Palmerston, later in his career, described this decision as a 'tremendous blunder' on the part of that British government. He wrote:

> It is true that Russia alone prevented at that time the occupation of Constantinople by Ibrahim or at least some general break-up in consequence of his advance: I … think that no British Cabinet at any period of the history of England ever made so great a mistake in regard to foreign affairs as did the Cabinet of Lord Grey in refusing assistance and protection to the Sultan.

Russian intervention in 1833, as Palmerston acknowledged, solved, if only temporarily, the problem which Ellis and Palmerston had identified. In 1839–40 the problem was solved more permanently, this time with the participation of Great Britain. Mehemet Ali did not become an independent sovereign, or move his capital from Cairo to Baghdad. Syria and Mesopotamia remained within the Ottoman Empire. Russian intervention in 1833, however, also had the effect of exacerbating, or of making more difficult to solve, the second of the British Empire's Eastern Questions – namely how to attack the Russian Empire with a good possibility of defeating it.

❖

When the Russians retired from Constantinople in 1833 they did so having obtained, through the Treaty of Unkiar-Skelessi, a particular relationship with the Ottoman Empire. As a reward for rescuing the Ottoman Empire from the Egyptians, they had secured an obligation on the part of the Ottoman Empire to close the Dardanelles Strait to foreign warships if requested by Russia to do so. Did this not make it impossible for Great Britain to get at Russia physically? Did this not make it impossible for Great Britain to bring pressure to bear, in order to stop Russia advancing, not into the Ottoman Empire itself but behind the screen, or stopper, of the Treaty of Unkiar-Skelessi, into Transcaspia, Persia, the Khanates and towards Afghanistan and ultimately India?

In September 1834 Palmerston had the British ambassador in Constantinople put the following question to the Ottoman government: 'Supposing Russia and England happened to find themselves at war over a problem and at a time when Turkey had no quarrel with England, would the Bosporus and the Dardanelles be opened to Russia and closed to England, or would they be closed alike to Russia and England?' After consulting the Russian ambassador, the Turkish Foreign Minister announced that the two Straits would remain closed as long as Turkey was at peace.

Information about what Russia was doing, and might do, behind the barrier to Great Britain that was the Dardanelles, began to reach Palmerston well before the Treaty of Unkiar-Skelessi was signed. In August 1832 Palmerston had evinced his concern at rumoured Russian designs on Khiva, the possession of which would place them, he said, 'nearly in command of the navigation of rivers which lead down to the very frontier of our Indian Empire'. In the same year a British lieutenant had gone from Persia on a special mission to Khiva. His report concluded that the obstacles to a Russian invasion of India were so few that it would amount to little more than the sending of a caravan. Palmerston took these matters increasingly seriously. In 1835 he sent Captain Charles Stoddart to Persia to make a military survey of part of the Persian Empire. In the same year John MacNeill wrote his book *Progress and Present Position of Russia in the East*, in which he argued that Russian foreign policy was based on a pre-conceived design that in Asia as elsewhere called for subversion and conquest and that India would give Russia a counterbalance to British commercial superiority. At the very least Russia could annihilate British commerce in Central Asia, and force Britain to have her Indian revenues diminished and her expenses increased. In February 1836 Palmerston appointed MacNeill minister to Persia. In 1837 another military report concluded that 'a Russian army, equipped for the invasion of India, could find its way in two or three campaigns to the banks of the Indus'. Also in 1837 Lord Durham, British ambassador in St Petersburg, secured access to and forwarded to London documents regarding Russia's Asiatic plans which he had obtained surreptitiously from the Russian ministries of Finance and Commerce. Some concerned projects for commercial and political expansion at the south-east corner of the Caspian Sea. Astrabad was the objective.

In the autumn of 1837 Tsar Nicholas I paid his first visit to this area, and the Asiatic Committee of the Russian government adopted resolutions which the Tsar approved on 27 September 1837 for establishing a foothold at Astrabad (now Gorgān). Commerce with Persia was to be extended under government subsidy; access to Astrabad would be made from Astrakan, already an important Russian commercial depot. By 1838 Palmerston regarded Astrabad as possessing unequalled opportunities for political purposes. From there the communications between Tehran in Persia and Herat in Afghanistan could be cut. Russia could thus dominate the policies of both countries. She had established direct relations with Afghanistan in 1836.

In April 1838 Palmerston learned of a projected large Russian expedition to Bukhara, under the command of the governor of Orenburg. He immediately instructed MacNeill to dispatch a secret agent to the ruler of Bukhara to warn of the Russians' intentions. In May of the same year Palmerston believed Russia to be backing the Persian army's siege of Herat. He instructed MacNeill to advise the Shah of Persia to give up the siege, as it showed 'a spirit of hostility towards British India'. In July MacNeill reported his belief that Russia had a greater facility for attack on India than ever. All this led, in October 1838, to Palmerston haranguing the Russian ambassador, Pozzo di Borgo. Palmerston complained of the growth of the Russian fleet; he denounced the Russian conquest of the Caucasus, and he dwelt on the Russian threat to India. He returned to these themes, and especially the

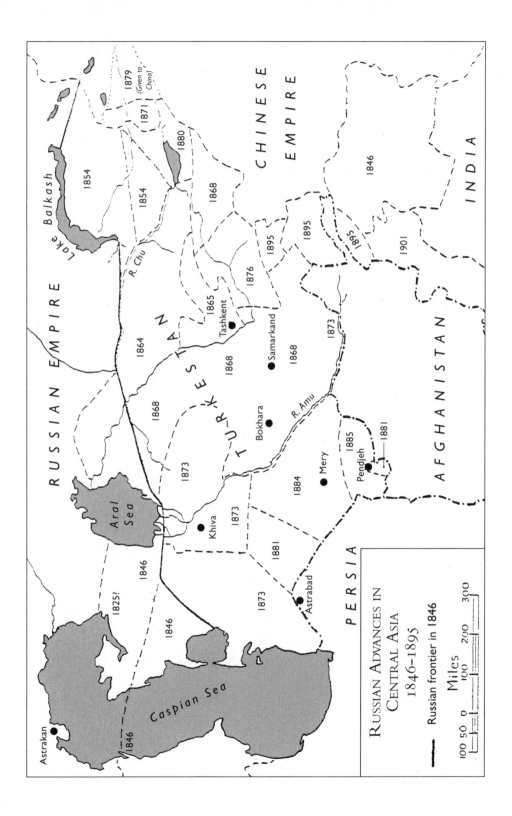

RUSSIAN ADVANCES IN
CENTRAL ASIA
1846–1895

—— Russian frontier in 1846

Miles

100 50 0   100   200   300

latter one, in the same company, a fortnight later. He accused Russia of instigating Persia to menace the Indian frontier by her alliance with Afghan chieftains; he indicted Russia for wanting to exterminate the Circassians. No wonder that, in September 1838, the Ottoman government was asking the French ambassador in Constantinople for advice as to what to do if an Anglo-Russian war over Persia resulted in a renewal of British demands to admit British warships into the Dardanelles.

At the root of Palmerston's furious language towards Pozzo di Borgo lay sheer frustration. The British could do nothing about the region in question. They had not the means to invade and occupy Persia, as MacNeill wanted. It was one thing, in a dispute with Persia over the siege of Herat, for Britain to occupy the island of Karak in the Persian Gulf; it was quite another thing to put direct pressure on the Russian Empire. Whilst ambassador to St Petersburg, Lord Durham identified three souces of Russian weakness: Poland, the Caucasus, and the navy. There was no way in which the British Empire could utilise the Polish weakness. And so long as the Dardanelles could be closed, there was no way of utilising the Caucasus weakness and the naval weakness, and playing to the British Empire's own naval strength. Hence Palmerston's frustration. As Nesselrode observed, on receiving Pozzo di Borgo's reports of Palmerston's harangues:

> It appears that England fears us at all the points at which she feels vulnerable, and, in order to defeat the designs which she persists in attributing to us, she seeks to create enemies for us everywhere and tries to lead us into trouble with our most intimate allies.

As Nesselrode recognised, the trouble was that Persia was an 'immediate neighbour' of Russia, and at the same time could not but be regarded by Great Britain as 'a barrier for the securing of British India against attack'; the same applied to Afghanistan.

The frustration felt by Palmerston in particular throughout the 1830s was not matched in terms of relief when Russia announced itself prepared to forego the renewal of the Treaty of Unkiar-Skelessi. What replaced that treaty was the Convention for the Pacification of the Levant of July 1840, which when signed by France became the Straits Convention of July 1841. These new treaties stipulated, and made it a matter of international law, that the strait of the Dardanelles remain closed to foreign warships as long as the Ottoman Empire was at peace, and that the same rule applied to the strait of the Bosporus. Palmerston, typically, maintained that this change was a great achievement on his part, even though it had been offered to him on a plate by Nesselrode. Others were to question whether Great Britain won or lost more by closed as compared with open straits. Lord Salisbury, who dominated British foreign and imperial policy in the third quarter of the century, was of the opinion that, on account of the existing British naval supremacy, she lost more by her exclusion from the Euxine than Russia lost by having her Black Sea fleet confined to the Black Sea.

For Great Britain the problem of access to Russia, and of how to damage her seriously, remained, and Palmerston continued to chafe at it. In 1840, even as the Russians were explaining that their current expedition to Khiva was not intended to establish a garrison and base there or to counter British India's expedition into Afghanistan, but was to 'establish tranquillity for the future', Palmerston answered that Russia seemed merely to be taking a different road to India.

Whenever he was Foreign Secretary in the 1840s Palmerston chafed at this problem. When he became Prime Minister, during the Crimean War, he believed that he had a chance to dispose, once and for all, of the Russian threat to India. This is why he wanted that war to go on for another year; and also why he envisaged a 'redrawing of the European map' which would include restoring Finland to Sweden, giving Russia's Baltic provinces to Prussia, independence for Poland, giving Moldavia and Wallachia to Austria, and restoring the Crimea and Georgia to the Ottoman Empire. Palmerston's new appointments to India were just as extreme – Smith and Seymour wanted to go on the offensive in Asia, to turn the Caspian into a Persian lake, and with British help create a naval squadron on it which would 'blockade the mouths of the Volga, prevent supplies and troops being sent from Astrakan to Baku, put a stop to the trade of Russia with Central Asia, and encourage the tribes of Central Asia to throw off the Russian yoke'.

In January 1856 the British Cabinet favoured an expedition to the eastern side of the Black Sea, an expedition which one minister, the Duke of Argyll, rightly described as having 'an Anglo-Indian aspect'. In March 1856 Palmerston urged on the French the desirability of Russia's recognising the independence of the whole area between the frontier of the Ottoman Empire and the river Kuban. And in April 1856, at the Peace Congress in Paris, the British delegation did try to achieve, as one of the conditions of peace, the independence of the Caucasus.

❖

In conclusion, for the British Empire, the maintenance of the Ottoman Empire was not an end in itself. The end being sought was victory in the Great Game in Asia, and the preservation of British rule in India.

Support of the Ottoman Empire was part of the means to those ends. Edward Ingram in a series of works has, in my view most effectively, shown that, after the Russian dominance over Persia achieved by the Treaty of Turkmenchai of March 1828, the Great Game in Asia was a game that the British Empire could never win, a game the inevitable outcome of which it could merely try to delay. The British Empire's delaying tactics were to include the *rapprochement* of 1906 and *entente* of September 1907 with Russia, and the declaration of war on the German Empire in August 1914.

4

PROMISE AND COMPROMISE: 1848

By Article II of the Treaty of Alliance and Friendship between Great Britain, Austria, Prussia and Russia, signed at Paris on 20 November 1815, those four powers bound themselves 'to maintain in full vigour and, should it be necessary, with the whole of their forces', their mutual obligation, embodied in the treaty of 11 April 1814, forever to exclude Napoleon Bonaparte and his family from supreme power in France. Nor was this all. Article II continued:

> And as the same Revolutionary Principles which upheld the last criminal usurpation might again, under other forms, convulse France, and thereby endanger the repose of other States; under these circumstances, the High Contracting Parties solemnly admitting it to be their duty to redouble their watchfulness for the tranquillity and interests of their people, engage, in case so unfortunate an event should again occur, to concert amongst themselves ... the measures which they may judge necessary to be pursued for the safety of their respective States, and for the general Tranquillity of Europe.

At the end of February 1848 there was no expectation that a Bonaparte would seize supreme power in France. That supreme power, however, had been seized by revolutionaries, had been taken away from the Orléanist monarchy of Louis Philippe, and had been embodied in a republican regime. This development understandably inspired fears that there would be a repetition of the 1790s, that France would move again from revolution to foreign wars. Within a few days there was reason for further concern, this time about the validity and force of the arrangements made at the Congress of Vienna, arrangements which had already undergone some alteration – the separation of Belgium and Holland in the course of the 1830s, for instance, and the Austrian seizure of the Free City of Kraków in 1846. For on 5 March 1848 Lamartine, Foreign Minister of the new Second French Republic, issued a manifesto. He declared:

The treaties of 1815 no longer exist as law in the eyes of the French republic; nevertheless, the territorial delineations of these treaties are a fact which she does recognise as a basis and as a point of departure in her relations with other nations.

Lamartine tried to soften this potential blow by then stating:

But if the treaties of 1815 now exist only as facts to be modified by common accord, and if the Republic declares her mission to be to arrive by regular and pacific means at a modification of them, the good sense, moderation, conscience, and prudence of the Republic do exist, and are for Europe a better and more noble guarantee than the letter of these treaties, which have already been so often violated or modified by Europe.

Despite the reference to 'regular and pacific means', 'modification', at the very least, of the treaties of 1815, did appear to be the future policy of the new France. Whether she would display 'good sense, moderation, conscience, and prudence' remained to be seen. Confidence that the status quo would be maintained was further diminished by other passages in Lamartine's manifesto:

If it seems to us that the hour of the reconstruction of some oppressed nationalities in Europe, or elsewhere, has come in the decrees of providence; if Switzerland, our faithful ally since the time of Francis I, were to be limited or menaced ...; if the independent states of Italy were invaded; if limits or obstacles were imposed on their internal transformation; or if their right to ally themselves together to consolidate their Italian homeland were challenged by armed might, the French Republic would feel she would have the right to arm herself to protect these legitimate movements for the growth of peoples' nationalities.

Lamartine went on to claim that France would merely set an example, merely exercise, 'by the glow of her ideas, by the spectacle of order and peace which she hopes to give the world, the only honest kind of proselytism, proselytism of the mind and spirit'. He claimed, 'This is not war.... This is not agitation against Europe.... This means not setting the world aflame, but shining on the horizon of peoples in order to act as their guide'. To others, these were distinctions so fine as to be meaningless. To Austria, for example, all kinds of proselytism were bad, and it was not possible to distinguish between encouragement and incitement.

Lamartine's manifesto ended by defining 'liberty, equality and fraternity', as applied to French foreign policy, as 'the freeing of France from the chains which weighed upon her principles and dignity; the recuperation of the position she must occupy among the great European Powers; finally, the declaration of friendship and alliance of all peoples'. Much remained to be defined, especially as far as 'liberty' and 'equality' were concerned. Lamartine's final sentiment was that 'if France is conscious of her part in the civilising and liberal mission of the times, not one of her words signifies *war*. If Europe is prudent and just, not one of her words does not signify *peace*.'

❖

Even as this manifesto was being written, similar sentiments were being expressed in Great Britain. Contrary to the impression given by H.W.V. Temperley and L.M. Penson on page 155 of *Foundations of British Foreign Policy 1792–1902* (London, 1938), where it is asserted that 'Palmerston was urging the upholding of treaties', the British government announced that it would not become involved in Italy even if France intervened beyond the Alps. Britain would guarantee the existence of Belgium, but did not feel bound by the treaties of 1815 to help Austria retain her northern Italian provinces. In conversations with members of the diplomatic corps Palmerston distinguished between treaties of guarantee and mere treaties. Having been a signatory in the latter case gave a right to intervene, he maintained, but imposed no obligation to do so. It was otherwise with a guarantee: this involved the obligation of maintaining the state of possession. Palmerston pointed out that guarantees had been given by Britain to the King of Prussia for the province of Saxony in 1815, and to Switzerland in 1815 and to Belgium in 1839 for their neutrality and integrity. That was all. Britain had not guaranteed Lombardy to Austria, or the Rhine provinces to Prussia. Palmerston was quite emphatic about this, and recounted in a despatch of 14 March to Westmorland in Berlin what he had and had not said:

> I did not say 'that England would unflinchingly maintain the arrangement of the Treaty of Vienna', but on the contrary I especially guarded myself against being understood to make any declaration as to what England would or would not do in any case which has not yet happened.... I pointed out that the Treaty of Vienna of 1815 contains no guarantees except in regard to the portion of Saxony which was allotted to Prussia, and in regard to some of the arrangements connected with Switzerland.

Although on 2 June, as the war declared in the last week of March by King Charles Albert of Sardinia against Austria progressed, Palmerston warned the French that Her Majesty's government would 'seriously oppose' any territorial changes in the treaties of 1815 and 'would not be indifferent to a French army crossing the Alps and even simply occupying Savoy', his fundamental attitude remained unchanged. He wrote privately to King Leopold of the Belgians on 15 June:

> I cannot regret the expulsion of the Austrians from Italy.... Italy was to [Austria] the heel of Achilles, and not the shield of Ajax. The Alps are her natural barrier and her best defence. I should wish to see the whole of Northern Italy united into one kingdom, comprehending Piedmont, Genoa, Lombardy, Venice, Parma and Modena; and Bologna would, in that case, sooner or later unite itself either to that State or to Tuscany.

Such a northern Italian kingdom would have great merits, according to Palmerston: if such a kingdom came into being there would be, interposed between France and Austria, 'a neutral State strong enough to make itself respected, and sympathising in its habits and character neither with France nor with Austria'.

❖

For Lamartine the outbreak of war between Sardinia and Austria offered the French the opportunity to re-acquire Savoy and Nice. These provinces might come as territorial compensation demanded from a victorious Sardinia, or as the price of French aid to a Sardinia which might otherwise be defeated. As he told the Constituent Assembly's Committee on Foreign Affairs in July, 'in forming the Army of the Alps he had some view to finding a compensation for France for any changes on the other side of the Alps, in the possession of Nice and Savoy'. On 1 May Lamartine informed the British ambassador that France would not object to a settlement of the Italian question by which Sardinia acquired Lombardy, but in that case 'France might well expect some small compensation in the way of security, if so powerful a neighbour as Sardinia would then become was established upon her Eastern Frontier within forty miles of Lyons'. The treaties of 1815, he went on, 'had left so untenable a position for France on the side of Lyons ... that it could not be thought unreasonable, if, when the independence of Italy was assured with the free consent of France, she should expect some addition in that quarter which would not amount in all to half a million souls'. Lamartine further pressed this argument at secret sessions of the Executive Commission on 19 and 20 May, saying that, as a statesman, he:

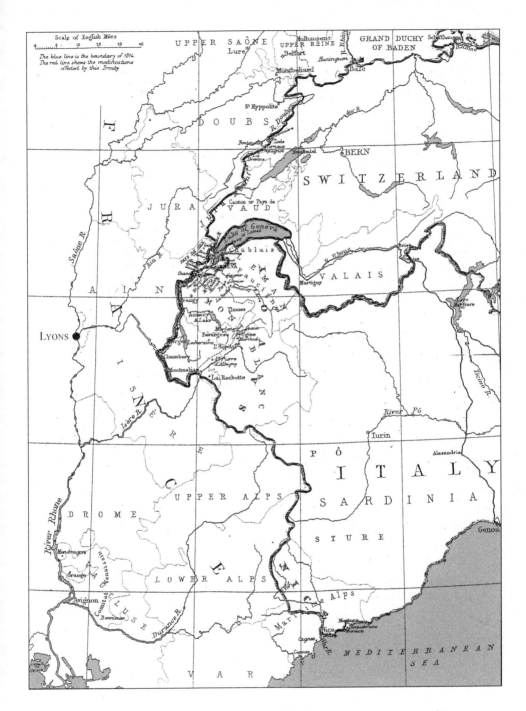

The Franco-Piedmontese frontier as established by the Second Peace of Paris, 20 November 1815.

had to foresee the results of the formation of a strong kingdom [in Northern Italy], allying itself later on with Austria against France, in control of all the passes of the Alps, the doors of France, as a result of the treaties of the second invasion [1815], and freeing them to enemy armies overflowing into France. It was therefore impossible to consent to the concentration of several Italian states, without claiming back what had even been left to us by the first treaties of 1814, a line of frontiers which would be defensive, not offensive, for the two nations, which would assure to each, by loyally established boundaries, complete security.

On 16 June the Minister of the Interior, Recurt, added his voice to that of Lamartine. Proposing the mobilisation of 300 battalions of the National Guard, Recurt stated that whilst the Executive Commission maintained the firm hope of preserving the peace, nevertheless, 'France could not possibly look on without precautions to redistributions of territories. She could not tolerate that an increase in power of her neighbours, without compensation for her, should reduce her own power.' On 19 June Bastide, who had been Foreign Minister since May but very much in the shadow of Lamartine, echoed his predecessor's sentiments of 1 May. He conceded to the British ambassador 'that it was true they might feel, when Piedmont [Sardinia] was no longer a second-rate Power but had monopolised the greatest part of Italy, that France could hardly view with the same unconcern her entrance into [France's] very centre within forty miles of Lyons'.

At the end of June Lamartine advised the Austrians to negotiate with Sardinia on the basis of an Austrian abandonment of Lombardy and Parma but retaining some control over Venetia through an 'independent' viceroyalty of an Austrian prince. Such an arrangement, he said, would allow the French Republic 'to rectify one of its frontiers broken after the Hundred Days and the second treaty of 1815, and he had been thinking of this for a long time'. Even after his fall from power, after June 1848, Lamartine continued to think along the same lines. He claimed to have warned Charles Albert that if Sardinia were victorious, if he were accepted as King of Italy, if Sardinia became a power of 26 million people instead of being a harmless nation of a few million subjects, the French would decide to strengthen against him their too thin and exposed border of the Alps from Lyons to Toulon. For:

this border, sufficient today, would not be strong enough to carry the weight of a nation of 26 million people ... which could eventually ally itself in turn to Austria against us.... Savoy and Nice will be remade in a French way. Any French government, be it monarchy or republic, which would let the House of Savoy conquer and govern 26 million close-knit and brave people without occupying the Alps would be a traitor to France.

At the very end of July 1848 the tide of battle in Italy turned, with the Austrian victory at Custozza. This, together with British promises to guarantee the integrity of Sardinian territory if the Austrians emerged victorious, and the Russian invasion of the Danubian principalities to deal with disorders that had broken out in Bucharest towards the end of June, placed the fate of areas other than Savoy and Nice higher on the international agenda. As early as 1 May Lamartine had hinted to Austria that she 'should find a compensation for the loss of her Italian states in the Danubian provinces'. Bastide took up this particular *baton* in mid-July. He suggested to the British that they and France support Austria 'in the east', so that Austria might become an effective barrier to Russian expansion there: 'it was for her dignity, perhaps for her preservation that, receiving whatever might be a fair compensation for her sacrifice of her Italian interests, she should ... concentrate her strength in that portion of her dominions, where she might, ere long, be so seriously threatened.' Towards the end of August Bastide declared that France wished to see Austria remain strong in Germany and in the east. The latter area was 'where the development of her riches and power call her':

> It is in this area that we wish her to move back her frontiers, rendering herself mistress of all the Lower Danube, stretching out her possessions as far as the Black Sea; and if ever the cabinet of Vienna wished to give this tendency to its policies, it could count upon the sincere and energetic support of France.

During the October uprising in Vienna Bastide tried again. Austria was wrong in trying to preserve her Italian provinces, he told the Austrian ambassador; Austria's 'true and most permanent interests were in the countries washed by the lower course of the Danube'. There, Austria was 'in rivalry with a Power whose ambitious views there are only too notorious'.

❖

The course of German history in the year 1848 added other possibilities to those already mentioned. Initially the French welcomed the March revolution in Berlin, for one of the first concessions granted by the King of Prussia was a promise to reconstruct a new Polish state out of Prussia's Polish possessions. This not only alienated Russia, and broke the alliance of the three northern powers; it also presented the ultimate prospect, much favoured by Talleyrand at Vienna in 1814–15, of a fully resuscitated Poland, which might form, as in previous centuries before the partitions of the later eighteenth century, a barrier against Russia as well as a potential ally to France, as also in the past. The French government hastened to assure the Prussians that if Russia attacked them and invaded their territory over any seizure of Posen (now Poznań), France would give them armed support.

As the policies devised by the Frankfurt Parliament were elaborated and put into practice, however, French perceptions changed. As was the case in regard to the Italian question, the French became much more defensive, much more concerned about the adverse impact on themselves that certain developments would have. At the end of July Bastide wrote that whilst German unity might well result in a democratisation of Germany,

> Unity will also make this people of 40 million souls a redoutable Power for Germany's neighbours, which is not the case today; and, therefore, I do not see it as being in our interest to desire this unity and even less to encourage it. The invading spirit of Germany is already not too reassuring.

A week later, on 5 August, he went into more detail:

> German unity is an excellent principle as long as it remains within the limits of democratic fraternity among the different peoples who compose the great Germanic family. However, if under the pretext of unity and fraternity, they wish to absorb Schleswig, which is Danish, Limbourg, which is Dutch, Lombardy and Venice, which are Italian, Poznań, which is Polish, and perhaps Alsace and Lorraine, German unity becomes a thing which must be combatted. Therefore, since this tendency is manifest, it is necessary, from now on, to encourage Prussia, Bavaria, and the other states to conserve their independence and their nationality.

The invasions to which he referred had completely disabused Bastide about 'the principle of nationalities'. The feeling of German nationality which promoted German unity encroached upon the rights of France's allies, and also menaced France herself 'in a part of her territory'. There was a clear parallel to be drawn between Schleswig – Holstein and Alsace – Lorraine. What was most alarming was the German pretension that any land inhabited by Germans, and any land in which the German language was spoken, belonged to Germany. If what Bastide described as 'the unitarians of Frankfurt' had their way, and unity on the basis of race and language was realised, France might not only lose Alsace and Lorraine, but have to face 'a single state of 45 million people at the very doorstep of France'. Accordingly, French policy reverted to its more traditional line of promoting German disunity. In effect, the French had come to prefer the principle of legitimacy to that of nationalism, and the maintenance of the status quo to revisionism.

Ironically enough, given the position taken up by the French in March, they had come round to share the Russian viewpoint. Towards the end of August the Russian Chancellor, Nesselrode, had warned them 'of the appearance in the middle of Europe of a compact and solid Power of 45 million men', something which could result in the 'violation of all equilibrium' in Europe.

❖

The events of the year 1848, a year in which revolutions challenged the existing regimes and forms of political authority and orthodoxy in several of the Great Powers – in France, Austria and Prussia – presented opportunities, raised hopes, and inspired fears. From the events of that year different lessons were learned by different individuals. Different problems were identified and perceived; different policies were devised and suggested to solve and counter them. For the French political commentator and writer Alexis de Tocqueville the lesson was that Germany must be unified; only then could western Europe, by means of an alliance between France and a united Germany, defend itself against the threat posed by Russia. As de Tocqueville wrote in his *Mémoires*:

> It is an ancient tradition of [French] diplomacy that one has to see that Germany remains divided between a great number of independent powers; and that was evident in fact when behind Germany nothing existed except Poland and a half-barbarian Russia; but is this still the case in our day? The answer which one has to give to this question depends on the answer which one has to give to another one: which is in our day what danger does Russia imply for the independence of Europe? I happen to think that our occident is threatened to fall, sooner or later, under the yoke or at least under the direct and irrestistible influence of the tsars, and I believe that our first interest is to favour the union of all the Germanic races in order to oppose this menace. The state of the world is new; we have yet to change our old principles and not to fear to fortify our neighbours so that they are in a position to push back one day, together with us, the common enemy.

For Tsar Nicholas I of Russia, on the other hand, the lesson was the reverse: the unification of Germany would endanger Europe; if it were to come about, France and Russia would have to combine their forces in order to meet and withstand the German menace. As he told a French diplomat in St Petersburg:

> If the unity of Germany, which you don't desire any more than we do, will come about, it will need a man to handle it even better than Napoleon did, and if this man should falter, this mass in arms would become threatening, and this would be your affair and ours.

5

RESPONSIBILITIES:
THE CRIMEAN WAR

J.A.S. Grenville, in *Europe Reshaped 1848–1878* (London, 1976), maintained (page 199) that there was 'little point in trying to divide the blame in some proportional way between those responsible for the [Crimean] war'. The present writer is inclined to differ, and to follow, on this occasion, the example set by H.W.V. Temperley in Appendix V of his book *England and the Near East: The Crimea* (London, 1936).

❖

In J.B.Conacher, *The Aberdeen Coalition 1852–1855: A Study in Mid-Nineteenth-Century Party Politics* (Cambridge, 1968), there is a detailed chronology, or calendar, of diplomatic developments between January 1853 and April 1854 (Appendix E, pages 564–66). From this and other calendars, a number of things can be discerned. Firstly, Russian demands on the Ottoman government, delivered in the course of the Menshikov mission, which arrived in Constantinople on 2 March 1853 and left on 22 May. Secondly, further Russian pressure at the end of May 1853 in the shape of an ultimatum to the Ottoman government regarding the principalities of Moldavia and Wallachia, and Russia's occupation of those principalities, which began on 2 July. Thirdly, the meeting of a conference at Vienna from 24 July to 20 September, and the efforts it made to prevent the crisis from escalating. Fourthly, the role of the Ottoman government: its determined opposition not only to the initial Russian demands but also to all attempts at compromise devised subsequently – its rejection of the Vienna Note, for instance, on 20 August, and of British and Austrian efforts on 5 and 24 November. Fifthly, the Ottoman Empire's decision for war with Russia at the turn of September into October 1853, and its opening of hostilities with Russia on 23 October. Sixthly, a further five months of negotiations between the Great Powers, together with movements, especially of the British and French fleets, before Britain and France declared war on Russia on 27 and 28 March 1854.

Clearly the Crimean War took a long time to break out. Even the conversion of the Russo-Turkish war, which existed from October 1853, into the Crimean War, took half a year. In the study of crises which end in war the proposition is sometimes put forward that efforts to establish what might be called the decisive acts ought to be concentrated upon the last days of peace. For surely the acts or decisions which made a peaceful outcome impossible are likely to be found towards the end of a war-in-sight crisis, especially a long drawn-out one, rather than towards the beginning? In the case of the outbreak of the Crimean War, however, it is as well not to be quite so categorical. It will be maintained here that the diplomatic calendar that has been drawn upon does not go back far enough; that it should go back to July 1852, perhaps even to May of that year. It will also be maintained that this and other diplomatic calendars are not as comprehensive and detailed as they should be.

To take the latter point, about the comprehensive nature of the diplomatic calendar, first. Attention should be paid to the entries for 13 and 14 June 1853: 'British fleet arrives at Besika Bay'; 'French fleet joins British at Besika Bay'. Now where do these entries, or rather these fleet movements, come from? Why the change from the position of 19 and 20 March, when the French acted alone in sending a fleet from Toulon to the Aegean, and the British did not accompany them? The question is of importance, for there is no denying that the later, joint, Anglo-French fleet movements encouraged the Ottoman government to resist the diplomatic pressure being exerted on her by Russia, and to contemplate risking war with that country. The crucial period is not from 19/20 March to 13/14 June. It is from 19/20 March to 23 March 1853, and it involves a country, namely Belgium, which does not appear on any diplomatic calendar. On 23 February the French Foreign Minister, Drouyn de Lhuys, told a British diplomat in Paris that if Russia, Austria and Prussia, as a result of Russo-Austrian designs on the Ottoman Empire, should secure territorial gains, France would not remain content with what she had. Two weeks later, on 9 March, Drouyn told the British ambassador that France had as good a right to enter Belgium because she had complaints about the attitude towards her of the Belgian government, as had Austria to enter Switzerland, which it was rumoured that Austria might do. On 12 March Monsieur His de Butenval took up his duties as the new French minister to Belgium. On 22 March, the day Admiral Hamelin's fleet left Toulon for the eastern Mediterranean (having been ordered to get ready to do so on 20 March), de Butenval made it clear to the Belgian Foreign Minister that the outbreak of war in the East, between Russia and the Ottoman Empire, would be the signal for the beginning of hostilities between France and Belgium. de Butenval read out a despatch from Drouyn to the following effect: previously the Great Powers had concerted together in matters affecting the Eastern Question; now, a different system was in operation, as Russia and Austria seemed determined to act alone. So, according to Drouyn:

> France is compelled to look to her own interests, and to declare that upon the slightest infraction of existing treaties in the east, or in the event of a single Russian soldier crossing the Turkish frontier, France will consider herself released from every obligation imposed upon her by the treaties of 1815, and free in all respects to act as she thinks fit.

The Belgian government immediately communicated this threat to the British, and to all the other states which in 1839 had guaranteed their independence and integrity, and asked for protection. The British Foreign Secretary, Lord Clarendon, recommended in his reply that the Belgians take every precautionary step, including placing their main fortresses in a state of readiness, with stores and provisions enough to last until aid from England and her allies arrived. On the following day, 23 March 1853, Clarendon terminated the conversations initiated by the Tsar in January regarding the future of the Ottoman Empire. His stated reason for so doing was that complications in the east would reopen treaties binding western Europe. As he put it, the main object of Her Majesty's Government was the preservation of peace, and 'they desire to uphold the Turkish Empire, from their conviction that no question can be agitated in the east without becoming a source of discord in the west, and that every great question will assume a revolutionary character, and embrace a revision of the entire social system'. A European Congress on the Ottoman Empire was ruled out, again as Clarendon put it, because it would mean:

> the certainty that the treaties of 1815 must be open to revision, when France might be prepared to risk the chances of a European war to get rid of the obligations which she considers injurious to her national honour, and which having been imposed by victorious enemies, are a source of constant irritation to her.

This was the turning point.

Although the French had already achieved their objective, namely the splitting away of Great Britain from Russia, they maintained their pressure. An article in the French ministerial journal, *Le Pays*, stated on 24 March that 'if Russia, in contempt of treaties, can virtually seize Constantinople, other Powers might also invade any other weaker State which might be near them.... The first step towards this dismemberment of Turkey inevitably would lead to the remodelling of the whole map of Europe.' The British ambassador in Paris, Lord Cowley, reported on 26 March that Napoleon III and his ministers had several times made it clear that they regarded the treaties of 1815 as binding on the east as well as on the west, and that if Russia and Austria took something in the east, they (the French) would feel justified in taking something in the west. By this time, in fact on 25 March, Clarendon had already told the French ambassador in London, Walewski, that Great Britain would not be taking the part of Russia in opposition to France; the French government, said Clarendon, should know that 'it always has been and will be the policy of this country to maintain the Ottoman Empire'.

Official and public unity between France and Britain came at the end of May when joint orders were issued to advance their Mediterranean squadrons to the region of the Dardanelles, where they arrived on 13 and 14 June. On 25 June, his job there well and truly done, de Butenval was transferred from Brussels.

❖

To return from the question of the comprehensiveness of the diplomatic calendar to that of whether a better starting date might be July 1852, or even May 1852. In May 1852 a French warship, *Charlemagne*, was sent throught the Dardanelles to Constantinople, a violation of the Straits Convention of 1841. In July 1852 a French naval squadron was sent to Tripoli and proceeded to threaten to bombard the coast of Syria. At the same time, the French overnment raised the question of the guardianship of the keys to the Holy Places of Palestine. These moves on the part of the French, taken as a whole, constituted a championing of the Sultan of Turkey against the Tsar of Russia, and a challenge to the existing relationship between Russia and the Ottoman Empire. A note given by the Russian Foreign Minister, Nesselrode, to the British ambassador in St Petersburg, Sir Hamilton Seymour, dated 5 March 1853, recounts some of the Russian grievances which French actions had produced. It also makes clear what, from the Russian point of view, was the point of the Anglo-Russian conversations on the future of the Ottoman Empire which the British had raised no objections to throughout January, February and the first three weeks of March 1853. This *Note Verbale* began by maintaining that, in his conversations with the British ambassador, the Tsar was not thinking of proposing, in order to cover the eventuality of the fall of the Ottoman Empire, any plan by which Russia and England would dispose of it in advance. He had no thought of 'a ready-made system', 'still less a formal transaction to be concluded between the two cabinets'. The object of the exercise was rather to ascertain, so far as both powers were concerned, 'less what was wanted *than what was not wanted*; what would be contrary to English interests; what would be contrary to Russian interests; so that, if the case arose, each side could avoid actions *which contradicted those of the other*'. It was intended to be 'a simple exchange of opinions', not involving either schemes of partition or an agreement to be forced upon the other Powers. The *Note Verbale* continued:

> In presence of the uncertainty and weakness of the present state of affairs in Turkey, the English Cabinet expresses the desire that the greatest patience should be exercised towards the Porte. The Emperor is not conscious of ever having acted otherwise. The English Cabinet itself agrees on this.... But so that the Emperor should be able to continue to agree to this policy of patience – to abstain from all demonstrations, from peremptory language – it is necessary that this system be followed simultaneously by all the Powers. France has adopted a different one. It is through threats that she has obtained, against the letter of the treaties, the admission of a warship into the Dardanelles. It is at the mouth of cannon that she has twice put forward claims and demands for compensation at Tripoli, then at Constantinople. Again it is by intimidation that, in the contest over the Holy Places, she has brought about the annulment of the firman and of solemn promises which the Sultan had given the Emperor.

The *Note* regretted the silence of England in the face of 'these acts of overweening power', a silence which had resulted in the Porte's drawing the conclusion that it was only from France that she had everything to hope and fear, and could evade with impunity the claims of Russia and Austria. This in turn had brought Russia and Austria, against their will, to act by intimidation. The Russians begged Britain to exert herself to make the Ottoman Empire see reason:

> In place of uniting with France against the just claims of Russia, let her take care not to support or even to appear to support the resistance of the Ottoman Government. Let her be the first to invite the latter, as she herself thinks is essential, to treat its Christian subjects with more fairness and humanity. This will be the surest way of sparing the Emperor the obligation of exerting in Turkey those traditional rights of protection which he uses only unwillingly, and to postpone indefinitely the crisis which the Emperor and Her Majesty the Queen are equally anxious to guard against.

Only a few days before this was written, and whilst Menshikov was packing his bags for *his* mission of intimidation to Constantinople, Nicholas I had made some notes on Russian policy in the Near East. It is striking that, in considering how to secure the Russian objective, which was, basically, the exclusion of French influence from the area and the re-establishment of a sort of Russo-Austrian-British condominium, as in 1840, the Tsar expected no opposition from Great Britain, even if Russia launched a surprise attack on Constantinople. When considering the probable results of that particular action, he listed them as follows:

1. Turkey will give way.
2. She will not give way; destruction of Constantinople.
3. The defeated Turkish army retreats towards Gallipoli or Enos.
4. Occupation of Dardanelles.
5. The French send a fleet and an expeditionary Force. Conflicts with them.

No objection or opposition at all was expected from the British. Nicholas I ended his notes with a section dealing with the replacement of the Ottoman Empire. Under the sub-heading 'the least bad of all bad solutions', he continued:

(a) The Principalities and Bulgaria as far as Kistendj to Russia.
(b) Serbia and Bulgaria independent.
(c) coasts of Archipelago and Adriatic to Austria.
(d) Egypt to England; perhaps Cyprus and Rhodes.
(e) Crete to France.
(f) Islands of Archipelago to Greece.
(g) Constantinople a free city – Bosporus Russian garrison, Dardanelles Austrian garrison.
(h) complete freedom of trade.
(i) The Turkish Empire in Asia Minor.

It is as well to repeat that, for Nicholas I, this scheme for 'replacing' the Ottoman Empire was 'the least bad of all bad solutions'. It was not the most desirable outcome for Russia. The most desirable outcome for Russia was simply the re-establishment of Ottoman deference towards her. As the Tsar stated at the outset of his speculative notes: '1. Reparation. 2. Guarantees for the future. 3. Conservation of the position as it used to be.'

❖

What the French wanted out of the crisis had already been achieved by 23 March 1853 – the splitting apart of Russia and Great Britain. The French did not want, and were not prepared for, war. Indeed in February 1853 Napoleon III ordered reductions, not increases, in the French armed forces. Subsequently, the French did make certain efforts to resolve the crisis on a diplomatic plane. These efforts included a last-minute appeal from Napoleon III to Nicholas I. Even so, because she set the ball rolling by endeavouring to replace Russia in the affections of the Ottoman Empire, and because she successfully blackmailed Great Britain into becoming her accomplice in this, perhaps France was the power most responsible for the Crimean War.

Or perhaps Britain was. For it was the coalition government of Lord Aberdeen, an administration riven with faction and one that found it very difficult to arrive at unanimity, that succumbed to the French threat of 22 March 1853 to link the Eastern Question with the question of western Europe, and to rectify their northern frontiers at the expense of, and in contravention of, the treaties of 1815. This French *coup*, coming at a time when Nicholas I was not giving clear and unequivocal answers to questions about the ultimate fate and disposition of Constantinople and the Straits in his conversations with the British ambassador, led to a complete reversal of what British policy had been since 1844 at least. Perhaps afraid to ask Russia for help as regards Belgium because Russia might on this occasion have asked in return to determine even more fully what happened to Constantinople and the Straits, the British changed sides. This change of sides made possible everything that followed. In effect, this particular British administration turned out to be prepared to sacrifice its good relations with Russia (which had recently extended to Persian questions also) in order to keep France out of Belgium and from revising the Vienna settlement of 1815. For the sake of a quiet life and the maintenance of the status quo in the west of Europe it was prepared to go to war in the east of Europe. From late March 1853 the British government said that they would be fighting, if it came to war, for the integrity and independence of the Ottoman Empire, and so, in the end, they were. Fundamentally, however, and perversely, they were fighting against the power most capable of upholding the Vienna settlement, Russia (as demonstrated as recently as 1850), in order to preserve that settlement from a French challenge which the British, unaided, could not hope to repulse. Anglo-Russian relations did not recover until 1906–07, and not entirely even then.

It is no easy matter to allocate responsibility between the Ottoman Empire, Russia, France and Great Britain for the war that was fought mainly in the Crimea. The effort to do so, however, remains a valid one.

6

REDRAWING THE MAP: NAPOLEON III, 1849–66

The French word *remanier* means to 'recast', to 'redraw'. The concept of redrawing the map of Europe – of Europe as a whole, not just western Europe – was at the heart of Napoleon III's approach to foreign policy. In this respect he was absolutely consistent.

What would the map of Europe, as recast by Napoleon II, have looked like? Several versions exist. One, dated 1859/60, envisaged the following: Sardinia would have Venetia, Parma, Modena, the Romagna; there would be an enlarged Papal State at the expense of the King of Naples, who would be compensated with the regency of Tunis; the Duchess of Parma would receive Sicily; Prussia would absorb Hanover, Mecklenburg, Hesse, Waldeck, Anhalt and Lippe, and would cede the left bank of the Rhine to Belgium or Holland; Austria would give up Venetia to Sardinia, and Galicia to Russia, receiving in return Serbia, Bosnia, and Egypt; the King of Hanover would acquire Rumelia and the title King of Constantinople; the Duke of Mecklenburg would rule Bulgaria, Moldavia, and Wallachia; Great Britain would receive Cyprus and the valley of the Euphrates.

Another version, from May 1861, envisaged the reconstitution of an independent Poland, with the Saxon dynasty on the throne; Prussia would be compensated by extending its boundaries up to the frontier of Bohemia; Russia would get sovereignty over the shores of the Black Sea and an unassailable position in the Dardanelles; Austrian compensation for releasing Galicia back to Poland would be her annexation of the eastern shores of the Adriatic; Austria would give up Venetia but retain influence in Germany.

Yet another, two years later in 1863, also envisaged a reconstituted Poland under the King of Saxony, who would cede Saxony to Prussia; Prussia would give up Poznań to Poland, Silesia to Austria, the left bank of the Rhine to France, and receive Saxony, Hanover and the duchies north of the river Main; Austria would cede Venetia to Sardinia, a part of Galicia to Poland, and take in return a new frontier across Serbia along the Adriatic, plus Silesia and land south of the river Main in Germany;

France would cede nothing, but would acquire the left bank of the Rhine with the exception of Belgium out of deference to Britain; Sardinia would have Lombardy, Venetia, Tuscany, Parma, Piacenza, Bologna, Ferrara; Sardinia would restore the kingdom of the Two Sicilies to the King of Naples; the Ottoman Empire would be abolished – its Asiatic possessions would go to Russia, the line of the Adriatic to Austria, and Thessaly, Albania and Constantinople to Greece; the dispossessed kings and princes of Europe would go to the Americas, 'to civilise and monarchise the American republics, which would all follow the example of Mexico'.

The establishment of confederations would be a large element in this recasting. Napoleon III had a passion for confederation. He had schemes for a Slavonic principality consisting of Serbia, Montenegro, Herce-govina, and part of Bosnia, for instance, and for a Danubian confederation of Hungarian and Slavic peoples. He also had plans for a Scandinavian union. At one point in 1861 Gortachov, the Russian Chancellor, showed Bismarck a 'future map of Europe' from a French source in which the continent was divided into Iberian, Gallic, Italian, Greek and German confederations.

It is worth remarking that the above plans do reveal a readiness, on the part of Napoleon III, and well before 1866, to see a considerable increase in the power and influence of Prussia. They also reveal a distinct propensity to utilise, for the purposes of compensation and rearrangement, the lands of the Ottoman Empire, the power for whose independence the French had fought between 1854 and 1856, and whose integrity and independence the French had guaranteed in April 1856, both in the Peace of Paris and in a separate Triple Treaty with Great Britain and Austria.

During the Crimean War Napoleon III had suggested that Ottoman territory could be used to enlist allies against Russia. In 1853, even before the war broke out, he had confided to his ambasador in Constantinople: 'The idea of establishing Christianity where infidelity now exists has always had a charm for me – I could not regret such a change.' In March 1856 he stated that the Ottoman Empire could not last long, that 'the subject was constantly in my thoughts'. Also in 1856, he stated that he wished 'to see the coast of the Mediterranean in the hands of Christians alone', thus making the Mediterranean not 'un lac français' but 'un lac européen'. As it was, 'These were all magnificent countries rendered useless to humanity and civilisation by their abominable governments'.

Having raised in 1853–54 the possibility of an exchange by Austria of Lombardy for the Danubian principalities, in 1856 Napoleon III suggested a scheme by which the Duke of Modena and the Duchess of Parma would give up their duchies to Sardinia and succeed to the thrones of Wallachia and Moldavia. At the end of 1859, Napoleon III began urging Austria to take those principalities, or Egypt, or the Adriatic coast, as compensation for granting Venetia autonomy within an Italian confederation. Early in 1861, he thought Italy might purchase Venetia from Austria and Austria use the money to buy Bosnia and Hercegovina from the Ottoman Empire. It was more than once flatly asserted by French ministers and diplomatists that it was Napoleon III's firm intention, when circumstances permitted, 'to settle the Italian question in the East'.

❖

What were the motives that lay behind Napoleon III's insistence on a redrawing of the map of the whole of Europe? One motive was the maintenance of European peace through the pre-emptive solution of problems which if left to develop might well produce war between the Great Powers. This consideration goes back to the very beginning, to March 1849, when Louis Napoleon, as he then was, told the British ambassador to Paris: 'From the Sound [the Denmark Straits] to the Dardanelles, from Wallachia to Sicily and especially in the very heart and centre of Europe there were questions which were every day assuming a more menacing character.' Louis Napoleon claimed to foresee, and certainly forecast, that, if measures were not taken, cases for war might occur when least expected. As he put it to the British Foreign Secretary, Lord Malmesbury, again in 1849: 'the danger to Europe lay in the absolute necessity of modifying the treaties of 1815, which should be done before a war broke out'. As he continued to put it in 1866, in order to find solutions to the problems threatening to bring on war, he felt it necessary to involve all parties openly, to disengage them from the veil of diplomacy which covered them, and to give serious consideration to the legitimate wishes of sovereigns and peoples. As Palmerston recognised at the end of 1863, Napoleon III's idea was that the treaties of 1815 be examined article by article, that whatever required to be removed be removed, and the remainder be established as the 'Treaty of 1863–64'. Napoleon III praised the treaties of 1815, and their 'salutory result' – forty years of peace. He maintained that the bringing of them up to date, for by the middle of the century they were 'obsolete' in some respects, and therefore 'invalid', and because the makers of those treaties had not taken into account the 'wishes and aspirations of the people', 'the voice of nations', would ensure another such long period of peace.

An associated motive was to make France itself more defensible against invasion. Napoleon III said in November 1859 that the makers of the treaties of 1815 'well understood that to avoid a new expansion of France it was necessary to facilitate a future invasion by rolling back her frontiers far enough to allow the crossing of the Alps and of the Rhine without danger; that one had to be able to enter by way of Savoy and Luxembourg'. If he could remove 'what is dangerous to France' in those treaties, he could then dispense with the large army of 600,000 men which they forced him, he said, to maintain. 'The day when I shall have Savoy and Nice in the south and sufficient fortresses in the north, my mission will be accomplished', he said. He insisted that he had no wish to emulate his great-uncle, the first Napoleon: 'I have no ambitious views like the first Emperor.' For himself, 'it would not be a question of the Rhine frontier', rather merely 'a better boundary line in the direction of Metz, for example, since the present line was obviously drawn with hostile intent towards France'. After acquiring Savoy and Nice, he told the Belgian minister:

> It is necessary that France have a system of frontiers which will defend themselves. The acquisition of Savoy and Nice now covers her on the Italian side; the neutrality of Belgium guarantees her against an aggression coming from the North. It is, then, only from Mayence [Mainz] to Cologne that rectifications are indispensable.

It was a matter of '*small* rectifications', 'bits [*pouces*] of land only' – 'several square miles'. *Not* Mainz, *not* Cologne, for, as Napoleon III stated, 'If France were to go to Mayence, she would require also to go to Coblenz, and from thence to Cologne, and if once at Cologne she would be obliged to go to the Zuyder Zee, which would be committing over again the faults of the First Empire.'

Similarly, the confederations envisaged by Napoleon III also increased the defensibility of France. They would pose less of a threat to her than unitary governments would pose. Only in the cases of Poland, and to a lesser extent the Danubian principalities, was the national principle, and unitary government, to be allowed full rein. The national principle was certainly not supposed to apply in Italy, an end to which state Napoleon III was contemplating as early in its existence as 1861, when he suggested a tripartite solution there instead of what Garibaldi and the 1,000 had recently brought into being.

Napoleon III did appreciate, of course, that as a result of the changes he envisaged, French influence would grow. As he put it, 'our own influence will increase immensely.... The people who are our neighbours

THE RHINE FRONTIER

French frontier 1814 · · · · · ·
French frontier 1815 ——————
French frontier 1871 — — — —
Federal fortresses   Mainz

Miles
40   20   0   40   80

Zuider
See

HOLLAND

Rhine

BELGIUM

PRUSSIA

Liège

Aachen

Cologne

Koblenz

Moselle

Mainz

HESSE

LUXEMBOURG

Luxembourg

BAVARIA

Landau

Metz

Rastatt

BADEN

Strasbourg

FRANCE

Rhine

Lake Constance

on the Rhine, in Switzerland, in Belgium, will beg for our alliance – either through fear or sympathy.' He might have added 'Poland', and he might have added 'through gratitude'. The point is that he was not thinking of conquests as such, and that the increased influence that would accrue to France would be essentially local. It would not amount to hegemony, or to empire.

❖

How – through what mechanism and by what means – was the redrawing of the map of Europe to be achieved? In the thinking of Napoleon III, it was to be achieved, or realised, through the holding of a congress of the Great Powers of Europe. He proposed such a congress in 1856, in 1859, in 1863, in 1866, and in 1867. His alliances, which baffled both contemporaries and subsequent generations of historians, were geared to bringing about, or to advancing, this gathering, through which in turn to advance the cause of *remaniement*. Between 1853 and 1857 he cultivated Great Britain. From 1857 to 1863 he cultivated Great Britain and Russia. In the early 1860s, up to 1863, he cultivated Austria. Between 1864 and 1866 he cultivated Prussia. These different and overlapping alliances were means to an end. The consistent purpose of them was to make the Concert of Europe function, to bring the powers together to discuss and solve the most urgent problems facing them, and therefore Europe as a whole, and then to keep the powers together thereafter to regulate the new arrangements made.

Napoleon III returned again and again to the judgement that, although the Congress of Vienna had humbled France, it had given Europe forty years of peace. 'A new congress', he said, 'could produce like results.' What might come to pass, indeed, might be a new congress system, not necessarily based in Paris, but for which the French would, and deservedly, take the credit, for they would have set it in motion, and encouraged Europe to settle disputes in this way, short of wars that might otherwise follow. As a result, not only might France 'hold her own in the Councils of Europe', and be treated as an equal, which since 1815 had been her objective; but she might also assume a sort of *moral* ascendancy, or hegemony, over the continent. Moreover, as France would have helped to create the new arrangements and dispositions, she would be able to embrace and accept them as she had never been able to embrace and accept the dispositions of 1815 which had been *imposed* upon her.

❖

Napoleon III's policy, of redrawing the map of Europe through the mechanism of a congress, was stymied and brought to nothing by the opposition and suspicion of the other powers – Great Britain, Austria, Russia and Prussia. In March 1849 Palmerston wrote:

> This notion of a European Congress to settle all pending matters and to modify the Treaty of Vienna so as to adapt it to the interests and necessities of the present time sounds well enough to the ear, but would be difficult and somewhat dangerous in its execution.... On the whole, therefore, I should be for giving a civil but declining answer, pointing out the many difficulties which would arise in such a course.

In March 1856 Queen Victoria took it upon herself to caution Palmerston, now Prime Minister. She stated: 'We have every interest *not* to bring about a European Congress *pour la révision des traités*, which many people suspect the Emperor wishes to turn the present Conference [at Paris] into.' Clarendon, Palmerston's Foreign Secretary, reassured the Queen in the following month, having dissuaded Napoleon III from adding to the peacemaking at the end of the Crimean War by seeking a European Congress for 'the annulling of treaties that had become obsolete' and for a general *remaniement*. As Clarendon put it to the Emperor:

> That meant the Rhine for France which Prussia would not consent to, the reconstitution of Poland which Russia would not hear of, the expulsion of the Austrians from Italy to which they would never agree, the reform of the Diet [of the German Confederation] which Austria would require to have more subservient to her own interests and the carving out of the minor German states by way of compensation to Austria and Prussia.

Clarendon had begged Napoleon III 'to consider what interests and passions and hopes and fears would be excited by such a Congress and the extreme difficulty of carrying out any decisions it might come to except by coercion which might lead to general war.' To Palmerston Clarendon wrote:

> I see that the idea of a European Congress is germinating in the Emperor's mind, and with it the *arrondissement* [rounding-off] of the French frontier, the abolition of obsolete Treaties, and other such *remaniements* as may be necessary. I improvised a longish catalogue of dangers and difficulties that such a Congress would entail, unless its decisions were unanimous, which was not probable.

Queen Victoria's consort, Prince Albert, recounted similar experiences of Napoleon III in 1859. To the latter's attempts to persuade him that there was only one means of preventing the complications he foresaw, and that was that England and France should come to a previous understanding 'as to the reconstruction of the map of Europe', Prince Albert invariably replied:

> We in England maintained that there are no better means of bringing about the complications feared, than to tie one's hands against eventualities of the future, since by so doing the party who has an interest in change can morally compel the other to co-operate. To play such a part no British statesman would either now or at any future time consent.'

When Napoleon III said that he regretted 'these mistaken English theories' Albert, who was of course German, as was his wife, cut short the discussion, remarking that Napoleon III 'would find himself convinced to his cost of the correctness of our [English] principle'.

The Austrians were always adamantly opposed to Napoleon III's suggestions. As Count Buol, Austrian Foreign Minister at the time, put it in 1858:

> There were certain indications that France was desirous of submitting other questions which did not devolve from the Treaty of Paris [of 1856], and to this he must give his decided opposition.... He had an insuperable objection to the establishment of a permanent Conference at Paris, and to acknowledge a position to which France appeared to lay claim – of constituting herself the 'arbiter or great tribunal of Europe'.

The Austrians were to reject congresses in 1859–60 and again in 1865–66. So were the Prussians. The Russians, having got wind of Napoleon III's idea of exchanging the Danubian principalities for Venetia, declared in 1860 that nothing would induce them to consent. Similarly, in 1863, it was the intransigence of Gortachov that vitiated in advance Napoleon III's proposed appeal to the treaties of 1815 in the case of Poland. The former members of the Quadruple Alliance were, in effect, leagued together against French revisionism, long after the destruction of the Quadruple Alliance itself by the outbreak of the Crimean War, and against such a *de facto* combination the French were unable to prevail.

7

RESPONSIBILITIES:
THE FRANCO-PRUSSIAN WAR

On the eve of the Austro-Prussian war, Napoleon III hoped that it would lead to a tripartite Germany, with the hegemony of Prussia established in north Germany, a confederation of the south German states, and a still-powerful Austria. Best of all would be that such an outcome, including some modest but tangible gain for France in the shape of the restoration of the boundaries of 1814, should be confirmed by the Concert of Europe through the holding of a congress. In June 1866 he declared emphatically to the British ambassador that he would never permit 'the formation of a Great German Power uniting under one sceptre a population of 70 millions'. Although both before and after the battle of Sadowa, which took place on 3 July and effectively ended the war, Bismarck refused to entertain the idea of a congress, he made it clear to the French, by 11 July, that Prussia would halt at the river Main and offer reasonable terms of peace to Austria. The immediate creation of a German power of 70 million was not, therefore, an immediate problem, and Napoleon III left the conduct of French policy in the hands of Drouyn de Lhuys and retired to Vichy to recuperate from ill-health. In the absence of the Emperor the French Foreign Ministry demanded at Berlin that France receive the boundaries of 1814 as well as the Bavarian and Hessian territories on the left bank of the Rhine, and that Prussian troops be withdrawn from garrisoning the fortress of Luxembourg. On returning to Paris, Napoleon III repudiated his Foreign Minister, whose demands had been rejected immediately by Bismarck, and declared that the true interest of France lay 'not in a meagre increase of territory but in helping Germany to establish herself in a manner most favourable to our interests and to those of Europe'. The resignation of Drouyn de Lhuys was accepted on 20 August.

Napoleon III went on to authorise his ambassador in Berlin, Benedetti, to negotiate a *modus vivendi* which would, in effect, create a Franco-Prussian alliance. By 23 August a treaty had been drafted. In Article I Napoleon III recognised the acquisitions made by Prussia in the war against Austria and her allies within the former German

Confederation, and committed himself to support the preservation of the new North German Confederation. In article II the King of Prussia promised to help France to acquire Luxembourg. In Article III Napoleon III agreed not to oppose a federal union of the North German Confederation with the south German states (with the exception of Austria), a union which might be based on a common parliament whilst respecting the sovereignty of the latter states. In Article IV the King of Prussia agreed to give armed support to France, should she decide to conquer Belgium, against any power which, in this event, declared war upon France. Article V declared the above arrangements to constitute an offensive and defensive alliance. Although this treaty, a copy of which Benedetti gave to Bismarck on 29 August, was never ratified, the episode as a whole marked a high point in Franco-Prussian relations, suggesting as it did that France could even envisage with equanimity a united, albeit federal, Germany, especially if France received compensation in the form of Luxembourg and Belgium.

Napoleon III's equanimity lasted until the spring of the following year. Then, on 19 March 1867, Bismarck released the details of defensive treaties made between Prussia and Baden, Bavaria, and Württemburg. Bismarck followed up this move, which coincided with the agreement of the King of Holland (who was also Grand Duke of Luxembourg) to sell the duchy to France – something towards which both France and Prussia had hitherto been working – with an announcement in the Reichstag on 1 April that Prussia could no longer support this transaction because of the hostility of German public feeling towards it. In the course of the ensuing crisis over the fate of the Grand Duchy of Luxembourg, Bismarck threatened to mobilise the Prussian army. In June, he announced another step towards German political union in a remodelling of the Zollverein which admitted deputies from the south German states to the North German parliament.

These developments helped promote a change in the outlook of Napoleon III both as regards the concept of the concert of Europe and as regards the best solution, from the point of view of French interests, of the German problem. This change was in the nature of a reversion to the position he had maintained before the Austro-Prussian war. In practical terms, it became a bid to maintain the status quo. The possibility of an Austro-French alliance for the preservation of the status quo was brought up by Napoleon III at a meeting with Franz Josef at Salzburg in August 1867. In November Napoleon III declared: 'We must openly accept the changes that have come about on the other side of the Rhine, and proclaim that as long as our interests and our dignity shall not be threatened, we shall not interfere in those changes which are wrought by

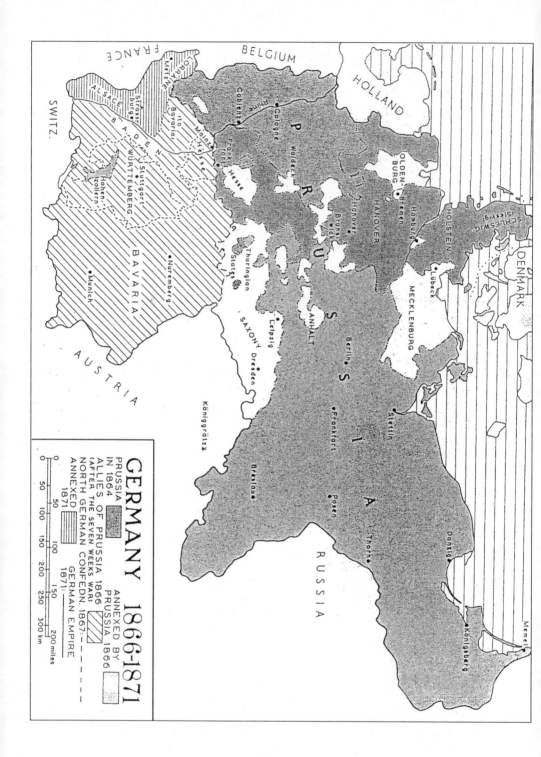

GERMANY 1866-1871

PRUSSIA IN 1864

ANNEXED BY PRUSSIA 1866

ALLIES OF PRUSSIA 1866 (AFTER THE SEVEN WEEKS WAR)

ANNEXED BY PRUSSIA 1866

NORTH GERMAN CONFEDN. 1867:

ANNEXED 1871

GERMAN EMPIRE 1871:

0   50   100   150   200   250   300 km
0   50   100   150   200 miles

the will of the people.' He went on, in 1868, to envisage a congress 'to consecrate the present status quo, limiting it to boundaries determined upon together'. In April he tried to get the British government to discourage Prussian designs on the south German states. In October he was reported by the British ambassador as revealing that his object was 'to calm public opinion in France, and the means of doing this were to be a sort of collective confirmation by Europe of the Treaty of Prague'. Whilst France could accept the Treaty of Prague, made at the end of the Austro-Prussian war, 'on the other hand they expect that southern Germany shall be allowed to reconstruct herself as the states may think best for their own interests, that the southern fortresses shall not be occupied by northern troops, and that Austria shall not be further molested'. A memorandum drawn up by Napoleon III's first minister, Eugène Rouher, made it clear that Prussia would have to formally pledge herself for ten years to respect the status quo in Germany as created and defined by the Treaty of Prague.

Towards the end of 1868 Napoleon III became convinced that a congress was unlikely to be engineered for the purpose he had in mind. There was an alternative, however, and on 31 December 1868, at a meeting in Paris with a representative of the King of Italy, Napoleon III proposed an offensive and defensive alliance between Austria, Italy and France: 'I think it right', he said, 'that Austria ask for territorial compensation and I am ready to work towards the reaching of a complete accord among the three Powers.' The British ambassador was confided in at the end of January 1869:

> The only arrangement that could make a settlement of the German question, satisfy France, and restore confidence in peace – was the neutralisation of the states south of the Main. Their military connection with Prussia should be dissolved, and they should be placed on the same footing as Belgium.

❖

In the course of the discussions of 1868 on a congress the Austrians had expressed the reservation that a guarantee of the status quo would be a direct *halte là* to Prussia. No other construction of this policy of Napoleon III is possible. The same construction was placed on the policy of the Second Empire as a whole by Sir Robert Morier, a member of the British diplomatic corps who was stationed at Berlin, and then at Frankfurt-with-Darmstadt, Stuttgart, and Munich in the 1860s and 1870s. In a letter of 6 January 1871 he wrote:

The true *raison d'être* of the [Franco-Prussian] war may be defined as follows: it was undertaken by France to maintain her claim to an exceptional and privileged position in Europe, in virtue of which exceptional and privileged position no continental nation was allowed the right of bettering its position without leave asked of and tribute paid to France in the shape of territorial expansion and 'improved frontiers'.... By ingeniously acting as *accoucheur* in the case of Italy, Napoleon satisfied French vanity and secured the regulation fee – increased territory and a regulated frontier. But how about Germany? There was the rub. Would she pay tribute? I myself believe that a very small tribute *just to save the principle* would have sufficed. *But the principle must be saved*: on this point ... there was the most complete unanimity of opinion amongst all Frenchmen.... That the north and south of Germany should unite without the consent of France and without an equivalent to France was simply a thing that could not be.

Morier went on to say that he had informed the British Foreign Secretary, Lord Clarendon, in April 1870, that everyone in Germany felt that to proceed with the work of unification would mean war with France, whilst not to proceed with it meant risking the falling apart of what had been accomplished in 1866:

On the one hand, France said: If Prussia gives but her little finger to Baden, that is war with us; on the other, it was becoming impossible for Prussia to continue turning a deaf ear to the solicitations of Baden to be admitted into the North German Confederation without abdicating her position in Germany and definitely breaking with the national party. Bismarck frankly told the leaders of the national party that to concede their most moderate wishes was to declare war to France. The North German Parliament of 1867 would die a natural death in the summer [1870], the new elections would take place in the autumn, the demand that the national question should with the new Parliament advance a step was universal; but there France stood, like the angel with the fiery sword at the gates of Paradise, barring the entrance of the German nation into its imperial palace. *Messieurs, l'entrée est interdite!* Bismarck was being driven up into a corner.

So far as the last, post–Austro-Prussian war, phase of the Second Empire is concerned, it would appear that, at least as far as Napoleon III himself was concerned, Morier's reading of French policy was correct.

❖

On 2 January 1870 Emile Ollivier took office as Minister of Justice and of Religions in a new French administration. Despite the rather unprepossessing title there is no doubt that he was the first minister, a position towards which he had been working throughout the 1860s. In the debates of 14–18 March 1867 in the French parliament Ollivier had stated that the French should accept as a *fait accompli* the new greater Prussia that had come into being in 1866:

> The only wise, intelligent, and decent course is to accept without pusillanimity, to accept without anxiety, to accept with confidence a work which, I am convinced, is not directed against us. Yes, gentlemen, Germany will join in friendship with France the day France ceases to threaten it.

Instead of being regarded as France's hereditary enemy, he continued, echoing de Tocqueville, Germany should be viewed as 'our rampart, our veritable *avant garde* against autocratic Russia'.

He repeated these sentiments early in 1870. On 1 February he was reported by the British ambassador as seeing German unity as a whole 'as an irrevocable fact' and as feeling that France could accept it 'with neither peril nor diminution'. In March he declared in the French Chamber that he would not oppose the unification of north and south Germany whether it was brought about by the will of the people or by Prussian conquest:

> Have not the treaties of alliance unified Germany militarily and has not the renewal of the Zollverein united it economically? German unity against us is accomplished: what still remains to be done, political unity, is purely Prussia's business, and it will bring it more difficulties than strength. What interest have we in preventing the democrats of Württemburg and the ultramontanes of Bavaria from going to annoy Bismarck in his parliaments, since in any case when it comes to a war all Germany will be against us?

This speech was, effectively, a disavowal of the new Foreign Minister, Comte Daru, one of whose first actions had been to issue a circular, without cabinet approval, declaring that France would oppose the unification of Germany, and almost exactly replicates Napoleon III's treatment of Drouyn de Lhuys in August 1866.

Although Ollivier was clearly more relaxed about the prospect of German political unity than were some of his colleagues and than was the Emperor himself, on other scores he was not, and could not afford to be, any more than could any French politician of the era. French public opinion, at least as represented by the French press, which was under less regulation in the years after Sadowa than before, and which was increasingly febrile so far as the position of France in Europe was concerned, was one influence. Inextricably intermixed with this was the question of the future of the regime of Napoleon III itself. In the debates of 14–18 March 1867 the official view, which Ollivier shared, that as a threefold division of Germany had replaced the German Confederation France's position was improved, by no means carried the day – something which was not lost on Bismarck. At the beginning of the crisis over Luxembourg, Napoleon III pointed out to the Prussian ambassador that 'his own existence as sovereign of France would be imperilled if he were to submit to such a rebuff' as appeared to be in the offing. He went on to mention to the British ambassador 'the irritation and alarm which the successes of Prussia had aroused in the French nation', elements which might, he claimed, be calmed by the cession of Luxembourg to France. Bismarck had already pointed out, in a long interview with the British ambassador to Berlin, Lord Loftus, on 13 April, that the question was not really that of the possession of Luxembourg: 'The question was whether the internal position of France did not render it necessary to the Emperor Napoleon to seek a war; Luxembourg therefore was but the pretext'; in Bismarck's view, Napoleon III himself was indisposed to war and anxious for peace, 'but ... there were some members of his Court and advisers who considered that the existence of his dynasty depended on his finding a diversion for public opinion'. Bismarck was not alone in detecting this mood, and these considerations, as far as French foreign policy was concerned. In March 1868 the Russian ambassador to Berlin showed him a despatch in which French intentions were discussed and the conviction voiced that France would wait until Austria had sufficiently recovered her strength and was adequately rearmed, and would then seek an occasion for war with Prussia. In Bismarck's view this forecast, 'judging from the prevailing mood in Paris and Vienna', was 'not at all improbable'. In October 1868 Lord Clarendon recalled a conversation, earlier in the year, in the course of which Napoleon III had insisted that, were there any infraction of the status quo, 'the irritation of France, and above all that of the army, would know no bounds'. In January 1869 the French Foreign Minister La Valette said that any marked step of Prussia towards the annexation of the south German states 'would so excite public opinion in France, that whatever might be the wishes of the Government, war would be inevitable'. In the following month Napoleon III told Marshal Niel, whom he had placed in charge of the reorganisation of the French army: 'France feels herself diminished by the success of Prussia; she would like to find the occasion to establish her influence under the best possible conditions and without arousing all the passions in Germany.'

On this latter occasion Napoleon III had in mind only the acquisition of Belgium – something which in March 1869 Bismarck was instrumental in squashing by giving the impression that Britain and Prussia would be at one in opposing it. At least since April 1867 Napoleon III's Spanish-born wife, the Empress Eugénie, had had wider-ranging plans, described by the Austrian ambassador as 'castles in Spain'. As she increasingly stridently put it, 'France is losing her rank among the nations' as a consequence of Prussian expansion, 'she must win it back or die'.

The perceived, or imagined, 'diminishment' of Napoleon III's regime in the face of developments outside of France was complemented, and increasingly so after 1866, by internal challenges. Behind the campaign mounted by Ollivier to transform the Empire into a more parliamentary system by uniting 'the forces of conservatism' was the feeling, and fear, that 'the revolution was threatening'. Napoleon III made the necessary domestic, constitutional, concessions, and the 'Liberal Empire' – delayed as long as possible by right-wing Bonapartists like the Empress, who believed that 'real strength comes from consistency' – came into being in January 1870. The French political entity was now, however, an unhappy *ménage*. The right-wing elements detested the new regime. The left-wing elements wanted more radical changes. In these circumstances, it was the less likely that any concessions could be made on the foreign policy front, whether by Napoleon III or by any of his ministers.

This was the situation that Ollivier inherited. This helps to account for the touchiness noticed immediately by the British ambassador, who reported on 30 January 1870 that Ollivier 'was particularly alive to the importance of not exposing France to the appearance of being slighted – in fact he would not conceal from me that, under present circumstances, a public rebuff from Prussia would be fatal – "*Un échec*", he said, "*c'est la guerre*".' The reason given was that 'We who have to render an account to Parliament and the country are less than the former Government able to put up with any wound to the national pride. Our main object is peace but we must show firmness and spirit or we shall not be able to cope with Revolution and Socialism at home'.

From Ollivier's point of view, the situation deteriorated, and the problems were compounded following a plebiscite held on 8 May which, although it won a majority in the country, destroyed his majority in Parliament. On 6 May Lord Lyons had written: 'A war unmistakably provoked by Prussia would be hailed by many as a welcome diversion from internal difficulties. So far as I can judge, Ollivier is not the man to shrink from one.' On 12 May the Austrian ambassador, Kleindwart, reported Ollivier as saying:

> You know that I am a partisan of a peace policy ... but should Bismarck
> ... throw himself lightly into some new risk, should he seek a new reason
> for activity and renown ... he will see that under my auspices the impulse
> to fight will come immediately in the country and that I can
> accommodate myself as easily to war as to peace.

On 15 May there was a cabinet reshuffle which left Ollivier as a figurehead in the interests of a compromise with the parliamentary left, but which brought in the principal spokesman of the right, Antoine Duc de Gramont, as Foreign Minister. Prior to this, as ambassador in Vienna, Gramont had been active in seeking an alliance with Austria, arguing that it was a mistake to identify Prussia with German nationalism and more accurate to see her as pursuing a 'Greater Prussian' policy, which should be opposed.

Into this volatile cocktail of French politics and paranoia there came, at the end of June, the news that Prince Leopold of Hohenzollern-Sigmaringen, the heir to the junior, and Catholic, branch of the Prussian royal family, had accepted a Spanish offer to become King of Spain. Speculation and rumours about such a possibility had been rife for some time, and had escalated following a speech by the Prime Minister of Spain, Prim, in the Cortes, on 11 June. On that occasion the French ambassador in Madrid, Baron Mercier de l'Ostende, had guessed correctly when he whispered to his neighbour in the audience, 'It is Leopold of Hohenzollern in question.' Even before Leopold's acceptance of the offer of the Spanish throne had been confirmed, Napoleon III proposed, on 29 June, sending the French fleet from Cherbourg to intercept any Prussian vessel that might try to smuggle Leopold into Spain. And clearly more than a mere interception was envisaged, for the Minister of the Navy telegraphed to the Commander at Cherbourg on the same day: 'What do you have available in: boots, stockings, gloves, undervests, hats for a northern campaign?' On 4 July Ollivier and Gramont pressed the Prussian ambassador, Herr von Werther, not only for a withdrawal of the candidature, but for a guarantee that it would never be renewed. Gramont's language was threatening in the extreme: 'if the affair goes through and the Prince is elected – we shall destroy him; he would not remain King for six months.' Two days later, with opinion in Paris running high, and men 'putting their heads together over this question and saying it will be a second Sadowa, France should not let this happen to her' (as King Wilhelm of Prussia was informed by a relative), Ollivier's and Gramont's language was made public. In a statement in the French Chamber Gramont declared:

> We do not believe that respect for the rights of a neighbouring people obliges us to permit a foreign Power, by placing one of its princes on the throne of Charles V, to disturb to our detriment the present equilibrium of Europe, and to place the interests and honour of France in peril.

His concluding words were drafted by Ollivier, who clearly wished to appear no less strong than his Foreign Minister: France hoped for a peaceful withdrawal of the candidature, but 'if it turns out otherwise, strengthened by your support, gentlemen, and that of the nation, we shall know how to fulfil our duty without hesitation and without weakness'. The Chamber so obviously welcomed these words as a virtual declaration of war that Ollivier himself then rose to say: 'The government wants peace; it passionately wants peace, but with honour.' Of his own performance Gramont admitted to the British ambassador: 'Milder language would have rendered it more easy to treat both with Prussia and with Spain. (But) the nation was so strongly roused upon this question, that its will could not be resisted or trifled with. Nothing less than what he said would have satisfied the public. His speech was in fact, as regarded the interior of France, absolutely necessary; and diplomatic considerations must yield to public safety at home.' On the same day the Austrian ambassador reported the Empress Eugénie as saying: 'It will be very difficult for Bismarck to come out of the affair without either giving way to us completely or proving equal to taking the matter further. If he yields, he will do so under the threat of our attitude – a humiliation from which he will only recover with difficulty.' On the following day, 7 July, Benedetti was instructed to obtain a Prussian retraction through the King of Prussia; and a threat to break off relations with Spain was made. On 8 July the Austrian ambassador reported to Vienna an assertion of his own to Gramont, and Gramont's reply. The assertion was: 'You have jumped at the chance of either scoring a diplomatic success or of fighting a war on a ground where no German national feeling can oppose you.' The reply was: 'You put it exactly.' By 9 July reports were reaching Bismarck that the French were making preparations and intended a *coup de main*. On 11 July he arranged to dine with von Roon, the Prussian Minister for War, on the following evening. On the same day Ollivier wrote to Napoleon III to say that voices from both the left and the right in the Chamber had asserted that 'the Hohenzollern affair should be considered as merely an incident, and even if its solution should be favourable one must not stop there but rather raise the question of the

Treaty of Prague and resolutely place Prussia between an accepted congress or war.' On 12 July news reached Paris that Leopold's father, Prince Karl Anton, had retracted the candidature on his son's behalf. Benedetti was then instructed to press the King of Prussia to guarantee that it would never be renewed. On 14 July the French Council of Ministers met throughout the day and into the evening. Napoleon III said at one point that even if there was no 'avowable reason for war', a conflict would have to be accepted 'in order to follow the wishes of the country' – or, in other words, in order to avoid his own deposition. Gramont threatened to resign rather than to subscribe to a revival of the idea of a congress. He too had advanced too far to retreat with credibility. These latter declarations occurred in the knowledge that Benedetti had *not* been insulted by the King of Prussia. At 9 a.m. on 15 July the Council reconvened and decided unanimously to declare war on Prussia.

❖

So far as the unification of Germany was concerned Bismarck arrived, at an early stage in his career as Minister-President of Prussia, at a *modus operandi*. On Christmas Day 1862 he wrote that the road to the realisation of the aspirations of Prussia had been opened by the Zollverein:

> This institution, upon which the common customs system of its members rests, would afford ... the most effectual basis for the common handling of the economic and eventually of the political interests of the German states.... The alterations to be undertaken, whatever specific form they may take, must aim at introducing majority decisions binding on the minority and at establishing an assembly representative of the peoples of the Zollverein states. To this assembly would fall the task of mediating in the disagreements between the governments and of replacing the need to gain the agreement of all the Parliaments in the individual states.

Even at this stage, it was to the period after 1 January 1866 that Bismarck looked for the realisation of Prussia's intentions. The interval would, he said, 'be filled by diplomatic conflicts over the shaping of the period following 1865'.

After the Austro-Prussian war Bismarck took up again this approach to unification. The war itself had automatically ended the Zollverein, although the peace treaties signed by the south German states with Prussia in August 1866 provided that the old Zollverein should continue for six months. Article 33 of the constitution of the new North German Confederation provided that it should form a single area for tariff purposes, and Bismarck was eager to extend this area so as to include the south German states. In a speech in the North German Parliament on 11 March 1867 he said:

> I think ... that as soon as we have completed the North German constitution, we should make overtures to the south German governments for conferences with us, to consider how we may attain a permanent, organic Zollverein instead of one that can be denounced every twelve years.... Should the Zollverein continue with its present scope, the creation of organic institutions, by means of which south Germany can participate in legislating on tariff questions, is quite unavoidable.

Bismarck did not wish to underrate what he had in mind by describing it as simply a customs parliament:

> It is difficult to believe that such a common legislative institution, if once created, could avoid gradually appropriating to itself most of the remaining things that come under the heading of economic welfare and much formal legislation such as that on commercial procedure, or could avoid bringing into use regulations in these affairs common to the whole of Germany.

A conference of the Customs Union states was convened at Berlin in July 1867, and new tariff treaties were made with the south German states. A Customs Parliament, elected by universal suffrage, and a Customs Federal Council were the Prussian-dominated institutions of a new Zollverein. In November 1867 Bismarck wrote that 'for the interest of Germany as a whole that course seems to be most beneficial which will most quickly lead the south German states voluntarily into the North German Confederation'. He acknowledged that 'everything turns upon the direction in which public opinion in south Germany evolves and the speed with which it does so'. In December, the month in which elections began for the Customs Parliament which was due to meet in the spring of 1868, he expressed the hope that the new assembly 'will be inclined to prepare the extension to the south German states, according to the treaties, of the laws which have already been enacted for the North German Confederation, or are in the process of being enacted, namely, those on citizenship, passports, and civil procedure'.

Bismarck's hopes of speedy progress were dashed by the results of the elections in the south German states. It was made clear to Bismarck that his policy of extending economic unity to political unity lacked a popular base in Baden, Bavaria, Hesse, and Württemburg. In the immediate aftermath of these disappointing results Bismarck appeared relatively phlegmatic. He told the Minister of War of Württemburg, Suckow, in May:

> We all have national unity at heart, but for the calculating politician the necessary aim precedes the desirable one. First let us build our house and extend it afterwards. If Germany were to attain her national aim within the nineteenth century, that would appear to me something great enough. If it were to be within ten or perhaps five years that would be something miraculous, an uncovenanted blessing from God!

In the following February, of 1869, Bismarck gave to Werthern, his representative in Munich, his opinion that it was self-evident that 'German unity at this moment is not a ripe fruit'.

Lothar Gall has argued (in *Bismarck, the White Revolutionary*, London, 1986, i.342), partly on the strength of another of Bismarck's opinions expressed to Werthern on this occasion, namely that he thought it 'probable that German unity will be forwarded through violent events', that Bismarck's policy, or rather his tactics, changed as a result of the setback of 1868; that, from that point, he decided to 'await an opportunity of making some progress on the back of a mobilisation of national feeling triggered off from outside'. Whether Bismarck actively sought foreign complications in order to advance the cause of German unity is, however, quite another matter. Indeed, Bismarck said precisely this in the very same communication to Werthern: 'It is quite another matter to bring about such a violent catastrophe and to bear responsibility for the choice of the time for it. Such arbitrary interventions in the development of history – interventions governed only by subjective reasons – have always had as their consequence only the striking down of unripe fruit.' Another reason against *inducing* or promoting change was the likelihood that this would permanently alienate Bavaria and Württemburg. As Bismarck put this to King William in November 1869:

> We cannot accelerate [the national unification of Germany] unless unexpected events in Europe, such as some upheaval in France or a war of other Great Powers among themselves, offer us an unsought opportunity to do so. Apart from such events, every recognisable attempt of Prussia to determine the decision of the south German princes, by pressure or agitation, will have as its consequence the opposite of the result sought, and will endanger our immediate aim ... to keep, first the

Bavarian Government, and secondly the Württemburg Government, in such a political direction that as long as the status quo lasts, neither Cabinet will co-operate with Paris or Vienna nor find a pretext ... to loosen or even to break the alliances that have been concluded.... If, feeling that we are superior to France in war, which I do not doubt, we were to encourage the impatient policy [of Baden] both peace with France, and, which I think would be worse, our relationship with Bavaria and Württemburg would be destroyed, since even our friends in these two countries will not tolerate being *forced* by Baden, their smaller neighbour, into a policy which sooner or later they would embark upon voluntarily.

A war with France, therefore, was not the answer to this particular problem.

❖

In March 1869 and again in the following May the French government expressed to Bismarck a degree of concern lest Prussia give 'a king of any sort' to the Spaniards, from the throne of which country the Bourbons had been swept by a revolution in the autumn of 1868. Bismarck took up the matter of filling the vacant Spanish throne, and with a Prussian prince, only in March 1870. He did so having been informed by the Spanish Prime Minister that if Spain failed to secure a Hohenzollern they would elect a Bavarian or a Habsburg prince. Bismarck considered these latter possibilities as extremely damaging for Prussia. As he put it in a letter to Wilhelm I on 9 March 1870:

> In the event of a [Prussian] rejection, the wishes of the Spaniards would probably turn to Bavaria. If Prince Adalbert's line or the Ducal line there accepted the offer, Spain would have a ruling house which looked for support to France and Rome, maintaining contact with anti-national elements in Germany and affording them a secure if remote rallying point. The same tendency to enter into relations with Rome, France and Austria with the approval of native ultramontane reactionaries would take place in Spain under Carlist rule. We should then consistently have to regard her as belonging to the ranks of our adversaries.

Whilst a Hohenzollern as King of Spain would increase the prestige of Prussia, both inside Germany and in Europe as a whole, a Bavarian or Habsburg prince would increase the prestige and consciousness of the separate identity and history of the south German states, and would encourage the existing trend of south German opinion in its direction away from Prussia towards continued political independence and greater reliance on Austria. The Austro-Hungarian Foreign Minister, Count Beust, a Saxon, had been greatly encouraged by the results of the elections for the Customs Parliament in 1868 – so much so that he had been active in trying, and not without success, to revive the tendency to favour a Greater German solution of the German question, one that included Austria, as opposed to Bismarck's lesser German solution. Since late in 1868 Bismarck and Beust had been engaged, through the inspired press of Prussia and Austria, in a campaign of mutual disparagement.

Bismarck's pressure on Wilhelm I and on the family of Leopold to accept the Spanish throne was not designed primarily to produce a war with France. It was, rather, a defensive move to maintain Prussia's position in relation to southern Germany, to prevent the status quo there from further changing in her disfavour. When Prince Karl Anton objected to the accepting of the offer of the Spanish throne on the grounds that to accept might give rise to complications with France, Versen, one of Bismarck's intermediaries with the Spanish, replied: 'Bismarck says that is just what he is looking for.' Such 'complications' with France as Bismarck was here credited with seeking, and which, by this time (Versen's diary entry was for 19 June 1870), he could be sure that the French reaction would be sufficient to produce, would improve Prussia's relations with the south German states at the expense of those of anyone else but particularly of Austria. What Bismarck could not possibly have predicted with certainty was that the French reaction would be so extreme as to produce a declaration of war upon Prussia.

❖

The Europe of July 1870 placed the responsibility for the Franco-Prussian war squarely upon the shoulders of the French, and rightly so. Whilst Bismarck's *volte face* of April 1867 over Luxembourg might have been more carefully explained and less abruptly announced, it did not merit the French over-reaction of demands for the stopping of the German political clock at August 1866. Given what, in August 1866, the French were prepared to see happen in Germany, theirs was by far the greater *volte face*, and by far the more provocative stance. It was followed, moreover, on the part of the French Foreign Ministry and certain ambassadors, especially Gramont in Vienna, by a search for allies for a future war – a search in which Bismarck, for his part, never indulged, as he had done before 1866 in respect of Italy in particular. In March 1868 it was the Russians who had approached Bismarck, and offered to station 100,000 of their troops on the Austrian frontier, 'to keep Austria in check and prevent her from taking an active part' in a war declared by

France upon Prussia. This Russian offer was made in order to obtain a similar amount of Prussian support should Russia be threatened by Austria and France, as a result of movements of the Eastern Question. Whilst Bismarck welcomed this understanding, he made it clear that he would not go beyond *entente* into alliance:

> The conclusion of a treaty of alliance to meet the case of war could, in fact, lead to such a war, because the alliance could not remain secret, and knowledge of it would prompt the formation of counter-alliances on the other side, which would necessarily raise the tension step by step, until at last war resulted, without anyone wanting it. Experience shows that such a preoccupation is not unjustified, also that the maintenance of secrecy about specific written documents is very difficult.

Twelve months later, in February and March 1869, it was with a view simply to maintaining this *entente* that Bismarck allowed himself to tell the Russian ambassador that, should war break out in the Balkans between Russia and Austria, Prussia would eliminate French support of Austria by provoking a French attack on Prussia. This could easily be done, he maintained: 'Troop concentrations, national manifestations in Germany and Italy, incidents connected with our relations with Belgium, even with Spain, would offer us opportunity for diversions which might bring about our entrance into the fray without giving it the appearance of an aggressive cabinet war.' In the course of reassuring Russia in this way, and keeping open the line to St Petersburg, Bismarck did recognise the importance of French public opinion, and the difficulties the French government would have in resisting it; but he stressed once again that he had no wish to initiate anything – Prussian relations with the south German states were far too fluid for anything other than defensive action to be envisaged.

Finally, how unprepared in diplomatic terms Prussia was may be further illustrated by Bismarck's last-minute appeal on 14 July to the Tsar. On 13 July Bismarck told Gortachov, the Russian Chancellor, who had arrived in Berlin *en route* to a spa in south Germany, that on the 12th, at a council composed mainly of the Prussian military, all but he had voted for an immediate declaration of war as a response to the arrogant language of the French. According to Bismarck, neither reason nor religion allowed the bringing forward of war; the outcome of war was always in the hands of a higher power; and a precipitate decision for war would pre-empt developments which could occur from one moment to the next. On the following day, 14 July, Bismarck appealed directly to the Tsar: if the Great Powers did not make energetic moves at Paris in favour of peace, and if war broke out and Austria took part, would Alexander let Prussia be erased from the map at the risk of seeing French armies in Berlin and in Poznań? This was a wise if belated improvisation on Bismarck's part, for by the beginning of August the Austro-Hungarian government was feverishly preparing to intervene on the side of a victorious France. Only the initial Prussian victories of 4 August prevented this and the large-scale war that might otherwise have ensued.

8

THE PROBLEMS FOR
GERMANY IN THE 1870S

The German Empire that came into existence in 1871 is usually presented, and regarded, as the strongest of the European Powers from then on, as the dominant force on the continent of Europe, as the hub around which European diplomacy revolved. The German Chancellor, Otto von Bismarck, is usually presented and regarded as the prime mover and principal manipulator in the diplomatic sphere.

The impression that the German Empire was the strongest of the Great Powers is strengthened by the knowledge that Bismarck turned down three overtures from Austria-Hungary for an alliance with Germany in the course of the decade – in September 1872, November 1876 and April 1878. His doing so makes the new German Empire appear strong, independent, and in no need of any ally or any help to maintain its position. The impression is strengthened still further by certain contemporary comments about the German, or Bismarckian, system of government. Having received several reports from a senior British diplomat, the British Foreign Secretary Lord Derby concluded in April 1875:

> It seems impossible to doubt that the possession of absolute power, acting on a nature always impulsive and violent, has developed in the German statesman a tendency like that shown by the first Napoleon between 1805 and 1812: a tendency difficult to describe in exact terms, but which is the disease of despotism. Not only can he bear no opposition: not only is resistance to his wishes a crime, even on the part of foreign and independent States, but mere acquiescence in his authority is not enough. It must be exercised and felt at every moment and in every place. Nothing must be done in Europe in which he does not at least seem to take the lead.

In the face of this impression, what is one to make of Bismarck's speaking to another British diplomat, Odo Russell, Ambassador to Berlin, in March 1875, of 'the danger to Germany', and, on being asked from what quarter it could possibly come, answering: 'from the union of France, Austria, and Russia'? What is one to make of the declaration on 16 April 1875 by Count Munster, Bismarck's ambassador to London, that 'France has virtually only one frontier to defend. Germany is assailable on all sides'? Was Lord Derby correct in pressing on the French, as he did at this time, the view that 'the German military preparations are quite as much the result of fear as of fresh aggressive designs'?

The argument in this chapter is that, in the 1870s, Germany was not the dominant power in Europe; that she faced, indeed, severe problems; and that Bismarck was driven from pillar to post in a desperate search for solutions to these problems. What Lord Derby described as 'the disease of despotism' might more accurately be regarded as the frustration of impotence. This is especially true of the war panic in Berlin in the spring of 1875, which resulted from the lack of control over the general situation that a recent reconciliation between Austria-Hungary and Italy represented to Bismarck. My cue is taken from something said to Lord Derby in May 1876 by Colonel Mansfield, the British minister to Romania from 1876 to 1878. What Mansfield said was that 'the chief gainer by the war of 1870 has been not Germany, but Russia. Russia has now an ally always ready against the Germans; and Bismarck lives in continual fear of a Russo-French coalition.'

❖

At this stage, some remarks on the German army are called for. No one would deny that the *Prussian* army, which had won the war of 1870, was and remained a formidable military machine. What must not be underestimated, however, and what emerges very clearly from Arden Bucholz's recent work *Moltke, Schlieffen and Prussian War Planning* (1991), is that the creation of an equally efficient army for the new German Empire as a whole involved the integration of the armies of the former North German Confederation and of the south German states with the Prussian systems of recruitment, training, manoeuvres, tactics, equipment etc. Manuals had to be rewritten, maps had to be redrawn; even a common language had to be devised. All this was no easy task, and it took many years, perhaps the whole decade, to accomplish, given the separate military traditions and cultures that had to be moulded into one.

The attitude of the Russian Empire, to both western and eastern European affairs, must now be briefly delineated. The affairs of western Europe meant, to the Russians, the relations between France and Germany. Until 1870 the Russians had preferred a dualistic solution of the German Question which would leave Prussia in control in Germany north of the river Main and Austria predominant in south Germany. During the Franco-Prussian war the Russians tried to save France from further humiliation and dismemberment. As Bismarck refused to submit the peace settlement to any outside vetting, the Russians failed in this. They reasserted themselves in this respect, however, when in September 1872 the Russian Chancellor Gortachov made it clear to Bismarck that in Russia's view the limits of German expansion and aggression in the west had been reached. Gortachov stated: 'Russia had no interest in the weakness of France; on the contrary, he wished for a strong and prudent France, *une France forte et sage*.' Two years later, in 1874, Gortachov instructed his representative in Paris, Count Orlov, to say: 'France has nothing to fear from Germany at present, because Russia is virtually mistress of the situation, and Russia is resolved that the peace of Europe shall not be broken.' As the British ambassador to Berlin reported this, on 28 November 1874:

> It has given great offence in official, military and court circles in Berlin, where since the creation of the German Empire the former assumption of superiority over Prussia by Russia is no longer admitted.

In the following May, in a crisis in Franco-German relations which was partly a result of pressure from the 'war party' of Chief of the General Staff Moltke, War Minister Kameke and Radowitz, who was on the staff of the Wilhelmstrasse, and partly an effort on Bismarck's part to reassert German influence after the setback of late 1874, the Russians intervened again. The Tsar went to Berlin, determined to insist on the maintenance of peace, and prepared to threaten a rupture with Germany. Gortachov went so far as to demand from Bismarck something akin to what the French had demanded from Prussia in July 1870 as regards the Hohenzollern candidature, namely a categorical promise that Germany would never go to war against France in the future. The British ambassador in Berlin described this episode as 'Bismarck having had the humiliation before all the world to be bound over to keep the peace by Russia'. The British Foreign Secretary agreed that this was 'a heavy blow to Bismarck'.

So far as the affairs of eastern Europe were concerned the Russians made their position clear in August and September 1872. In Berlin Gortachov told the Austro-Hungarian Foreign Minister, Count Andrassy, and the British Ambassador, that if there was a rising on the part of the Christian subjects of the Ottoman Empire, Russia would not tolerate the forcible intervention of Austria-Hungary: 'Active interference by Austria in the provinces of the Danube ... would become the starting-point of a conflict' between Russia and Austria-Hungary.

The fact that Russian declarations and assertions about both eastern and western Europe were made at *Berlin* reveals another dimension so far as the role and position of Russia are concerned. For the visit paid by Emperor Franz Josef to Berlin in August 1872 was to reciprocate that of Wilhelm I to Vienna earlier in the year. The Russians invited themselves to Berlin. As Bismarck put it: 'Gortachov forced himself upon us with his scribes, for the Tsar to assert by his presence and that of his heir the traditional protectorate of Russia over Prussia.' Gortachov phrased essentially the same sentiment slightly differently, telling Odo Russell that he 'had insisted on his august master joining the Emperors of Germany and Austria to complete what would have been incomplete without him'. One result of the Russian action was the demolition of the hopes that Andrassy had entertained of an Austro-Hungarian-German alliance.

In May 1873 Wilhelm I went to see the Tsar in St Petersburg, and a Russo-German military convention was ratified. This provided that if either Russia or Germany were attacked by another power, the other would come to its aid with 200,000 men. Despite having been told by Bismarck that this convention should be kept secret from Austria-Hungary, the Tsar proceeded to visit Franz Josef at Schönbrunn in Bohemia (near Ostrava, Czech Republic) the following month, where a Russo-Austro-Hungarian agreement was made to the effect that 'in case an aggression coming from a third Power should threaten to compromise the peace of Europe, their Majesties mutually engage to come to a preliminary understanding between themselves, without seeking or contracting new alliances, in order to agree as to the line of conduct to be followed; if, as a result of this understanding a military action should become necessary, it would be governed by a special convention to be concluded between their Majesties.' The Germans subscribed to this latter, and less specific, arrangement in October, when Wilhelm I visited Franz Josef in Vienna. It has become known as the Three Emperors' League. The Germans' own convention with Russia went by the board. The Russians, whether destroying or creating, remained firmly in the driving seat. They had effectively won the struggle between themselves and the German Empire for diplomatic dominance.

This conclusion is reinforced by Gortachov's attitude in December 1879, six years after the Three Emperors' League first came into being, towards a reconstitution of it: if Russia was not the principal associate, as she was before, but only serving as a clerk, he wanted nothing to do with it. Just four months earlier, in August 1879, the Tsar had reverted to the tone he had maintained in the spring of 1875, warning Wilhelm I of the grave consequences of a breach between Russia and Germany, and reminding him of the service he (the Tsar) had rendered Prussia in 1870, and of the debt incurred by the latter as a result. This was a final, and fatal, attempt to assert 'the traditional protectorate of Russia over Prussia' which had been such a feature of the decade.

❖

Even before the Eastern Question began to be asked in mid-1875, when there were revolts in the Balkans against Ottoman rule, Bismarck had become afraid of coalitions against the German Empire. He manifested this fear in November 1874, saying that whilst he wanted to see Austria-Hungary and Russia on good terms, he did not want to see them on terms so intimate that they might unite against Germany. In February 1875 he renewed complaints about the 'excessive civilities' shown by Russia towards France. Lord Derby recorded that Bismarck thought that Russia, Austria-Hungary and France 'may at any time combine against him'. On 20 May 1875, after his humiliation by the Tsar and Gortachov, Bismarck was reported by Andrassy as being 'troubled with something like monomania on the subject of conspiracies to murder him, and plots against the German Empire'.

These fears were exacerbated by events in the Balkans from July 1875. In February 1876 Odo Russell reported from Berlin that what Bismarck most feared 'is a too close intimacy between Austria and Russia: since these Powers united could at any time reckon on help from France, and so make a coalition against Germany'. The coming together of Austria-Hungary and Russia in their agreement at Reichstadt in July 1876 did nothing for Bismarck's peace of mind. Lord Derby in October 1876 thought that Bismarck 'would probably be glad of a quarrel that would avert during some years that which he most fears – a Franco-Russian coalition against Germany'. At the end of January 1877 Russell reported that Bismarck 'is again alarmed at the French armaments and at the growing intimacy with Russia.... He dreams of coalitions against Germany'. Lord Derby told the Russian ambassador, Shouvalov, that Bismarck's object was evident – it was 'to entangle Russia in war, to weaken her for years to come, and to prevent the possibility of a Franco-Russian alliance'. Reports to the same effect were made throughout that spring and into the early summer of 1877. At the end of May Russell recorded that Bismarck was 'strangely haunted by constant apprehensions of an alliance of the Catholic powers against Germany – as also with the idea of a Franco-Russian coalition'.

❖

On at least three occasions in the second half of the decade Bismarck made overtures to Great Britain for an alliance. The first two occasions, if not the third, may be taken as evidence of his, and Germany's, insecurity. The first overture began in December 1875 and lasted into February 1876. The British ambassador, who received it, explained Bismarck's change of front by his conviction that the Three Emperors' League, from Germany's point of view, was a failure, that Austria–Hungary and Russia had drawn together, and that in May of the previous year Russia 'had the satisfaction of binding over Germany to keep the peace'. Bismarck had told him: 'Allied to Russia and Austria alone, Germany can be dragged by them against her wish and will into war. United with England to prevent war in the East, Germany regains her independence and her control over Russia and Austria'.

The second overture came at the end of January 1877. According to Russell, Bismarck wanted an offensive and defensive alliance between Germany and Great Britain, 'which would forever secure Germany against French designs, and release him from the necessity of courting Russian friendship'. Given Lord Derby's negative reaction, Bismarck regretted in March that he 'must now yield to Russian caprices, as it is indispensable that he should have an ally to neutralise possible coalitions against Germany'.

The enquiries of September 1879 were a different matter. By then, the Austro-German Alliance was already being negotiated. Those enquiries were probably made at the behest of, and to indulge, Austria-Hungary.

The overtures to the British government were not the only overtures for alliances that Bismarck made, but arguably they were the most important. In January 1877 he toyed with the idea of an alliance with Austria-Hungary, but did not pursue the matter. In December 1877 he may even have sounded out the French as regards the possibility of a deal whereby Germany would take Belgium, and return the provinces of Alsace and Lorraine to France. Although the British Prime Minister, Disraeli, was so anxious to become embroiled, and to play a role, in European affairs, that in October 1876 he was considering giving Bismarck an assurance or guarantee that Alsace and Lorraine should remain within the German Empire, nothing came of Bismarck's overtures to Britain. They were handled by the Foreign Secretary, Lord Derby, who in effect ignored them. Mixed in with them, as far as Derby was concerned, were efforts to set Britain against Russia. At the beginning of June 1877, for instance, Bismarck went so far as to suggest a British seizure of the Dardanelles, which would certainly have had that effect. Derby, less susceptible to this sort of encouragement than Disraeli, had no more to do with these schemes than with Bismarck's attempts to create trouble between Britain and France (Russia's putative ally, in Bismarck's eyes) by advocating the British occupation of Egypt, which he did in November 1876.

As a war between Russia and the Ottoman Empire approached, and then developed, Bismarck's only cause for celebration, given his failure to bring Great Britain into play and his appreciation that some sort of agreement must have been arrived at between Austria-Hungary and Russia, lay in the prospect and then the actuality of Russian setbacks in the campaign against the Ottoman Empire. In January 1877 Lord Derby noted the undisguised delight of the German government at the prospect of an unsuccessful, or at least of a troublesome and costly, Russian campaign. Derby went on: 'The reason is obvious: the one event really feared at Berlin is the not improbable one of a Russo–French combination against Germany.' At the end of August and the beginning of September 1877 Bismarck was positively 'exultant' at the dire situation Russia was then in, and at the revelation that the Russian armies were weaker and less efficient than had been generally supposed. In February 1878 Bismarck did not conceal his pleasure at the prospect of an Anglo-Russian war, and argued that if Britain did not wish to see a Russian protectorate over the Ottoman Empire, she must go to war with Russia.

❖

At the end of 1875 and again towards the end of 1876, Bismarck stated the problem posed for Germany by developments in the Balkans. In December 1875 he told the British ambassador:

> Germany could not well afford to let Austria and Russia become too intimate behind her back – nor could she let them quarrel with safety to herself. In the event of a quarrel between them, public opinion and sympathy would probably side with Austria, which would make a rancorous and dangerous enemy of Russia, who would then find in France a willing ally to injure Germany. If on the other hand Germany took the part of Russia the consequences might be fatal to the very existence of Austria, who would fall to pieces like a ship on a sandbank. There remained neutrality – but neutrality would be impossible for Germany if her allies quarrelled.

In October 1876 Bismarck wrote to Schweinitz, his ambassador in St Petersburg, in similar terms:

> It cannot correspond to our interests to see the position of Russia seriously and permanently injured by a coalition of the rest of Europe, if

fortune is unfavourable to Russian arms. But it would affect the interests of Germany just as deeply, if the Austrian monarchy was so endangered in its position as an European Power or in its independence, that one of the factors with which we have to reckon in the European balance of power threatened to fall out for the future.

As Bismarck put it during his first bid for a British alliance, as recorded in Russell's dispatch to Lord Derby of 1 February 1876, the problem for the German Empire was that a moment might come when she was neither able to agree with both Russia and Austria-Hungary, nor to stand aloof and be neutral. At such a moment, Germany would have to take one side or the other. Understandably, in these circumstances, Bismarck preferred to push Great Britain forward against Russia, to spare himself the necessity to choose.

Bismarck failed, both in 1876 and 1877, to secure the British alliance that he needed. He also failed to interest Lord Derby in taking up the policy of a peaceful partition of the Ottoman Empire which would satisfy the powers most concerned (Russia and Austria-Hungary) and thus prevent their going to war over it. In these circumstances, and at a point two and a half months after the outbreak of hostilities between Russia and the Ottoman Empire, Bismarck reviewed and revised his solutions to the problems facing the German Empire. At Kissingen on 15 June 1877 he produced the following:

A French newspaper said recently of me that I had '*le cauchemar des coalitions*'; this kind of nightmare will be a very justified one for a German minister to have for a long time to come, if not indeed for ever. Coalitions against us could be formed on the basis of the western Powers with the addition of Austria, or – perhaps more dangerous still – on a Russian–Austrian–French basis; a great intimacy between any two of the three last – named Powers would give the third of them the means to exercise very effective pressure on us at any time. In view of these dangers – which might become real not immediately but in the course of years – I would regard it as desirable from our point of view if the present Near Eastern crisis led to:

1. The gravitation of Russian and Austrian interests, and thus of their mutual rivalries, towards the east;
2. The adoption by Russia of a strongly defensive position in the Near East and on her coastline, so causing her to need our alliance;
3. A status quo satisfactory to England and Russia, which would give them the same interest in maintaining the present situation as we have ourselves;

4. The dissolution of the bonds between England and France (which will always remain hostile to us) because of Egypt and the Mediterranean;
5. A relationship between Russia and Austria which would make it difficult for both to set up the anti-German conspiracy to which centralistic or clerical elements in Austria might feel tempted.

Bismarck broke off at this point, unfortunately, before elaborating in detail the picture he had in mind, which was: 'not that of any territorial acquisition, but that of a general political situation in which all Powers except France need us, and are prevented as far as possible from forming coalitions against us by virtue of their relations to one another.'

Bismarck's fears of coalitions against Germany remained a feature of his outlook. A summary made in November 1878 of his remarks over the previous two years contained much to the effect that Germany was hated by neighbours who might unite against her as soon as their hands were free, and who therefore had to be kept on bad terms with each other. Keeping the 'eastern sore' between Austria-Hungary and Russia open in order to frustrate the unity of the powers against Germany was not really the solution, however. It did not eliminate the dangers of the sore becoming *too* open, and resulting in an Austro-Russian clash; or even, in view of the possibility of such a clash, an Austro-Russian reconciliation. In the first case, Germany would have to make a choice; in the second she would be isolated.

In August 1879 Bismarck decided that the best solution, albeit a solution far from perfect, to the foreign political problems of the German Empire, was an alliance with Austria-Hungary. What clinched this decision was the news, which reached Bismarck on 12 August, that Andrassy intended to resign as Austro-Hungarian Foreign Minister. It was this which caused Bismarck to do what he had been so reluctant to do for so long, and, in effect, to take sides. Austro-Hungarian foreign policy in the hands of anyone other than Andrassy had long concerned Bismarck. In January 1876, for instance, he said that the danger he apprehended most in Austria-Hungary was the downfall of the present administration: 'Andrassy, as a Hungarian, resisted the annexationist policy the Slav party were urging on the Emperor, but if he fell, we must be prepared to deal with an annexation policy in Austria and its consequences in Russia.' Bismarck went on to tell the British ambassador the following month:

As matters now stand, he hears from Vienna that Count Andrassy's position is threatened by the Court Military Party, headed by the Archduke Albrecht, and by the anti-Hungarian party led by Herr von

Schmerling. It is evident that a change of policy, or a change of ministry, in Austria might alter her present relations with Russia and Germany overnight, and he therefore earnestly hopes that Her Majesty's Government will use their moral influence in Vienna to keep Count Andrassy in office, if such be possible.

Two weeks later Bismarck went into more detail:

Unfortunately Germany had enemies in Austria near the Throne always at work to excite their Emperor's suspicions. Besides the Poles, the Czechs, and the Slavs generally, the Ultramontanes were anti-German in sentiment. The latter were as favourable as the former to an annexation policy, because they hoped to eradicate the Mahommedan element and make Roman Catholic provinces of Bosnia and Hercegovina, which the Hungarians alone could prevent.

The November 1878 summary reveals the continued presence of this element – a change of government in Austria-Hungary could with astonishing rapidity bring Germanophobe and Ultramontane elements to the helm and in their wake a rapprochement with France. Any such rapprochement would make of Germany a supplicant of Russia, and re-establish the traditional protectorate of Russia over Prussia, which Bismarck had had to endure for so long. The Tsar's use, later in August 1879 than the news of Andrassy's intention to resign, of the language of the senior partner, and his reminder of debts owed by Germany to Russia in connection with the Franco-Prussian war, only confirmed Bismarck's decision to make sure of Austria-Hungary whilst Andrassy was still in charge. Bismarck was still in the grip of his *cauchemar des coalitions*. Opting for Austria-Hungary would at least remove, or delay for the duration of the alliance, the still not unrealistic prospect, in Bismarck's eyes, of an Austro-Russian alliance, with which the vengeful French might associate themselves.

On Bismarck's part, then, the Austro-German Alliance was in the nature of a confession of weakness. In this respect, it faithfully represented the international problems of the new German Empire in the first decade of its existence, and made a fitting end to that decade. Only the relative, and revealed, weakness of Russia after the Russo-Turkish war made it possible for Bismarck to do at the end of the decade what he had been afraid to do hitherto for fear of alienating Russia altogether.

Bismarck's eventual 'least bad solution' had one incidental merit: it aligned the policy of the German Empire with the sentiment of its population. Even in 1869, as regards the policy to be pursued by Prussia if France and Austria attacked Russia, Bismarck had remarked on the unpopularity in Germany of Prussian support for Russia. In late 1875 he had noted once again, as has been seen, that German public opinion and sympathy would probably side with Austria-Hungary rather than with Russia. In January 1878 he made the same observation, to the British ambassdor. This underlying appreciation of certain constraints on purely Cabinet, or purely dynastic, diplomacy may well have made a contribution to his final decision.

9

GERMANY AND THE EUROPEAN
POWERS IN THE 1880s

In December 1875 Bismarck had said that if Russia was allowed to go to war with Austria-Hungary, the latter 'would go to pieces like a ship on a sandbank'. This expression cannot fail to bring to mind Bismarck's earlier description of Austria, in the 1860s, as 'a worm-eaten galleon'. It is not the least of the ironies of Great Power relations that Bismarck, who in the 1860s directed considerable effort towards breaking the connection between that 'worm-eaten galleon' and what he then termed the 'trim Prussian frigate', should in October 1879 have attached the new German battleship to a vessel, albeit since 1867 the dual monarchy of Austria-Hungary, in such a relative state of decay.

In the vocabulary of historians of diplomacy and international relations, as in that of the ministers and diplomatists responsible for such affairs of state, the expression 'horse and rider', to describe the relationship between allies, is frequently encountered. The 'rider' of the 'horse' is supposed to be the one in control of the alliance. Whether, in the years of Bismarck and of his Austro-Hungarian counterparts Haymerle and Kalnocky, Germany or Austria-Hungary was the 'rider' or the 'horse' in the Dual Alliance is one of the sub-plots – perhaps the main sub-plot – of what follows. Another sub-plot is that there is always the risk in these matters that the initiative, and therefore in effect the control, will go to the physically weaker partner, simply by virtue of weakness and need of assistance from the stronger in order to maintain position and even existence.

The first point to make is that, in the autumn of 1879 it was Bismarck who approached Andrassy for an alliance, and not the other way round. The threatening demeanour of Russia in the summer of 1879 had annoyed and unnerved Bismarck. It was in the unenviable role of supplicant that he approached Andrassy, and this placed the latter in the driving seat. Bismarck had wanted a simple defensive alliance against all comers. He had also wanted a public alliance, which would be placed before and accepted by the parliaments of the German Empire and the Austro-Hungarian monarchy. Bismarck's idea was that such publicity would allow the populations of the two allies, and especially the population of Austria-Hungary, to understand the value of the treaty and to become accustomed to the fact of its existence. As a result, it would be easier for the two governments to support each other if they had to than if the existence of the treaty was only revealed at a time of crisis and with war in sight. Such a public treaty, of course, would also have an educative effect elsewhere – in Russia, for instance, which would know in advance the mutual obligations to which Germany and Austria-Hungary had committed themselves. It was Andrassy who insisted that the alliance should have the more purely anti-Russian character that it did have, providing for Germany and Austria-Hungary to join together against a Russian attack. And it was Andrassy who insisted on the alliance being secret (although Wilhelm I also wished for this). It took Bismarck nearly ten years before he finally convinced Austria-Hungary to publish the text of the alliance, which she did in February 1888.

Andrassy's successor, Haymerle, was just as awkward a customer, from Bismarck's point of view. Haymerle was not prepared to relinquish in any respect the character and thrust of the relationship established by Andrassy. This was demonstrated when, in the summer of 1880, the Russians approached Bismarck in an effort to put together something resembling the League of the Three Emperors. Their basic reasons for so doing have been best presented by W.N. Medlicott in an article published in *Transactions of the Royal Historical Society* in 1945. From the Russian sources used by Medlicott it is clear that the Russians were convinced that the intimacy established between Germany and Austria-Hungary in October 1879 (Wilhelm I had insisted on showing a copy of the preamble of the alliance to the Tsar) bore a character of marked hostility towards Russia. So far as Giers, Gortachov's successor, was concerned, Russia had to choose between a serious and solid *rapprochement* with Great Britain, or else a return into a relationship with Germany and Austria-Hungary. An approach to Great Britain might be met with the demand that Britain be granted access to the Black Sea, which would reverse a position which Russia had successfully maintained at the Congress of Berlin. More significantly, in Giers' view, such a rapprochement would worsen Russia's relations with the two German powers. The latter had common frontiers with Russia, and were in a position to throw 2 million men across these frontiers. If that occurred, a British alliance would serve no useful purpose: '*L'Angleterre était loin*'. The Russian intention was to alter the perceived character of the relationship between Germany and Austria-Hungary so as to make it more negative and defensive. Needing to recuperate after their considerable exertions against the Ottoman Empire in the war of 1877, the Russians said, of their membership, once achieved, of the Drei-Kaiser-Bund: 'It guarantees us against Germany and saves us from a conflict in the immediate future with Austria.' Here, fear was the key – fear of the German powers and their current military capability if acting together. The most feared enemy was thus embraced, for the duration of her own relative military weakness, by Russia. It was an embrace in which there was no warmth.

Whether, even before the conclusion of the alliance of October 1879, Bismarck had envisaged a reconstitution of the League of the Three Emperors, this time with Germany instead of Russia at the centre of it, remains debatable. At the end of October 1879, the Dual Alliance having been made, a distinctly more relaxed Bismarck described German-Russian-Austro-Hungarian relations as follows: 'If one [i.e. Germany] were going through a wood with a dear friend who suddenly exhibited signs of madness [i.e. Russia], one did well to put a revolver [i.e. Austria-Hungary] in one's pocket.' Suitably armed, Bismarck from the end of 1879 had given some support to Russia on the several commissions implementing the terms of the Berlin Treaty of 1878. Moreover the policy of the new British government, led by Gladstone, which took office in April 1880, seemed to Bismarck to be so anti-Turkish that a new phase of crisis might arise in the Near East – especially if any sort of Anglo-Russian understanding was arrived at. For several reasons, therefore, Bismarck was not unresponsive to the Russian overtures.

The conditions made by Haymerle for responding to the Russians, however, were very stringent. Before permitting any negotiations to commence, Haymerle extracted from Bismarck a ministerial declaration on the relationship between the Dual Alliance and the prospective Drei-Kaiser-Bund. This read as follows:

> That the prospective Triple Agreement can under no circumstances prejudice [Germany's and Austria-Hungary's] Treaty of Alliance of 7 October 1879; the latter, on the contrary, remains binding, as if the former did not exist, and shall be executed according to its contents and the intentions of the two treaty-making Powers; that the Treaty of 7 October 1879 therefore continues to determine the relations of the two Powers without undergoing limitation or alteration in any point whatsoever through the prospective new treaty with Russia.

Once negotiations began, Haymerle rejected a clause suggested by Bismarck whereby a quarrel between any two of the three parties would be mediated by the third. He also rejected Austro-Hungarian neutrality in the case of a Russian invasion of Romania. And he insisted on a duration for three years only of any agreement made.

At the very same time as the Drei-Kaiser-Bund was signed, in June 1881, Haymerle concluded an alliance between Austria-Hungary and Serbia, which he had been negotiating simultaneously and without reference to Bismarck, and which had, like the Dual Alliance, at least as far as Austria-Hungary was concerned, an anti-Russian thrust. In the following year, 1882, Haymerle's successor Kalnocky put pressure on Bismarck to agree to an alliance between Austria-Hungary, Germany and Italy. Bismarck initially resisted. He succumbed, in the end, for the reasons he gave in May 1882: 'the sole point for us was to relieve our ally Austria as much as possible from the burden of covering her Italian frontier in the event of war.' The war envisaged here was one between Austria-Hungary and Russia. Finally, in October 1883, Austria-Hungary made another anti-Russian alliance, this time with Romania. In acceding to this, Bismarck agreed to regard action by Austria-Hungary in defence of Romania against Russia as bringing the Dual Alliance of October 1879 into operation. Bismarck thus conceded to Kalnocky in 1883 what he had managed to refuse to Haymerle in 1881, and adopted the Austro-Hungarian line and position that a Russian attack on Romania was to be regarded in the same way as a Russian attack on Austria-Hungary herself. It is fair to conclude that between 1879 and 1884, when the Drei-Kaiser-Bund was renewed for a further three years, Austria-Hungary rather than Germany was the dominant partner within the Dual Alliance.

❖

In August 1885 the British asked Bismarck to mediate between themselves and Russia over a dispute concerning the northern frontier of Afghanistan – the Pendjeh incident. In the course of this request the British Prime Minister and Foreign Secretary, Lord Salisbury, professed to be 'favourable to an alliance between [Germany and Great Britain] in the fullest sense of the term'. In response, Bismarck maintained that 'it was in the interest of Germany to be on good and friendly terms with both England and Russia, and arbitration would be sure to alienate one if not both of them'. Bismarck's son, Herbert, put the dilemma of Germany more explicitly: 'what we have to think of is the danger of a coalition against us of Russia and France ... the water is too hot for us to put our finger in it.' As Sir Philip Currie of the Foreign Office summarised the German reply, it was the fear of a Russo–French coalition against Germany which had determined Bismarck to do nothing that might fan into flames the smouldering hatred of the Russian nation against Germany.

At the end of September 1885 Currie, who was Salisbury's envoy in this matter, met Bismarck in person at Friedrichsruh. According to Currie, Bismarck promised support of England against France, and said that if ever the differences between England and France were pushed to the brink of war, he would not allow the war to take place. On the other hand, in an Anglo-Russian war he could only promise neutrality. This was because 'however victorious the German armies might be it would take a very long time to bring Russia to terms'. Beyond this, the main reason was that Bismarck's chief preoccupation must be to prevent a quarrel between Russia and Austria-Hungary. For, as Currie reported:

> if Russia and Austria went to war and Germany remained neutral, the losing Power would have an undying hatred for her, and would look out for opportunities of revenge. He could not say which side would win, 'perhaps Russia', but the result, if Austria lost, would be her total annihilation or her falling under the influence of Russia who might purchase her alliance by territorial concessions. Neither alternative would suit him. He would not annex the German provinces of Austria – there were too many discordant nationalities in them and too many Catholics and the unity of Germany would be impaired by such an accesion of hostile elements. On the other hand, he could not have Russia at Vienna.

This particular episode helps to make clear a number of things. It illustrates Bismarck's reasons for his fundamental commitment to Austria-Hungary: not only 'the smouldering hatred of the Russian nation for Germany', but also the danger to the unity of the German Empire of having to absorb the German provinces of Austria-Hungary if the latter, as was only to be expected, was defeated by Russia. It also illustrates the impossibility of Britain's doing anything to oppose Russia without the assistance both of the Ottoman Empire and of a continental ally of the military status of the new Germany. (This British offer, to a continental power, of an alliance 'in the fullest sense of the term', is usually elided from the history of British foreign policy, which is unfortunate. For Bismarck's refusal to help Great Britain *in extremis* against Russia left an indelible impression upon Lord Salisbury. Salisbury was never again to look to Germany for assistance against Russia, having come to the understandable conclusion that the considerations governing Bismarck's rejection of his overture would govern the outlook of all German governments and German Chancellors. In future, for Salisbury and for the sake of British interests, there had to be either a partition of the Ottoman Empire, or an Anglo-Russian agreement, or both.)

❖

The Drei-Kaiser-Bund was a fair-weather system. During the negotiation that led up to it, it had been agreed that, in view of the hostility of German public opinion to Russia and the hostility of Russian public opinion towards Germany, no inkling of its existence should be allowed to leak out. It was not to survive its renewal of 1884 for long, for in September 1885 the unification of Bulgaria with Eastern Rumelia took place, and led to open rivalry between Austria-Hungary and Russia. The prospect of war grew closer, and was closest of all in the autumn of 1887. It placed Bismarck very much on the spot. At the beginning of this latest Balkan crisis Bismarck noticed, and deplored, the disposition of Austria-Hungary, under Kalnocky, to try to bring Bulgaria within her sphere of influence, in contravention not only of the Drei-Kaiser-Bund but also of the provisions of the Treaty of Berlin, according to which the Austro-Hungarian sphere was the western Balkans only – Serbia and Bosnia. He noted in November 1885 that the Dual Alliance 'is a defensive [alliance], not a business partnership set up for profit'.

As Austria-Hungary showed great reluctance to share this point of view, Bismarck had to go to considerable lengths in efforts to persuade Kalnocky not to take Germany for granted. In December 1886 Bismarck warned Kalnocky that the German army, concentrated in areas where it could defend Germany against France, could not be spared for a Balkan war. On 11 January 1887 he asserted in the Reichstag that no one would be able to force Germany into a conflict with Russia over the Bulgarian question – that in no event would Germany place herself at the disposal of Austria-Hungary. On 20 August 1887 Bismarck warned Kalnocky that German public opinion would not allow Germany to wage war against Russia over Bulgaria. The Eastern Question was an endurance contest, he said: 'He who can wait, wins.' When, early in October 1887, a report reached Bismarck to the effect that Kalnocky, in talks with the Ottoman Empire, had claimed that 'in the moment of danger Germany will be on the side of Austria-Hungary', Bismarck minuted: 'If we, engaged in a war with France, are strong enough for this.' Bismarck then wrote, on 26 October, to his ambassador at Constantinople (who was an advocate of a war against Russia): 'The idea that in the moment of danger Germany would be on Austria's side is correct in theory, but in practice we will not have much to spare for the support of Austria.' In despatches to Vienna of 15 and 27 December 1887 Bismarck again suggested that if a war broke out between Russia and Austria-Hungary it was a German declaration of war against France that would follow, rather than an attack on Russia. The implication was, of course, that Austria-Hungary would be left to fend for herself.

In the end, after all these prevarications and attempts to lay false trails, Bismarck had to make concessions to the Austro-Hungarian point of view. On 24 January 1888 he assured her that if Russian military preparations went so far as to leave no doubt about Russia's aggressive intentions, Germany would mobilise to ward off an attack by Russia on Austria-Hungary. This, which was in line with the obligations incurred on 7 October 1879, was what Kalnocky had been counting on throughout.

❖

Throughout the autumn of 1887 negotiations had been proceeding for an agreement between Austria-Hungary, Italy and Great Britain. These negotiations had Bismarck's blessing. They serve to bring out, and to reinforce, what has already been said about the Dual Alliance and the relationship between Germany and Austria-Hungary.

In reply to insistent questioning from Lord Salisbury, Bismarck stated that 'Germany has a real interest in maintaining Austria's position as a Great Power.... It would be a mistake for England to consider possible a change in German policy, which is prompted by such compelling interests.' He went on:

> The existence of Austria as a strong and independent Great Power is a necessity for Germany.... We shall avoid war with Russia so far as that is compatible with our honour and with our security, and so far as the independence of Austria-Hungary, whose existence as a Great Power is a necessity of the first order for us, is not placed in question.... German policy will always be obliged to enter into the line of combat should the independence of Austria-Hungary be menaced by a Russian aggression.

After receiving this, and after seeing the text of the Dual Alliance, Lord Salisbury wrote: 'It sufficiently establishes that Germany *must* take the side of Austria in *any* war between Austria and Russia.' Under these circumstances, and only under these circumstances, would Salisbury allow Great Britain to commit itself to the Mediterranean *entente*. Early in 1888, commenting on what some diplomatists described as Bismarck's 'double game' of assuring the Tsar of German friendship whilst encouraging this Mediterranean grouping against Russia, Salisbury remained convinced of the correctness of his interpretation of Bismarck's policy:

> It may be she is deceiving us as well as Russia, but I lean strongly to the other belief – that Austria is a necessity to her and that all other motives

in European politics are made to bend to that necessity. She cannot afford to be flanked on the south by a Power less friendly than Austria.

❖

Comments made by Bismarck on despatches that he received are one of the most rewarding sources so far as understanding the real 'inwardness' of his policy is concerned. As the text of the second Mediterranean Agreement was being finalised, Bismarck appended the following remark to a despatch from Hatzfeldt, his ambassador in London: 'for the sake of our own existence we cannot do without either England or Austria, as effective Great Powers – Russia's duplicity.' When on 12 November 1887 Hatzfeldt reported Salisbury's concern lest Prince Wilhelm, whose Russian sympathies were no secret, might in due course adopt an anti-British and pro-Russian policy, Bismarck responded:

Impossible. We could never follow a policy which would end in our isolation, the moment Russia chose. We cannot be left alone depending on Russia's friendship after all that has happened since '78, nor can we quarrel with Austria, England and Italy, with whom the German alliance is popular. The idea of our working for an alliance with Russia and putting ourselves at the mercy of their humours in St Petersburg!

When Salisbury suggested a written declaration that Germany approved of the eight points of this second Mediterranean Agreement, Bismarck commented: 'The fact that our policy is founded on the impossibility of isolating ourselves with Russia and of being dependent on her, is stronger than any "approval" of the Points.'

Having sought out an alliance with Austria-Hungary in 1879, Bismarck had to hang on to it, in order to avoid being at the mercy of the whims and humours of the Russians, which might include changing partners and leaving Germany stranded in an isolation which Bismarck was unable to contemplate with any degree of equanimity.

Midway between the two Mediterranean Agreements, in June 1887, Bismarck made a separate treaty, the Reinsurance Treaty, with Russia. In that negotiation, Bismarck made a point of revealing to the Russians the text of the Dual Alliance. This revelation was designed to deter the Russians from taking too strong a line with Austria-Hungary, in the knowledge of the limits to which Germany could go in her relations with Russia. Bismarck took other precautions. He stopped German financial credits to Russia, hoping thereby to undermine the credibility of the warmongers in the councils of the Tsar. And in November 1887 he announced increases in the size of the German army. Bismarck regarded the terms of the Reinsurance Treaty itself as 'fairly inconsequential' – in a crisis they would 'keep the Russians off our necks for an additional six to eight weeks'.

Had Russia not been deterred, on this occasion, Austria-Hungary would in all probability have succeeded in calling Bismarck's bluff about the French priorities of the German army. However little connection there was between the Reichstag, elected by universal suffrage, and German governments, appointed by the Emperor on the advice of the Chancellor, German public opinion would have had a say, perhaps the decisive say, in the matter; and the sort of legalistic distinctions that Bismarck had been attempting to make between the attacker and the attacked, between intervention in the initial and intervention in the later stages of a war between Russia and Austria-Hungary, would have gone by the board. Germany would not have been able to stand aloof until Austria-Hungary was on the point of annihilation, or the Russian armies were at the gates of Vienna.

To a considerable extent, then, it can be argued that the German Empire had been taken prisoner by Austria-Hungary, the weaker of the two partners, by virtue of Austria-Hungary's weakness and of the indispensability of her continued existence to the stronger partner. To a considerable extent the roles of 'rider' and 'horse' had been reversed, or had turned out not to be what they had seemed. The German Empire, even under Bismarck, was not untrammelled master of the fate of Europe, or even of her own fate.

10

THE MAKING OF THE FRANCO-RUSSIAN ALLIANCE

In his book *The Fateful Alliance: France, Russia and the Coming of the First World War*, published in 1984, George Kennan, a former adviser to the US State Department, claimed that of all the alliances made before 1914, it was the Franco-Russian Alliance which contributed most to the outbreak of war in 1914. For my present purpose it is not necessary to dispute or to support that particular claim. What I am more concerned to do here is to explore differing explanations put forward to account for the making of the Franco-Russian Alliance. There are three schools of thought on this matter: long-term, medium-term and short-term; they will be dealt with in that order.

❖

In 1879 Bismarck had told Andrassy something from which the latter drew the following conclusion: to a Russo-French alliance the natural counterpoise was an Austro-German alliance. Does not the reverse follow? Does not an Austro-German alliance, such as was concluded in October 1879, in principle and in theory at least, produce a Franco-Russian alliance?

Even before October 1879, of course, Bismarck had projected, or imagined, joint action by Russia and France against Germany. Given the attitude protective of France displayed by Russia in 1872 and 1874–5, and given the hostility of France towards Germany which was a basic consideration in Bismarck's foreign policy after 1871, it is not difficult to understand why, in 1877 for instance, he should ask the British ambassador what Great Britain's attitude would be if Germany 'was unjustly attacked by Russia and France'; nor his asking again in August 1879 what would be the British attitude towards France if German support of Austria-Hungary in the east resulted in a war between Germany and Russia.

After October 1879 remarks positing this particular grouping of France and Russia multiply and become more widespread. In February 1887, for instance, the British Ambassador in Vienna, Paget, wrote to

Lord Salisbury: 'We have nothing to fear from Austria, Germany, Italy, Turkey – everything to fear from an accession of strength by France and Russia.' In November 1887 Bismarck himself wrote to Salisbury:

> We [i.e.Germany] must consider as *permanent* the danger of seeing our peace troubled by France and Russia. Our policy as a result will tend necessarily to assure to us the allies which offer themselves in view of the prospect of having to fight simultaneously our two powerful neighbours.

In the following month Bismarck admitted to the Prussian War Minister that 'in the not too distant future we shall have to survive a war against France and Russia simultaneously'. In February 1888 the British Ambassador in Paris, Lord Lytton, wrote to Salisbury: 'the French are constantly sounding me about England's relations with the German Powers and Italy on the one hand, and Russia and France on the other.' And on 27 March 1888 Salisbury wrote to the Duke of Edinburgh: 'The Germans are always impressing on me that the sole chance of Italy being able to help Austria in the event of an attack by Russia on Austria, would be that her coasts should be protected by us from a French naval attack.'

In view of such contemporary comment and interpretation, one might be forgiven for wondering quite what difference the formal signing of a treaty of alliance between Russia and France could make to the situation. One is also inclined to wonder whether, in what Salisbury in December 1888 called Bismarck's 'ceaseless efforts to build up diplomatic breakwaters against France and Russia', the German Chancellor was not mainly responsible for bringing it about.

In 1890, shortly after Bismarck's resignation, his successor Caprivi invited the whole of the German diplomatic establishment to comment on the question of renewing one item of the Bismarckian legacy, the Reinsurance Treaty. Not a single individual came to the defence of this device. What the German diplomatic corps as a whole wanted was a 'calm, clear-cut, honourable policy', 'a single, calm policy'. To maintain the secret treaty with Russia, argued Holstein, an official in the Wilhelmstrasse, was to give the Russians 'a weapon effectively to arouse mistrust against us among our allies'. Radowitz advised: 'Hold fast to the Triple Alliance, and avoid everything which could arouse mistrust against it, especially in Vienna. Do not go further in a separate treaty with Russia than is compatible with our relations with Austria.' Reuss wrote from Vienna that the merest suspicion about Germany's trustworthiness would be enough to alienate Austria-Hungary permanently. Several comments replicated the views of the ambassador in London, Hatzfeldt, who maintained that in a serious crisis Russia and France would act together, whether a written agreement existed between them or not. Caprivi agreed. In deciding not to pursue a renewal of the Reinsurance Treaty, he revealed that he was prepared to run the risk of a Russian alliance with France. In effect, he took it for granted that a Franco-Russian alliance already existed, that a formal treaty between those two powers was not necessary.

❖

In 1885 the German government had expelled about 30,000 Russian citizens from the Prussian eastern provinces in the course of a policy of forcible Germanisation, allied to a sharpening of policies for the protection of German agriculture. In May 1887 the Russian Government retaliated by forbidding foreigners in their Polish provinces to acquire land, or to pass it on by inheritance, or to be bailiffs. Nine out of ten of the foreigners in the Polish provinces of Russia had German citizenship.

On the same day as that on which the Reinsurance Treaty was signed, 29 June 1887, a campaign commenced in the German press against Russian bonds and state credit. The point made was that German bondholders might well be dispossessed as suddenly and unilaterally as had been the German landowners in the Russian Empire. On 16 October Bismarck issued from the Wilhelmstrasse an instruction to the heads of all Prussian Departments that in future foreign paper money could not be accepted in certain financial transactions in which government officials were involved. In November 1887 the German capital market was deliberately and effectively closed to Russia. Partly under the influence of this sharpened crisis in German-Russian relations as well as the prospect of a Franco-German war, which Boulangism in France had enabled Bismarck to exaggerate, the Reichstag passed in the same month a law enabling the size of the German army to be raised to 600,000 men.

The protectionist policies of Russia had halved German industrial exports between 1880 and 1887 and increased Russian exports to Germany to over three times the value of German exports to Russia. The financial measures taken against Russia enabled Bismarck to draw the teeth of his preventive warmongers, who included Generals Moltke and Waldersee, who argued that at least the strategic railways planned by Russia in Poland should not be built with German capital. Bismarck also hoped, by intimidating Russia in this way, to ease the position of Austria-Hungary in relation to Bulgarian affairs by weakening the war party in Russia. The latter, thought Bismarck, would have an easier time if credit was readily forthcoming: as Bismarck's son Herbert told the Austro-

Hungarian diplomat Aehrenthal six months later: 'Germany was working steadily to keep Russia's credit low in order to have a calming effect on her willingness for war and if possible to delay matters.'

As regards the financial repercussions, however, Bismarck would appear to have miscalculated. In July 1887 he maintained 'that France is no market for Russian paper', and that the success of Russian financial agents in Paris 'will remain a pious hope'. His own pious hope was not fulfilled. The French welcomed the Russian bonds, took over in 1888 one important loan, made another in 1890, and by 1895 had made a profit of over 600 million francs. In 1893 Giers, the Russian Foreign Minister, was to tell the German ambassador in St Petersburg: 'Prince Bismarck drove us into the arms of France, especially with his financial measures.'

Giers' comment would appear to settle the matter decisively in favour of the medium-term explanation. However, given that Giers himself, in 1890, secured the consent of the Tsar to a renewal for six years of the Reinsurance Treaty with Germany, something the Russians formally proposed on 17 March, his remark of 1893 cannot be regarded as definitive. Might it not rather be the case that it was the failure of Bismarck's successor to renew the Reinsurance Treaty that was responsible for the making of the Franco-Russian Alliance? This was a view popularised by Bismarck himself between his enforced retirement and his death in 1898, and after that by the 'Bismarck school' of historians. Although Bismarck's claim that even at the end of the 1880s Russo-German relations were still good as a result of the Reinsurance Treaty is not borne out by the facts, it remains possible that the final cutting adrift of Russia, the German failure to spin out 'the line to St Petersburg', was crucial. Another possibility is that it was the uncertainty attaching to what German foreign policy might be after, or without, Bismarck, that made the difference, especially so far as the Russians were concerned. This is a factor difficult both to estimate and to underestimate. By the end of 1890 Lord Salisbury was saying: 'One misses the extraordinary penetration of the old man.' He would not have been alone in this. With Bismarck, after a time, you knew where you were: you didn't know where you were. This uncertainty had much to recommend it.

❖

Both the absence of Bismarck and the failure to renew the Reinsurance Treaty may be relevant to the short-term explanation for the making of the Franco-Russian Alliance. There is, however, an even shorter-term explanation. In late March and early April of 1891, almost a year after

Germany's refusal to renew the Reinsurance Treaty, the French government instructed its ambassador in St Petersburg to secure from the Russian government some concrete assurance for the future. In particular, they wanted to know what the attitude of Russia would be in the case of a war between Germany and France. There was no answer. The French Ambassador was rebuffed, and was immediately recalled to Paris. Four months later, on 20 July 1891, the Russian Foreign Minister, Giers, invited the French to begin negotiations for a closer relationship between themselves and Russia.

So what happened, between early April and late July 1891, to account for this *volte face* on the part of the Russian government? Why, in April, should Giers be confident that, as he put it, 'France is at our feet', whilst in July he should decide to take the initiative himself in approaching France? Why should the Tsar, who in autumn 1890 had told Kaiser Wilhelm II that he would never make an alliance with a republic, have agreed to Giers' new policy?

What had happened was that, on 6 May 1891, the Triple Alliance of Germany, Austria-Hungary, and Italy had been renewed. This was disappointment enough for both France and Russia, both of whom had been making efforts to wean Italy away from the Triple Alliance. What was even worse, however, was that the impression was given that Great Britain had acceded to, and in effect become a member of, the Triple Alliance. This impression was mainly the work of the Italians. Rudini, the Italian Prime Minister, gave an interview which was published in *The Times* on 14 April, in which he 'laid great stress on his firm conviction that Italy ought never to come into conflict with Great Britain.... Great Britain and Italy ought to be found on the same side.' Similar statements were made in the Italian Chamber of Deputies on 14 May, probably at the instigation of the Italian Foreign Office. Chiala, for one, stressed the importance of the agreement of 1887 between Britain and Italy, and cited Depretis' declaration that Italy's position was secured by land and sea, so long as Italy and England stood by the Central Powers. In articles published by the *Corriere della Sera* on 6 and 7 June, the deputy Ferraris, a friend of Rudini, stated that the Triple Alliance might be regarded as having been renewed, and continued: 'England engages to defend Italy even in case the latter becomes involved in a war resulting from her obligations to the Triple Alliance. This disposition is especially important because, by it, England indirectly enters the Triple Alliance, which thereby becomes quadruple.' Reports of such statements seemed to confirm the interpretations placed by Prince Napoleon on remarks by King Umberto of Italy and published in the French press on 3 June. King Umberto's words were:

> I have nothing to fear for the security of the Italian coasts, for I have had a formal promise from the Cabinet of St James that the English Fleet will ally itself with mine, should the necessity arise, in order to protect Italy against all maritime operations.

On Prince Napoleon's saying that this was tantamount to adhesion to the Triple Alliance on the part of England, the King of Italy replied: 'I have nothing more to say to you about it. But I can state that the English and Italian governments have exchanged despatches which contain certain definite engagements, and I have full confidence in the written word of the English government.'

In London, Salisbury was clearly unprepared for the Italian interpretation of what had transpired. Questions were asked in the House of Commons, and Salisbury refused an invitation to go to Italy precisely because of what he called 'the extraordinary stories as to special engagements between Italy and England' which were circulating. He laboured in vain, however, to correct the impression that had come to prevail. On 16 June 1891 he lamented that 'we have been unable so to frame our answers as to avoid giving the impression that we are more "Tripliste" than people thought; and France is consequently out of humour.' This was an understatement. Both the French and the Russians were seriously alarmed. With the Kaiser paying a state visit to England in July, and the British Mediterranean squadron paying visits to Fiume and Venice and being honoured by Franz Josef and King Umberto, this alarm seemed fully justified. Salisbury tried again to reassure the French, by telling them that nothing had changed, that Britain's interest in the status quo benefited France as regards Tunis, that it was moreover a general interest which included the Adriatic and the Black Sea, and that Britain had for years been restraining Italy wherever possible, had been engaged 'in keeping the Italians within bounds'. None of this had the desired effect. French and Russian representatives throughout Europe were unanimous. Their reports were full of phrases that implied that the renewal of the Triple Alliance meant also 'the entry of Great Britain into the concert of the Central Powers', that it represented the 'accession more or less direct of Great Britain to the Triple Alliance', or Britain's having become 'a satellite of the Triple Alliance'. On 4 July the *Neue Freie Presse* commented:

> The mighty sea power, England, feels called upon to unite its great interest in the status quo in the Mediterranean with the interest in peace of the three continental Powers, and this union, even without the form of a written treaty, automatically turns against France and Russia, these

being the Powers which are dissatisfied with the present situation in Europe.

Both France and Russia were threatened by such an extended grouping. The French feared closer Anglo-Italian relations; the Russians feared a readiness on the part of Germany to subscribe to a British interpretation of the rule of the Straits. In the previous year, when the British had given Germany Heligoland in exchange for Zanzibar, Giers had complained to the German ambassador, Schweinitz: 'Germany, Austria, Italy were joined in alliance; the Triple Alliance Powers were showing every sign of trying to reach an agreement with Great Britain.' A year later, in mid-1891, it seemed that just that had finally been accomplished. It was in this context that the Russians and French met in August 1891 to discuss their respective positions in Europe and the world.

The French records of these meetings, and of further meetings in November 1891, reinforce the concern already expressed by the Russians about the Triple Alliance. Giers is reported as denouncing 'the manoeuvres of the Triple Alliance', and as stressing the need to counter them; he also noted that although that alliance appeared to be a defensive one, appearances might be deceptive – war could break out 'by surprise', and it would be as well to take steps in advance so as to be ready for that eventuality. From this followed the obligation for both France and Russia to mobilise if Germany or Austria-Hungary did so. Giers is also recorded as stating what the Franco-Russian entente had already accomplished, and what, in his mind at least, it was designed to deal with: 'There was no longer', he said, 'any question of the hegemony of Germany – the equilibrium had been re-established in Europe'. In other words, the Franco-Russian Alliance was a step taken to redress the diplomatic balance of power, which with the renewal of the Triple Alliance and Great Britain's apparently close connection with it, had seemed to be too much in favour of the Central Powers.

For ten years, since 1882, Giers can be found referring to the importance of France not only as a balance to Germany and Austria-Hungary in Europe, but also to Great Britain in Africa and Asia. He thought that Russia occupied a pivotal position – that she should neither withdraw completely from international affairs nor pursue aggressive policies which would tend, as in 1877–78, to produce coalitions against her. This was the keynote of Russian policy in his time. Throughout these years, however, he had foreseen a time when Russia might need to add herself to France as a counterpoise to Germany. In his judgement, that time had arrived with the renewal of the Triple Alliance in 1891, or, to put it another way, with the failure of the Triple Alliance to break up. Giers hoped that, as a result of the now formalised relationship with France, the war that he believed would eventually come would at the very least be delayed. The Franco-Russian Alliance, then, was intended to end the *de facto* and diplomatic hegemony of Germany in Europe. Giers believed that it did just that.

❖

Having put forward three contending explanations for the coming into existence of the Franco-Russian Alliance, it must be said, in conclusion, that it is quite possible to combine elements of the three explanations, which are by no means mutually exclusive. There is such a thing, moreover, as the cumulative effect of diverse, and separate, developments.

11

LORD SALISBURY'S GRAND DESIGN: FROM NEAR EAST TO MIDDLE EAST

It will become clear that the attitude of Robert, third Marquess of Salisbury, towards the Ottoman Empire had much in common with that of Napoleon III. As already demonstrated in Chapter 6, Napoleon III regarded the Ottoman dominions as areas where compensation could be found for those displaced by alterations in the map of western Europe, as statelets where minor princelings could occupy themselves. He also regarded this process as a means whereby to accomplish the re-Christianisation of eastern Europe in particular. Salisbury similarly, as brought out in the most definitive biography of him that we are ever likely to have – that by E.D. Steele published in 1999 – wished to see, on religious grounds, the reduction of Ottoman power as a long stride towards the westernisation of the Orient and the erosion of what he regarded as a 'false religion'. As he developed as a statesman, and as the international system developed in his time, he also came to appreciate that a peaceful partition of the Ottoman Empire would do much to satisfy, and keep occupied, the Great Powers of Europe: this would make the competing alliances, which he believed had become too numerous, more or less redundant, in the sense that they would be the less likely to be called into play.

❖

The third Marquess of Salisbury had two stints as Secretary of State for India before becoming British Foreign Secretary for the first time on 2 April 1878. The second, and longer, of these stints began in February 1874, and included the build-up to and the crisis at the end of the Russo–Turkish war of 1877. Salisbury was the British delegate to a conference which met in Constantinople in December 1876 to try to defuse the situation. In the course of this experience he became increasingly convinced of what he called 'the deplorable folly of the Crimean War'. To his cabinet colleague Lord Carnarvon on 11 January 1877 he expressed two hopes: that the Constantinople Conference had 'made it impossible that we should spend any more English blood in sustaining the Turkish Empire', and that 'it will make English statesmen buckle to the task of devising some other means of securing the road to India'. To Lord Lytton, the Viceroy of India, in a letter of 9 March 1877, he condemned British policy, past and present, for being 'to float lazily downstream, occasionally putting out a diplomatic boat-hook to avoid collisions', and revealed himself as altogether more adventurous and pro-active than his colleagues:

> I should like to move a little faster. I feel convinced that the old policy ... of defending English interests by sustaining the Ottoman dynasty has become impracticable, and I think that the time has come for defending English interests in a more direct way by some territorial arrangement. I fear that when we come to do the same thing some years later, one of two things will have happened. Either France will have recovered her position and be jealous of any extension of our power in the Mediterranean, or Germany will have become a naval power. Either of these contingencies will make it difficult for us to provide ourselves with a *pied-à-terre*, in place of that which we shall infallibly lose at Constantinople.... But these are dreams.

To the Prime Minister, Disraeli, a few days later, he expressed his fears that Austrian permission had been granted for a Russian campaign against the Ottoman Empire and that Russia would insist on 'some territorial result' which she could find in these circumstances only 'on the side of Asia' – perhaps in Armenia, which would provide access to the Euphrates valley as a point on the route to the head of the Persian Gulf. On 15 June 1877 he delivered to Lytton the view which, 'after two years' study of the subject', now commended itself to him:

> I would have devoted my whole efforts to securing the waterway to India – by the acquisition of Egypt or of Crete, and would in no way have discouraged the obliteration of Turkey. But the worst of our policy has been that it has not been a consistent whole on either side. A bit of each train of thought has been embedded in it, surrounded by a thick mass of general inertia.

In March 1878, whilst the British government was considering how to deal with the Treaty of San Stephano which had ended the Russo-Turkish war, Salisbury reminded Disraeli that he was 'not a believer in the possibility of setting the Turkish Government on its legs again, as a genuine reliable power'. Advising against the adoption of 'any line of policy which may stake England's security in those seas on Turkish efficiency', he listed amongst his own personal desiderata 'Two naval stations for England – say Lemnos and Cyprus, with an occupation, at least temporary, of some place like Scanderoon [Alexandretta].'

❖

As Foreign Secretary from April 1878 Salisbury did do something along some of these lines. The Cyprus Convention, which he negotiated, did provide a *pied-à-terre* of sorts, in return for a British commitment to defend by force of arms the Ottoman territories in Asia as defined by the Congress of Berlin. This commitment, together with his scheme for installing British consuls to administer the provinces of Asia Minor, and the consideration given to the building of a railway from the Gulf of Iskanderoon to the Euphrates, suggest that Salisbury was not yet prepared to pursue 'the obliteration of Turkey'. Salisbury regarded the Gladstone government's occupation of Egypt in 1882 as following from policy failures over the previous two years; it nevertheless fitted his template of June 1877 as a necessary step in the direction of 'securing the waterway to India'.

Between June 1885 and February 1886 Salisbury was both Prime Minister and Foreign Secretary. He became Prime Minister for the second time in June 1886, and occupied that office and the post of Foreign Secretary from January 1887 until August 1892. In the Balkan crisis of autumn 1886 he stood firm against the Chancellor of the Exchequer, Lord Randolph Churchill, who was rather inclined, for financial reasons, to let Russia have Constantinople. Salisbury now resisted this for purely party-political reasons. As he explained to his Chancellor on 1 October 1886:

> I consider the loss of Constantinople would be the ruin of our party, and a heavy blow to the country.... My belief is that the main strength of the Tory party both in the richer and poorer classes lies in its association with the honour of the country. It is quite true that if, in order to save that honour, we have to run into expense we shall suffer for it as a party – that is human nature. But what I contend is that we shall suffer as a party more – much more – if the loss of Constantinople stands on our record.

Towards the end of this period in office, in June 1892, Salisbury received a report from the Directors of Naval and Military Intelligence which caused him to revert to his original approach whilst Secretary of State for India in 1874–78. The report was written in the context of what appeared to be a *rapprochement* between France and Russia, together with the development by Russia of a modern Black Sea fleet. The question examined was that of a possible Russian attempt to seize Constantinople and what British naval and military action would be required to deal with such an attempt. The pessimistic conclusion was that 'Great Britain, unsupported, cannot prevent the *coup de main* without endangering her general naval position'. Salisbury registered the import of this finding as follows:

> The protection of Constantinople from Russian conquest has been the turning point of the policy of Great Britain for at least forty years, and to a certain extent for forty years before that. It has been constantly assumed, both in England and abroad, that this protection of Constantinople was the special interest of Great Britain. It is our principal, if not our only, interest in the Mediterranean Sea; for if Russia were mistress of Constantinople, and of the influence which Constantinople has in the Levant, the route to India through the Suez Canal would be so much exposed as not to be available except in times of the profoundest peace. There is no need to dwell on the effect which the Russian possession of Constantinople would have upon the Oriental mind, and upon our position in India, which is so largely dependent on prestige.

In Salisbury's view the report raised two 'very great questions' which the Government had to answer as soon as possible. 'In the first place', he wrote, 'it is a question whether any advantage arises from keeping a fleet in the Mediterranean at all.' The other consideration was that 'our foreign policy requires to be speedily and avowedly revised'. As he put it:

> At present, it is supposed that the fall of Constantinople will be a great defeat for England. That defeat appears to be not a matter of speculation, but of absolute certainty, according to the opinion of these two distinguished officers.... It would surely be wise, in the interest of our own reputation, to let it be known as quickly as possible that we do not pretend to defend Constantinople, and that the protection of it from Russian attack is not, in our eyes, worthy of the sacrifices or the risks which such an effort would involve. At present, if the two officers in question are correct in their views, our policy is a policy of false pretences. If persisted in, it will involve discomfiture to all who trust in us, and infinite discredit to ourselves.

Salisbury left office two months later, which was not enough time to resolve 'this momentous question'. Whilst in opposition, however, certain familiar ideas began to germinate in his mind. In December 1894 he confided to Sir Philip Currie, who had been Permanent Under-Secretary at the Foreign Office from 1889 to 1893, and who was currently the ambassador at Constantinople:

> As far as I can judge, matters are coming to a crisis in your part of the world and the Turkish Empire will have to be reconsidered. I should myself very much prefer to give Russia the South and East of the Black Sea – and open the Dardanelles to all Powers; set up some kind of autonomy in Egypt; take for ourselves the southern slope of the Taurus with Syria and Mesopotamia – pay off the French with Tripoli and a haunch of Morocco – Italy with Albania, and Austria with Salonika. But alas! these are mere dreams – nobody agrees with me.

❖

Salisbury took office again as Prime Minister and Foreign Secretary at the end of June 1895. Over the next eighteen months he attempted to translate his 'mere dreams' into reality. Revolts against Ottoman rule had already commenced in the province of Armenia, together with the inevitable countermeasures, and the prospect of such revolts spreading throughout the Ottoman Empire, and encouraging Russia in particular to intervene, as in the 1870s, could not be ruled out. Salisbury's first approach was to the German government. At the end of July 1895 he told the German ambassador that it was necessary to arrive at an understanding about a plan for the partition of the Ottoman Empire. He followed this up, at the end of August, by stating that what Britain coveted was not in the Mediterranean, but rather '*du côté de l'Euphrate*'. Also at the end of August, Salisbury instructed Currie to assume a menacing tone with the Ottoman Empire as regards Jeddah, on the Red Sea, and stated that 'the occupation of Jeddah may bring down the Turkish Empire with a run'. In November 1895 he delivered a speech at the Guildhall which foreign observers regarded as an incitement to the Armenians; this fitted in with what Salisbury had told Currie, and Lascelles the ambassador in Berlin, in September: 'Time is so much on our side that the excitement in Armenia, as it grows, becomes more and more distasteful to Russia. If we emphasise our demand by occupying some territory at Jeddah etc., it will add greatly to the excitement among the population, and to the alarm of Russia'; 'if [Russia] loses her head, she may make a desperate effort to reopen the Eastern Question and pacify Armenia after her own fashion.' Salisbury then asked the cabinet to give *carte blanche* to Currie as far as calling the Mediterranean fleet up to Constantinople was concerned. As Salisbury tried to persuade the First Lord of the Admiralty, Goschen: 'if we get there first we are a good deal the strongest and our views will be at all events very weighty in the ultimate arrangements that are made.' In the same letter, of 3 December 1895, Salisbury stressed that he himself was 'not at all a bigot to the policy of keeping Russia out of Constantinople'.

What Salisbury wanted very nearly did occur. In February 1896 Currie reported a conversation with the French ambassador at Constantinople, Cambon. Whilst talking of 'what might have been', Cambon had said:

> There was a moment, a very short one, when your fleet could have come in without opposition from any quarter, immediately after the outbreak [of disturbances] at Constantinople. If you had stated publicly that you were coming in simply to maintain order, and had invited Russia to do the same, she would have probably assented and would have ordered her Sebastopol fleet to co-operate with yours; and the other Powers would have followed suit.

Salisbury was certainly not so blindly and obstinately devoted to the policy of keeping Russia out of Constantinople – the policy of the Crimean War – that he was not prepared to try to devise and implement a better one. What he saw, in the state of the Ottoman Empire from the end of the year 1894, was a chance to put the clock back, to retrieve the mistake of the Crimean War, to avoid having to repeat that mistake in the future, and to transfer the focus of British interest from the eastern Mediterranean to the Persian Gulf. In September 1896, when he met the Tsar at Balmoral, Salisbury took the opportunity to refer Nicholas II to the proposals of 1853, and to encourage him to square Austria-Hungary with 'compensation and security' in return for the Russian occupation of Constantinople, to which Salisbury raised no objection provided it was made 'part of a general arrangement'.

As late as 23 November 1896 Salisbury was writing to Currie that 'if the cutting up of the Sultan becomes practical the sovereignty of the Straits may become both for us and Austria a question of compensation'. On 3 December Salisbury heard that Cambon in Constantinople believed that if the outlet of the Bosporus into the Black Sea were in Russian hands this 'would be generally acceptable as a solution'. On 20 December 1896 Salisbury heard that the Russian ambassador to Constantinople, Nelidov, who was then in St Petersburg, had revealed that his instructions did not specifically mention the integrity of the Ottoman Empire. On 22 December the German ambassador in London, Hatzfeldt, joked with Salisbury that the latter's interest in a rumoured Russian map dividing the Ottoman Empire showed that he wanted to know that his desires of August 1895 concerning 'l'Euphrate etc.' had been taken into account in St Petersburg according to his wishes. Hatzfeldt was rewarded with a nod of approval and '*un regard d'intelligence*' from Salisbury. Only British control over that more eastern part of the Middle East would counter the influence of Constantinople in the Levant and compensate for the substitution of Russian for Ottoman or anyone else's influence there. This was, as far as Salisbury was now concerned, *the* way to secure not just the route to India but also India itself. A continued occupation or a formal annexation of Egypt did not fulfill this requirement. Salisbury had been trying to get out of Egypt since at least 1887, in order to improve relations with France and to eliminate what he called Bismarckian *chantage*, and to be as a result in a position 'to snap our fingers at the world'. Salisbury had long appreciated that British public opinion would not easily relinquish Egypt – 'it has tasted the fleshpots and it will not let them go' – *unless* it received an even more substantial *pied à terre*. British control over East African coasts (which was what the reconquest of the Sudan, begun at the end of 1896, was really about, as it offered the prospect of a junction with a north–south railway from Uganda) was of more importance to the security of the British Empire, and to its communications, than any position in Egypt itself. '*Du côté de l'Euphrate*', 'the southern slope of the Taurus with Syria and Mesopotamia' was, in Salisbury's view, the best solution.

❖

Between mid-1895 and the end of 1896 Salisbury had seen himself, in effect, as Lord Aberdeen, Nicholas II as Nicholas I, and Currie as Sir Hamilton Seymour. He dreamt that it was to him as Prime Minister that Seymour had transmitted in 1853 the proposals of the Tsar for a 'reconsideration' of the Ottoman Empire, *and that he had accepted them*, had brought his cabinet along with him, and thereby avoided the Crimean War and indeed any subsequent war against Russia over the continued existence of the Ottoman Empire. Although he failed on this occasion to bring about his grand design, he did not lose sight of it by any means. In fact, in the first two months of 1898, he can be found trying to develop it into an even grander and more wide-ranging one. On 25 January 1898 he wrote to O'Conor, the ambassador to St Petersburg:

Our idea was this. The two Empires of China and Turkey are so weak that in all important matters they are constantly guided by the advice of Foreign Powers. In giving this advice Russia and England are constantly opposed, neutralising each other's efforts much more frequently than the real antagonism of their interests would justify; and this condition of things is not likely to diminish, but to increase. It is to remove or lessen this evil that we have thought that an understanding with Russia might benefit both nations. We contemplate no infraction of existing rights.... We aim at no partition of territory, but only a partition of preponderance. It is evident that both in respect to Turkey and China there are large portions which interest Russia much more than England and *vice versa*. Merely as an illustration, and binding myself to nothing, I would say that the portion of Turkey which drains into the Black Sea, together with the drainage valley of the Euphrates as far as Baghdad, interest Russia much more than England: whereas Turkish Africa, Arabia, and the valley of the Euphrates below Baghdad interest England much more than Russia. A similar distinction exists in China between the Valley of the Hoango with the territory north of it and the Valley of the Yangtze.

About all this, which is distinctly reminiscent of the outlook of Nesselrode in the 1840s (see Chapter 3 part II), O'Conor proceeded to see Nicholas II and his foreign policy advisers. On 7 February he reported that whilst the Russians were happy about the regions north of the Hoango and even with Tientsin and the Pechili coast of China, he had observed that Count Muraviev, the Russian Foreign Minister, 'has rather avoided referring to Asia Minor, Africa, Persian Gulf, etc.'. O'Conor thought the time had arrived 'to make it clearly understood that the arrangement between the two countries shall extend not only to China but to all the other regions where we have conflicting interests'.

This initiative of Salisbury's made no further progress. It is mentioned here simply to demonstrate the scale and daring of Salisbury's thinking on foreign and imperial affairs. The Russian ambassador in London, de Staal, had written to St Petersburg at one point in the Near Eastern crisis of 1895–97 that British statesmen rarely looked far ahead (*les hommes d'état anglais ont rarement la vision des choses lointaines*). This generalisation certainly did not apply to Salisbury, and on this score the representatives of the Great Powers in London were practically unanimous. Hatzfeldt, the German ambassador, said of Salisbury that he was a man 'who loves to examine the problems of the future and to discuss them'. Courcel, the French ambassador, wrote in June 1896 that Salisbury liked to see solutions, liked to see difficulties removed, liked to arrive at clear, well-defined situations, '*situations nettes*': 'the provisional, to which the English were all too habitually inclined, worried him and was a burden to him; he aspired to put an end to it'. Courcel also wrote that the possession of

Arabia and of the Persian Gulf would establish the uncontested primacy of England over the Muslim populations and would assure English rule over the whole of the littoral of the Indian Ocean, placing in her hands, like an almost uninterrupted chain, all the coasts and peninsulas from the Cape of Good Hope to the Straits of Singapore; the Mediterranean had lost for England the importance it had had over the last two centuries; once the railways in the valley of the Euphrates had been built, it was over that route to India that England would wish to exercise an influence beyond challenge.

This is what Osten-Sacken, the Russian ambassador in Berlin, had written in February 1896 – it was English control of the Red Sea that made her mistress of the Suez Canal; henceforward, English eyes were focused upon another route to India, '*celle de l'Euphrate et du golfe Persique*'. Salisbury could have put it better himself, but not much better.

12

THE PROBLEMS OF THE OTTOMAN EMPIRE, 1870–1908

In 1870 the Ottoman Empire occupied most of the Balkans, with the exception of Greece; all of Asia Minor; all of Syria and Mesopotamia; all of Arabia; and half of north Africa. It touched three continents. Its coastline stretched for several thousand miles through the Black Sea, the Aegean, the Adriatic, the Mediterranean, the Red Sea, the Persian Gulf, and the Indian Ocean. It was vulnerable to invasion by all the European powers except the German Empire; it faced problems with all the Balkan states and with numerous minor potentates in north Africa, the Middle East, Arabia and the Persian Gulf. The question here is: how did the Ottoman Empire survive as long as it did? In answer to this question there are five elements to be considered. The first element is the strength of the Ottoman Empire itself. The second is the faith of the other Great Powers in treaties guaranteeing its integrity and independence: their respect for them, their determination to uphold and enforce them, the extent to which they regarded them as binding, as part of 'the public law of Europe'. The third is alliances with other Great Powers. The fourth is alliances with minor powers. The fifth is the existence and exploitation of the rivalries between Great Powers and between minor ones.

❖

The Ottoman Empire always had 250,000 men under arms, drawn mainly from western and central Anatolia. It maintained seven armies, based at Constantinople, Edirne (Adrianople), Salonika, Sivas, Damascus, Baghdad and Yemen. Additional garrisons were stationed in Tripolitania and in Crete. On paper, the armies of the Ottoman Empire constituted a formidable force. On the ground, however, these armies could not easily be concentrated or brought together. For one thing poor internal communications were the norm, which meant either long marches or travel by sea. For another, to vacate the provinces or areas where garrisons were stationed might lead to problems there. As Abdul Hamid II, who ruled as Sultan from 1876 to 1908, put it:

The protection of the Balkan, Anatolian and Arabian frontiers, the maintenance of law and order in sensitive regions like the Yemen and Crete, support for the gendarmerie in suppressing brigandage in other provinces, and the collection of taxes in certain provinces all require troops.

Military expenditure was the largest single item in the budget of the Ottoman Empire. It amounted to some 40 per cent of the total. In the mid-1870s, total revenue was £17–18 million; of this, £14 million went on interest on foreign loans. So the 40 per cent of the budget which went towards military expenditure was only 40 per cent of £3–4 million. This was a situation which did not improve. In 1875, indeed, the bankruptcy of the state was declared. One result of this was the neglect of the navy from 1876 to 1908. Instead of a fleet, the Ottoman Empire relied on torpedoes, mines, and shore batteries. Foreign observers did admit that these cheaper methods had made the Dardanelles impregnable throughout the 1890s. The Dardanelles, however, although a vital spot, was not the only such spot. A great deal was left exposed. It was appreciated in Constantinople that naval powers such as Great Britain, France and later even Italy could use their sea power to encourage revolt and rebellion in far-flung provinces, especially in the Ottoman Empire's Arab territories.

❖

At the end of the London Conference which met in 1871 to deal with the Russian abrogation of the Black Sea neutrality clause of the Treaty of Paris of 1856 the Ottoman representative, Musurus, was commended for his work by the Sultan. Musurus replied that his job had been made that much easier by the Sultan himself, who in devoting 'all his solicitude to the organisation of his army and navy and to the improvement of the administration of his vast estates has shown how much he is aware that the maintenance of his rights of sovereignty and the integrity of his empire is more firmly assured when it is based on his own power and on the devotion of his people than when it rests basically on international guarantees'. The Sultan to whom Musurus was writing was Abdul Aziz. It might be said of Abdul Aziz that he carried the advice of Musurus rather too far, in that the large fleet he tried to build up before his death in 1876 was largely responsible for the state bankruptcy of 1875. What, however, of the point made by Musurus about international guarantees? What faith could be placed in them?

The position at the end of the London Conference of 1871 was as follows. The Ottoman Empire had lost the protection afforded to it by the neutralisation of the Black Sea. However, until the Russians decided to have a fleet in the Black Sea, and this was not until the 1890s, the situation remained, in practice, exactly the same. Moreover, important safeguards, embodied in international treaties, remained in force. The Danube barrier was intact: Russia was still excluded from the ranks of riverain powers. The reconfirmation of all the clauses of the Treaty of Paris except the one that neutralised the Black Sea suggested that all the powers continued to respect the territorial integrity of the Ottoman Empire and recognised that they should not interfere with its internal affairs. The Rule of the Straits had actually been strengthened to allow the Ottoman Empire to call in outside aid if it was threatened. The Triple Treaty of 15 April 1856, under which Great Britain, France and Austria agreed to supply military support to the Ottoman Empire, had not been challenged, and might be presumed to be still operative. The Great Powers of Europe, including Russia, had recognised their obligation not to abrogate unilaterally treaties to which they were signatories.

The whole occasion appeared to demonstrate that the rule of law still obtained, and that the umbrella placed over the Ottoman Empire in 1856 was still in place. Much as Lord Granville, the British Foreign Secretary, deplored the existence of the Triple Treaty, he did not deny that it was binding. He wrote: 'How very foolish it was of us to have concocted it. But there it is, with obligations as binding as were ever contracted.' He suggested getting the German Empire to subscribe to it. Granville's suggestion was vetoed by the Prime Minister, Gladstone, who stated in December 1870: 'stringent as it the Triple Treaty is in its terms, it does not appear to me to have much force as a covenant at present, when Turkey declares her own incapacity to fight except with (virtually) our money; guarantees as such seem to me to presuppose the capacity of any guaranteed State to fight for herself; and then to supply a further auxiliary defence.'

In the course of the next eight years, much was to change in respect of faith in treaties, and the change was along Gladstonian rather than Granvillian lines. Ominously, a British Parliamentary Blue Book of 1871, which listed 'treaties of guarantee under which this country is engaged to interfere by force of arms to attack or defend any government or nation', made no mention of the Triple Treaty. The agreement between Austria-Hungary and Russia at Budapest in January 1877 contained the following clause:

> If the [Austro-Hungarian] government is invited to cooperate in the putting into effect of the Treaty of 15 April 1856, it will decline to co-operate in the case provided for in the present convention and, without

contesting the validity of the said [1856] Treaty, will proclaim its neutrality.

In other words, Austria-Hungary and Russia were planning a partition of the Ottoman Empire – a direct assault on its integrity, as Austria-Hungary was allowing Russia to go to war with the Ottoman Empire in return for changes in the status of Bosnia and Hercegovina. The Triple Treaty was not to be allowed to stand in the way of these changes.

Given the attitude of Lord Derby, Granville's successor as British Foreign Secretary, an appeal to the Triple Treaty was more likely to come from France than from Great Britain. At the beginning of February 1877 Derby pointed out in the House of Lords that the Treaty of Paris, under which six powers undertook to respect the integrity and independence of the Ottoman Empire, and guaranteed in common the observance of this engagement, contained no promise to make its non-observance a *casus belli*. So far as the Treaty of Paris was concerned, said Derby, Great Britain was 'in no sense bound by a promise to fight for Turkey'. At the end of February 1877 Derby implied that the Triple Treaty, which had been devised to fill precisely that gap left by the Treaty of Paris, might itself be considered 'for practical purposes as null and void'. In Parliament on 19 April 1877 Derby continued in this vein:

> No treaties can or are intended to be eternal. They are framed with reference to existing circumstances, and though I do not say whether that is so or is not the case in regard to the Treaty of 1856, yet nothing has been more common in European diplomacy than the recognition of the fact that treaties do by the lapse of time and the force of events become obsolete.

Clearly, for Derby, Parliamentary Blue Books listing obligations were redundant, rather than required reading. His public statements, in effect, disposed of both the Treaty of Paris and the Triple Treaty, so far as Great Britain was concerned. Five days after Derby's statement of 19 April Russia declared war on the Ottoman Empire. Once war had broken out Derby maintained that, as the contracting powers to the Triple Treaty had allowed a violation of the integrity of the Ottoman Empire to take place, the moment for invoking that Treaty had passed! Two decades later Lord Salisbury was to minute: 'Remember the fall in 1877 of the tripartite guarantee of Turkey signed in 1856 by Austria, France, and England.' (One curiosity is that, on 30 March 1896, Salisbury's spokesman on foreign affairs in the House of Commons, Lord Curzon, stated that Great Britain was still bound by the Triple Treaty; whilst in

1899, under the same government, the Triple Treaty was omitted from another Parliamentary Blue Book listing 'parts of all treaties now existing and still obligatory as contain an undertaking entered into by Her Majesty with reference to the territory or government of any other Power'. It was a case of now you see it, now you don't. No wonder the Russian historian Gorianov concluded: 'History teaches us that Great Britain is one of those Powers who only observe the treaties they have signed when the latter coincide with their interests of the moment.'

The disinterested attitude of Lord Derby in the later 1870s was complemented by Bismarck's advocacy of schemes for a partition of the Ottoman Empire. Bismarck first sketched out his ideas in January and February 1876. His plan was that Austria–Hungary should take Bosnia and Hercegovina, that Russia should recover Bessarabia, that Britain should take Egypt, and that compensation for France and Italy should be found in north Africa. He elaborated further at the end of 1876, maintaining that the Ottoman Empire, as a political institution, was not worth great wars between the European powers. To avoid such wars, the powers must balance the alterations made at the expense of the Ottoman Empire. Bismarck again mentioned Bosnia and Hercegovina for Austria–Hungary, Egypt and Suez for Great Britain, on this occasion Syria for France, and an Anglo–Russian agreement which would leave Adrianople and Constantinople to the Turks. In July 1877 Bismarck told the British ambassador to Berlin, in response to enquiries made by Disraeli, that the powers would do well 'to force the question and settle it once for all': Russia and Austria–Hungary would 'take care of European Turkey'; England 'had better secure the road to India – and if France helped herself to something in the East he would be heartily glad'.

Partition, then, was the policy of Russia, Austria–Hungary, and Germany from the mid-1870s. At the Congress of Berlin, if not before, given Lord Derby's preparedness to accommodate Russia and Salisbury's attitudes as Secretary of State for India (see Chapter 11), it became that of Great Britain as well. The partition that duly took place at Berlin deprived the Ottoman Empire of two-thirds of its European possessions: Romania, Serbia and Montenegro were declared independent states, and each grew in size at the expense of the Ottoman Empire; Greece received Thessaly and part of Epirus; Russia retained southern Bessarabia; Britain took Cyprus; Austria–Hungary was in occupation of Bosnia and Hercegovina.

It could, of course, have been even worse for the Ottoman Empire. Bulgaria was not independent, merely autonomous and therefore still a tributary state, and did not include eastern Rumelia, another area made autonomous. From the Ottoman Empire's point of view, this was a distinct improvement on the terms extracted from it by Russia at the Treaty of San Stephano, which would have created a Greater Bulgaria including eastern Rumelia and with access to both the Black Sea and the Aegean. The Ottoman Empire still ruled directly over Albania, Macedonia, and much of Thrace, from its capital at Constantinople.

The new frontiers established by the Congress of Berlin did not render the Ottoman Empire any less vulnerable, for they did not always coincide with natural barriers. As Abdul Hamid II put it: 'Safe and definite frontiers were not defined for the Empire. Meadows and streams can never take the place of a clear and secure frontier.' The removal of Ottoman forces from Bulgaria and eastern Rumelia deprived the Ottoman Empire of the protection afforded by the Danube and by the Balkan range of mountains, and it no longer had any ports or harbours on the European shore of the Black Sea. The only tenable line of defence was at Çatalca, less than fifty miles from Constantinople itself. In 1886, however, Ottoman military control was re-established in the Rodop mountains as a result of the merger between Bulgaria and eastern Rumelia, although the consequence of this merger was that the Ottoman Empire henceforth faced a potential threat of Bulgarian invasion from two directions – south-east towards Adrianople and Constantinople, and south-west into Macedonia. In 1900 the Sultan's military advisers predicted that a Bulgarian invasion of Macedonia might reach Salonika in seven days. Salonika was all the more exposed as the Congress of Berlin had given Austria-Hungary a right of garrison in the Sandjak of Novi Pazar, which led to Salonika from the north. All the Sultan had was a promise on the part of Austria-Hungary to seek his permission before stationing garrisons south of the strategic Ragozna range of mountains, known as 'the gateway to Salonika'. On the Asian side, Russia's acquisition of the provinces of Kars and Ardahan, and her fortification of the Black Sea port of Batoum after 1886, placed her in a position to invade southwards towards Mosul, and thence towards both the Mediterranean (across Syria) and the Persian Gulf.

❖

It is against the background of the changes made at the Congress of Berlin that the remaining elements, of alliances with other Great Powers, of alliances with minor powers, and of exploiting rivalries between both, will be examined. It was not as if the Ottoman Empire, even in its truncated state after the Congress of Berlin, had nothing to offer to a potential ally. It had an army strong enough to count for something in a European war. (Bismarck minuted in October 1887, for instance: 'In a military sense Turkey's attitude for or against Russia makes a greater

THE BALKANS
1878-1908

Vienna

Graz

Budapest

RUSSIA

R Dniester

R Save

Agram (Zagreb)

R Prut

Bosnia

Belgrade

ROMANIA

R Danube

Sarajevo

SERBIA

Bucharest

Herze-
govina

Uvac

Nish

Bulgaria

Varna

MONTE
NEGRO

Novi Bazar

Mitrovitza

Sofia

Eastern
Roumelia

BLACK
SEA

ADRIATIC
SEA

Antivari

Üsküb

Philippopolis

Adrianople

Constantinople

O

T

T

Macedonia

O

M

Monastir

A

Albania

Salonika

E

M

P

I

R

N

E

Larissa

AEGEAN
SEA

GREECE

Athens

Frontiers of independent states
Frontier between the
Dual Monarchy and
the occupied territories
Boundaries inside the
Ottoman Empire
Railways

0   150
   Miles

0   Km   150

Crete

difference than England's.') The geographical position of the Ottoman Empire gave it the ability to intervene in certain conflicts. And it did control the Straits of the Dardanelles and the Bosporus, which were particularly important, if not indeed absolutely vital, in the case of hostilities between Great Britain and Russia. Some Russians seriously considered the option of such an alliance in 1885.

Great Britain, Russia, and Austria-Hungary were all potential allies for the Ottoman Empire. The latter's assessment of them will now be presented, in that order. Amongst those who helped determine the policy of the Ottoman Empire there were those who argued that the British and Ottoman Empires had a common interest in resisting Russian expansion in the Near East and Asia, and that Great Britain needed the Ottoman Empire as a barrier against Russia, needed the support of the Sultan as Caliph in dealing with its own Muslim subjects. To these arguments Abdul Hamid II replied, 'England does not have sufficient land forces'; he shared Lord Salisbury's view, expressed in 1887 to Bismarck, that British sea power would be of little assistance in repelling a Russian invasion by land of Asia or a Russia-supported attack by a Balkan state in Europe. As Abdul Hamid put it:

> As there is no need to explain, Russia is the Empire's neighbour, and whenever she wishes she can send powerful forces and occupy the Empire's Anatolian provinces as far as Mosul and Baghdad. Furthermore, although there exists in Bulgaria a party which is opposed to Russia, the greater part of the population looks to Russia and favours her. Similarly, the entire population of Montenegro is given over to her, and even a section of the population of Serbia and Romania is pro-Russian.

Or as one Grand Vizier put it: 'while admitting that Great Britain ... could attack the entire Russian Black Sea fleet, this would not suffice to prevent Russia's invasion towards the interior.'

It is worth remarking here that the Ottoman Empire of the last twenty-five years of the reign of Abdul Hamid II did *not* think that it had an alliance with Great Britain so far as its possessions in Asia were concerned, by virtue of the Cyprus Convention of 1878. The Convention did state that, 'If any attempt shall be made at any future time by Russia to take possession of further territories of His Majesty the Sultan in Asia as fixed by the Treaty of Berlin England engages to join the Sultan in defending them by force of arms'. But, at least by 1883, Abdul Hamid took this engagement as having lapsed – it having been dependent upon the implementation of reforms which he had never had any intention of implementing. It is not at all clear what took the British as long as it did to make this public – for it was only on 30 March 1896 that Lord Curzon told the House of Commons that, because the reforms which were a condition of Britain's pledge of military assistance for the defence of Turkey in Asia had not taken place, the British obligation had lapsed. Nor is it clear why, despite Curzon's announcement, the Cyprus Convention went on to be included in the 1899 Blue Book list of British treaty obligations and guarantees. This was yet another case of now you see it, now you don't. The possibly non-existent obligation was cancelled once again on 5 November 1914, this time by an Order in Council.

The Ottoman Empire after Abdul Hamid II, run by the Young Turkish Committee of Union and Progress, did approach Great Britain for an alliance at the end of 1908, and again in 1911. Although Winston Churchill was sympathetic on both occasions, as was the First Sea Lord, Sir John Fisher, the Foreign Office was not. By 1908 the Foreign Office had achieved a long-standing goal, an agreement with Russia, and had no wish to put this at risk. As the Foreign Secretary, Sir Edward Grey, wrote in August 1908 to the British ambassador in Constantinople: 'We cannot revert to the old policy of Lord Beaconsfield [Disraeli]'; Russia must not be given the impression 'that we are reverting to the old policy of supporting Turkey as a barrier against her'.

There were also, at Constantinople, those who argued that the Russian and Ottoman Empires had common interests as autocracies; that Russia should see that a strong and friendly Ottoman Empire was the best guarantee of her security in the Black Sea; and that after the loss of Cyprus in 1878 and of Egypt in 1882 to Great Britain the latter was more of a threat to the Ottoman Empire than was Russia. The counter-argument was that Russia's armies could not defend the Sultan's far-flung territories against British naval attacks. Kamil Pasha, who at the end of March 1878, even as the Peace of San Stephano was being negotiated, had discussed a Russo-Turkish alliance with the Grand Duke Nicholas, also pronounced on this fact of imperial life:

> In the event of war England will be able to incite neighbouring peoples against the Ottoman Empire and attack the Ottoman coasts with her fleet. Even if the Ottoman fleet was united with the Russian fleet, and even if they were able to block the entry of the British fleet into the Black Sea, it goes without saying that this would scarcely damage England's territory. Thus an alliance between the Ottoman and Russian Empires may be considered beneficial to Russia and extremely damaging to the Ottoman Empire.

Only if another naval power, such as France, joined a Russo-Turkish alliance would the latter make sense. In 1886 some Ottoman feelers were put out for such a project, but nothing eventuated.

To Abdul Hamid II, it appeared that neither Great Britain nor Russia could, alone, protect his empire against the other. Their different strengths cancelled them out. Abdul Hamid summed up the position, and dilemma, as he saw it, as follows:

> To whichever of these two Powers, England or Russia, the Ottoman Empire shows an inclination, it will encounter the other's violent hostility. Should it assume a course other than neutrality, it is clear that in the one case [i.e. an inclination towards Great Britain], the small Balkan governments of Serbia, Montenegro, and Greece – Russia's semi-vanguard – will attack, and by creating numerous difficulties, they will spread our force considerably. In the other case [i.e. an inclination towards Russia], however, the English will seek to force the Straits by sending their fleet to Besika in order to compel the Empire to ally with them, and they will try to create various troubles on the coasts of Anatolia and Syria.

Abdul Hamid no doubt learned about, and did not forget, contacts between the British and certain sheikhs and amirs on the periphery of the Ottoman Empire who wanted more independence from Constantinople even than they already had, as early as the late 1870s. The first professional consul of the British government at Jeddah, for instance, who took up his duties on 1 March 1879, had been in post only two weeks when he received an overture from Amir Hussein of the Hejaz. The British ambassador to Constantinople, returning there from a visit to Syria later in the year, was unwise (or wise) enough to tell the Sultan that whilst in Syria he had learned of the existence of an anti-Caliphate secret society, which aimed at establishing an Arab government. In London both the Foreign Office and the India Office thought that this sort of thing 'might possibly be turned to account at some future time'. On this particular occasion Abdul Hamid sent a special envoy into Arabia to investigate. Before that envoy completed his enquiries and returned, the Sultan had received further information. This was that two Englishmen had come from London to visit the Amir, and that the latter had taken them to a castle in Mecca where they stayed for a few days, holding secret talks. Abdul Hamid concluded that the participants intended to establish an 'Arab government in opposition to the Caliphate'. He put his foot down, and when Abdul Hamid II put his foot down, heads rolled. Even so, the British ambassador reported in March

1880 that the Sultan was still 'under some apprehension as to the communications between the British Government and the Amir.'

❖

During the winter of 1881–82 Abdul Hamid did propose an offensive and defensive alliance between the Ottoman Empire and the Central Powers. He sought political guarantees against Great Britain, Russia and France, and a military guarantee of the Balkans which only Austria-Hungary could provide. Germany and Austria-Hungary rejected this overture.

In 1887–88 the Ottoman Empire discussed the possibility of entry into both the Triple Alliance and the Anglo-Italian–Austro-Hungarian Mediterranean Agreements. Abdul Hamid decided not to pursue either alternative. His main objection was that neither Germany nor Austria-Hungary could protect the Ottoman Empire against a Russian invasion of Anatolia. All Abdul Hamid could do was to hope for a war between the Central Powers and Russia, and victory for the former over the latter. Such a war did not occur in his time. When it did occur, in 1914, the Young Turks immediately joined in on the side of the Central Powers.

❖

Alliances with Great Powers having been considered and, on the whole, having not been pursued, there remained the assistance that might be derived from minor powers. The latter can be divided into those to the east and those to the west. Abdul Hamid did make overtures to the Amir of Afghanistan during the Russo-Turkish war of 1877, but to no avail. As Caliph, he appealed for aid to all true followers of the Prophet. There was no response. In 1879 the Grand Vizier alluded to the possibility of an anti-Russian alliance between the Ottoman Empire, Persia and Great Britain. A similar constellation was projected in 1886. In the late 1890s Abdul Hamid suggested a confidential relationship between Persia and the Ottoman Empire, in which the Shah would retain full internal authority but place his armed forces under the control of the Sultan; a committee of clerics would be appointed to reconcile Sunni and Shiite religious doctrine, and thereby found the confederation on a basis of Islamic unity. Nothing came of any of the above speculations.

Rather more interest was displayed in the Balkan states that had secured their independence from the Ottoman Empire, or a large degree of autonomy. To have these states as allies would be by definition to secure the Ottoman Empire against aggression from them. It would also deprive potentially hostile Great Powers such as Austria-Hungary and Russia of opportunities to use them to further their own designs against the

Ottoman Empire. In theory, a ring of threatening neighbours could be transformed into a protective screen. The first serious initiative towards the west was in early 1886, for a military alliance with Bulgaria, which might lead to a broader scheme embracing Serbia, Romania and possibly Greece. As originally formulated by Abdul Hamid, the alliance would have brought about the military re-incorporation of Bulgaria into the Ottoman Empire; the Bulgarian army was to be considered part of the Ottoman army, and the Sultan was to be its Commander-in-Chief; they were to guard each others' frontiers in time of peace and mobilise together should war come. As concluded on 31 January 1886 the terms were less sweeping. It was agreed that in the event of external attack on Bulgaria or eastern Rumelia, the Sultan would place as many troops as necessary at the disposal of Bulgaria, and that Bulgaria would reciprocate in the event of external aggression against the European provinces of the Ottoman Empire. This alliance, which was an effort to redefine Ottoman-Bulgarian relations following the revolt of eastern Rumelia in 1885 and the war between Serbia and Bulgaria of the same year, was never ratified.

Ten years later, in 1897, Abdul Hamid put forward proposals for a series of parallel military understandings between the Ottoman Empire, Serbia, Romania and Bulgaria. These proposals were made before and after the Greco-Turkish war of April 1897, and were motivated in part with a view to isolating Greece, in which they were successful, but also with a view to securing the Ottoman Empire against Russia in the longer term. As one Ottoman official put it to a Serbian representative: 'As soon as Franz Josef dies, Russia will attack and smash the Austro-Hungarian monarchy. After that, Serbia and Bulgaria will be only two soup-spoonfuls for Russia. When she has swallowed *you*, then it will be our turn and then it will be all up with us.' This being the longer-term prospect, Abdul Hamid offered to defend Bulgaria, Serbia and Romania against external aggression, if they would reciprocate. Nothing came of this, because Serbia and Romania wanted an alliance *against* Bulgaria, not with her; because Serbia wanted concessions from the Ottoman Empire in favour of her co-nationals who were still within it; and because Bulgaria wanted autonomy for Albania and Macedonia and the transformation of the Ottoman Empire into a dual Ottoman-Bulgarian monarchy.

Ten years later, Abdul Hamid tried again. In 1907–08 he attempted to put together an arrangement with Serbia, Romania and Greece, which in the first instance would be directed against Bulgaria, as a result of the latter's exacerbation of Macedonian problems. This diplomacy was cut short by the Young Turk revolution of July 1908.

❖

From the foregoing, what can one conclude as to the reasons for the longevity of the Ottoman Empire? It did not survive through alliances with minor powers to the east or west, or through alliances with Great Powers as, in the end, none were made. It was the beneficiary, however, of rivalries between the successor and would-be successor states of the Balkans, and of differences of opinion amongst the Great Powers as to when, and with what, to replace it.

Although faith in and respect for treaties did not serve the Ottoman Empire well up to and including the Congress of Berlin, it could be argued that the final act of the Congress of Berlin had more force. Even on the principle adopted by Lord Derby in advance of the Congress, whatever it determined would not become obsolete for twenty years. At the Congress of Berlin Britain and Russia had put forward different interpretations of the Rule of the Straits. The Russian interpretation was embraced by Germany and Austria-Hungary in the Drei-Kaiser-Bund of 1881 which, renewed in 1884, lasted until 1887. This helped see the Ottoman Empire through the Pendjeh crisis of 1885, during which Great Britain pressed it to be allowed to attack Russia in the Black Sea. The Ottoman Empire, encouraged by the Drei-Kaiser-Bund, resisted British pressure, even though this stance raised the prospect of the permanent loss of Egypt. (The Sultan was not to know that Gladstone's government, on this occasion, considered the defence of the North-West Frontier of India so important that it considered pulling out of Egypt altogether in order to concentrate its resources on the more important objective.) In 1887 the Drei-Kaiser-Bund collapsed and was replaced by a grouping of the Mediterranean powers of Italy, Austria-Hungary and Spain, plus Great Britain. The Mediterranean Agreements, supported and encouraged by Bismarck, who regarded Britain as 'the cement' necessary to keep Italy and Austria-Hungary together, were designed to deter a Russian occupation of a Bulgaria now reunited with eastern Rumelia and in general to preserve the status quo in the Mediterranean and Black Seas. Clause 4 of the Agreement of December 1887 posited 'the independence of Turkey, as guardian of important European interests – the Caliphate, the freedom of the Straits etc., to be independent of all foreign preponderating influence.' Although the Ottoman Empire was not a party to these agreements, and did not know the precise terms of them, it did benefit from their emphasis on the status quo. Moreover, they lasted for ten years, into 1897, at which point Austria-Hungary and Russia made an agreement between themselves regarding the maintenance of the status quo in the Balkans. The operation of the Austro-Russian Agreement helped to internationalise the Macedonian problem. Muraviev and Lamsdorff for

Russia, and Goluchowski for Austria-Hungary, were determined not to let the small states of the region decide what should happen there. The Austro-Russian understanding in turn lasted ten years, until its breakdown in October 1908.

From the end of the Congress of Berlin it is as if the Great Powers of Europe were, on the whole, agreed that no further changes, beyond those already agreed upon, should be made, that the partition of the Ottoman Empire in Europe had gone as far as it should go. Although, in subsequent decades, one or another Great Power was momentarily tempted to go beyond the status quo, there was a basic appreciation that to do so risked embroiling Europe itself, the whole of Europe, in a great war. Tsar Alexander III might have stated flambuoyantly in September 1885, 'In my opinion we should have a single and unique aim: it is the occupation of Constantinople in order to establish ourselves once and for all in the Straits and to know that it will always be in our hands'. In practice, he knew this could not be done unilaterally. So did others. In mid-1888 the Russian ambassador in Constantinople, Nelidov, advised Giers to take advantage of a visit that the Kaiser might make to St Petersburg to ascertain the German attitude to a Russian *coup de main*: 'before risking a word, it is necessary to know whether Bismarck can and will go as far as is necessary for us.' After Bismarck, and especially after the conclusion of the Franco-Russian Alliance, it was for the Russians a question of the permission of France as well as that of Germany. The French made it clear in 1895–96 that they would not sanction a Russian *coup de main* against Constantinople and a further partition of the Ottoman Empire unless France received Alsace and Lorraine at the same time. This unacceptable demand, raising the stakes as it did, was the elegant French way of rendering a game that some Russians wished to play not worth the candle, although the intervention between 5 and 19 December 1896 of Witte and Pobedonestev, who shared the French view, to overturn a decision that some of their colleagues had taken, was crucial on this occasion.

The Congress of Berlin was brought back into play, three months later, by Lord Salisbury. In March 1897 he delivered a rebuke in the House of Lords to Kimberley, the spokesman of the Liberal Party on foreign affairs, and a former Foreign Secretary. Salisbury stated categorically that Great Britain would be 'no party to a violation of [the integrity of Turkey] without [the] authority [of the Concert, the federation of Europe] consecrated as [that integrity] is by congresses the most solemn, by negotiations the most important, by events which should have pressed their value upon every mind.' Given Salisbury's recent, and indeed enduring, interest in a partition of the Ottoman Empire which would have given the British Empire Syria and Mesopotamia (see Chapter 11), the key words here were 'without the authority of the Concert'. Having failed to get sufficient powers to go beyond the Treaty of Berlin in 1895–96, Salisbury, without of course disclosing what he had been attempting to do, now reoccupied the moral high ground of the maintenance of the status quo.

❖

After 1878, then, the Ottoman Empire could thank, at various times, but not simultaneously, all the Great Powers. It could thank Great Britain for her role in the Mediterranean Agreements. It could thank Austria-Hungary, whose alliance of 1883 with Romania helped keep Russia at a distance from the Ottoman Empire; which was also a party to the Mediterranean Agreements; which was flatly opposed to any change in the status of Constantinople in the years 1895 to 1897; and which then went on to make an understanding with Russia as regards the maintenance of the status quo in the Balkans. It could thank Italy, which was also a party to the Mediterranean Agreements, whatever designs she may have had upon Ottoman provinces in north Africa. It could thank Russia, whose definition of the Rule of the Straits she persuaded Germany and Austria-Hungary to share between 1881 and 1887; and which recognised that her acquisition of Constantinople required German assent in advance. It could thank France, who refused in December 1895 and again in December 1896 to back Nelidov's partition schemes. It could thank the German Empire, which in the person of Kaiser Wilhelm II refused in July 1895 to embrace the plans for a partition that Lord Salisbury was maturing; and which produced an impression of German interest in the maintenance of the Ottoman Empire as a result of the visits that Wilhelm II made to Constantinople in 1889 and to Damascus and Jerusalem in 1899, and as a result of the scheme elaborated in the early 1890s for a railway from Berlin to Baghdad. (From the point of view of Abdul Hamid II, the Baghdad Railway Project was designed to pull his empire more closely together, to increase central control over the peripheries by improving communications and making it easier both to collect taxes and to quash rebellions. The same motives applied to the spur railway to the Hejaz.)

The Ottoman Empire could also thank the first ruler of Bulgaria, Prince Alexander of Battenburg, who fell out with the Tsar in the early 1880s and adopted the Bulgarian, rather than the Russian, cause. It could thank the people of Bulgaria and eastern Rumelia, who reunited in 1885 and had no wish to readmit the Russians to a controlling influence in their affairs. It could thank both the Bulgarians and the Serbs – the former for repelling a Serbian attack in 1885, and the latter for attacking Bulgaria in the first place.

The Ottoman Empire could also thank itself, to some extent: its recognised ability to fight on the defensive, as demonstrated in the Russo-Turkish war of 1877, not only considerably weakened the Russians, but caused them to be in no hurry to repeat the experience; its fortifications of the Dardanelles made a forcing of the Straits a gamble so distinct that British cabinets in both the mid-1880s and the mid-1890s were most unwilling to contemplate doing so; its defeat of Greece, which had attacked it, in 1897, put at rest rumours of a wholesale decline and collapse at that time – the 'sick man of Europe' was not as sick as all that.

All the above elements are necessary to account for the survival and the longevity of the Ottoman Empire, historiographically the most neglected of the Great Powers.

13

THE ITALIAN PROBLEM IN INTERNATIONAL RELATIONS, 1882–1915

In May 1882 Sidney Sonnino, a deputy in the Italian parliament, stated that Italy ought to set herself the two goals of friendship with England and a hard and fast alliance with Germany and Austria-Hungary. He expressed the opinion that the friendship of Austria-Hungary in particular was the essential precondition for what he called 'a fruitful foreign policy' on Italy's part. The isolation that would obtain without such an arrangement, he said, would be equivalent to annihilation. Days later, on 20 May 1882, the Triple Alliance of Austria-Hungary, Germany and Italy was signed; it included a declaration that it could not be envisaged as being directed against Great Britain. On 26 April 1915 Baron Sonnino, then Italian Foreign Minister, signed the Pact of London, by which Italy agreed to declare war, within four weeks, on the Central Powers – Germany and Austria-Hungary.

For the historian of international relations, Sonnino personifies the problem, namely the change in Italy's allegiance between the point when her signature of the Triple Alliance, ostensibly, announced both her arrival and her acceptance, by acknowledged Great Powers, as a Great Power, and the point when she declared war upon the two states whose ally, technically, she still was.

❖

Before addressing the questions of when, and for what reasons, this change took place, it is not inappropriate to present certain features of the situation in which Italy found herself before she became a member of the Triple Alliance. In May 1874, for instance, the Austro-Hungarian Foreign Minister Count Andrassy made it clear that the Dual Monarchy was not disposed to view sympathetically any Italian claims on its land or its population:

> In effect, we could not cede Italy the people belonging to her by language without artificially provoking in those nationalities on the frontiers of the Empire, a centrifugal movement toward the sister

nationalities bordering our States. This movement would place us in the dilemma of resigning ourselves to the loss of these provinces, or, indeed, of incorporating the bordering countries within the Monarchy.

Andrassy went on, in October 1876, to warn Italy, through the Italian ambassador in Vienna, that 'no enlargement of our Monarchy ... could give Italy claim to compensation, and that we, at the first sign of an annexationist policy, would under no circumstances remain on the defensive but would proceed with the most resolute aggressive action'.

Further warnings were made in the spring and early summer of 1878, as the European powers made preparations for the Congress of Berlin. The Germans, who in August 1877 had rejected a request from the Italian Foreign Minister, Francesco Crispi, for an alliance against Austria-Hungary and France, informed the Italians in April 1878 that if they wished to count upon German friendship they must seek no irredentist compensation for Austria-Hungary's occupation of Bosnia and Hercegovina. The British, who in February 1878 had asked Italy if she would act with them if the presence of a combined fleet at Constantinople seemed desirable, and who at the end of March 1878 had sought Italian participation in an alliance with themselves and Austria-Hungary – on both occasions without securing the desired result – delivered at the beginning of June 1878 a strong warning to the same effect as the German one: if Italy took advantage of the occupation of Bosnia and Hercegovina by Austro-Hungarian troops to bring forward the question of the Trentino 'she would do so at her own risk and peril'; she would certainly be placing herself 'in opposition to England'.

The Italian government conceded the point made by Germany and Great Britain. Although initially the Italians tried to console themselves with the idea that if the Austro-Hungarian occupation of Bosnia and Hercegovina became permanent, requests for compensation might be made, they did not press the matter, and did not raise the question of compensation at the Congress of Berlin. The abandonment by the Italians of irredentist ambitions at the expense of Austria-Hungary was a price that had to be paid for membership of the Triple Alliance. The question for the Italians then became: what policy was to take the place of those ambitions?

❖

There is no doubt as to what, in the 1880s and 1890s, those contemporaries who had to deal with the foreign policy of successive Italian governments believed that policy to be. The Italians gained a reputation that immediately calls to mind Sonnino's use of the word 'fruitful' in May 1882. In November 1880 as in August 1877, Bismarck was reluctant to combine with Italy. To do so, he said, would encourage her to formulate exaggerated claims dictated by the international ambitions to which the Italian character was inclined. As late as 28 December 1881 Bismarck remained reluctant to embrace Italy. Apparently forgetting that in February 1878 he had told the British ambassador that if Austria-Hungary became involved in a war with Russia she would probably lose the Trentino, he stated that only Italy would benefit from any agreements made with her. In 1887 the British ambassador to Vienna wrote that the worst of having Italy as an ally, or associate, was that 'of course, she always wants something as a *pourboire*'. Salisbury agreed, and rejected an Italian proposal for an offensive and defensive alliance against France partly because, as he put it, 'the hypothesis cannot be admitted for a moment that Italy (would be) going to war without the prospect of compensation'. In 1888 as in 1887 Italy remained, for the British, 'an embarrassing ally'. Not only did Crispi, now once again Italian Prime Minister, long, in Salisbury's words, for some 'splashy interference in affairs', but he 'cost a good deal'. Salisbury went on:

> He [Crispi] has picked a quarrel with Zanzibar; he has given deadly offence to Turkey by affecting to have annexed Massowa [on the Red Sea] ... and by a singular stroke of genius he has contrived also to quarrel with Greece.... His singular propensity for breaking windows will get us into trouble before long.

Salisbury's explanation for all this, in a letter to Lord Dufferin of 28 December 1888, was that 'of course the Italians entered into the Triple Alliance for what they could get: and have shown an intelligible impatience to realise their investment'. He went on to say that Italy's 'demeanour' at that time was 'the result of her admission to the honour of fighting for two ancient dynasties'.

In January 1891 Salisbury produced a further analysis, of course from the British point of view:

> There is a misapprehension in the Italian way of looking at affairs which causes infinite trouble. They imagine that their alliance is a pearl of great price which we would sell much to secure: and on the strength of this belief they are constantly hinting that we should show our gratitude by large material concessions.
>
> I confess I do not take this view. To my mind the Italian alliance is an unprofitable, and even slightly onerous corollary of the German alliance.

Germany and Austria are very useful friends as regards Turkey, Russia, Egypt, and even France. *They* value the Italian alliance greatly, because it means many battalions to *them*; and for their sake, we value it too. But by itself, it makes our relations with France more difficult, and it is of no use anywhere else. Italy therefore thinks us unreasonable for not paying up.

Salisbury's remarks of 1888 and 1891 were his response to the ministry of Crispi which lasted from 1887 to 1891. Salisbury was scathing about Crispi, and determined to give him a very wide berth. Crispi might think that colonies were 'a necessity of modern life'; Salisbury simply found it 'difficult to guess what motive Crispi can have for the appropriation of barren territories which can never produce any trade, and which certainly confer no glory'. He regarded Crispi's colonial aspirations as 'misplaced and suicidal', and was positive that they would not be gratified at the cost of any solid sacrifices on Britain's part. Rather Britain would, as Salisbury confided to the French, direct her efforts towards 'keeping the Italians within bounds'. This British attitude was maintained by the Liberal government of Gladstone and Rosebery between August 1892 and the return of the Conservatives and Salisbury in July 1895, and by Salisbury subsequently, not least because Crispi had returned to office in 1893 and remained there until March 1896.

The attitude of the German government, after Bismarck, was much the same as that of Bismarck himself, and of the British. Bülow, for instance, who in the mid-1890s was German Ambassador in Rome before becoming Foreign Minister, spoke of the Italian desire for aggrandisement and said that it might manifest itself in any direction. In 1895, when Crispi asked the Central Powers for support, and especially for a formal engagement to acquire Tripoli for Italy, the Italians were told that the Triple Alliance was not to be regarded as '*une sorte de société d'acquets*' for the benefit of one of its members. In 1896 Passetti, the Austro-Hungarian ambassador in Rome, wrote that Italian statesmen were dominated by the desire to interfere in everything, by a thirst for new conquests, for resounding successes, and by the fear that they might be forestalled of prizes by action on the part of others.

There is undoubtedly a *prima facie* case for attributing the change of allegiance on the part of Italy to a desire to secure concessions. Further evidence might be adduced in the form of an agreement made with France in 1902 which gave Italy a free hand as regards Tripoli. This agreement, an exchange of letters between Prinetti, the Italian Foreign Minister, and Barrère the French Ambassador, in July 1902, was the end-product of a long drawn-out negotiation. The context for this negotiation was created by the assertion, early in 1896, of the then Italian

Foreign Minister the Duc de Sermoneta that, were he able to remake history, he would try to keep Italy out of major international combinations; as it was, he said, he would try to reduce, so far as possible, the inconveniences of those to which Italy already belonged. Sermoneta's assertion was followed up in 1900 by expressions of willingness on the part of the Prime Minister, Antonio di Rudini, and the Foreign Minister, Visconti Venosta, to alter the character of Italy's alliances with regard to France. In July 1902 it was agreed that France was free to extend her influence over Morocco, and that Italy was free to extend hers over Tripoli. The Italian government also declared that in the case where France was the object of either direct or indirect aggression on the part of one or several powers, Italy would maintain a strict neutrality. This was the price that Italy had to pay France in return for a free hand as regards Tripoli. The French had insisted that Italy demonstrate that she was a friendly power, disengaged from all political and military obligations against France.

To add to the *prima facie* case, there are the promises which Italy negotiated in the Pact of London of April 1915 in return for fighting with the Entente Powers against her own former allies: the Trentino, south Tirol, Trieste with Venezia Giulia, one third of Dalmatia and some Dalmatian islands; a virtual mandate over Albania, outright possession of Valona, the Bay of Saseno and the Dodecanese Islands; a substantial amount of Asia Minor, the whole of Libya, together with some other acquisitions in East Africa.

So can it be concluded that, in 1902, Italy sold out the Triple Alliance in return for what the British dismissively described as 'the vast sandpit' of a part of north Africa? Can it be concluded that Italy fought against her former allies from May 1915 in order to make her foreign policy as 'fruitful' as possible? Were concessions and acquisitions the keys to Italian foreign policy, and the explanation for her change of allegiance?

❖

There is rather more to be explored. Both Bismarck and Crispi, in 1882, remarked on the need of Italy, with her long and unfortified coastline, to be protected by the British Navy from her neighbour in the Mediterranean, France. Without the friendship or alliance of England, said Crispi, 'we would not be masters of our coasts'. Lord Salisbury, in 1888, wrote that

> the Germans are always impressing on me that the sole chance of Italy being able to help Austria in the event of an attack by Russia on Austria, would be that her coasts should be protected by us from a French naval

attack. Without our Naval Alliance, the Germans always maintain that Italy would count for nothing and be paralysed.

Caprivi, Bismarck's successor, wrote in a memorandum dated 23 April 1891:

> Italy can enter into no treaty directed against England; without England's friendship, Italy cannot move a step in the Mediterranean; the military value of Italy as an ally is mainly dependent on whether Great Britain is a fourth party to the [Triple] Alliance, and will relieve Italy of apprehensions about her coastline.

This was the consideration that governed what was known as Crispi's 'old habit of turning first to London in all questions affecting the Mediterranean and Africa'; that was responsible for the admission of Baron Blanc, the Italian Ambassador to London, in 1894, that there was 'nothing for it but to go with England as before'; and that lay behind Rudini's assertion in a speech of 1 July 1896 that 'the friendship of Great Britain was the necessary complement of the Triple Alliance'.

The change in the allegiance of Italy, which began in 1896, was kick-started by two things. One was the defeat, at Adowa in Abyssinia on 1 March 1896, of the 15,000 strong Italian Expeditionary Force – a defeat and humiliation which brought down the Crispi administration. The other was the Italian fear, at the same time, that an Anglo-French entente was imminent. Rudini, who took over as Prime Minister from Crispi, told his Triple Alliance partners later in March 1896 that, if Britain allied with France, Italy could not take it upon herself to make war against those two naval powers. Shortly afterwards Sermoneta, who remained Foreign Minister only until July, declared that Italy, given her geographical situation, and in particular the length of her Mediterranean coastline, could not take up arms simultaneously against these two powers. Rudini considered issuing an official note to the effect that Italy, in the case of England and France allying to open hostilities against one or both of the powers to which Italy was allied through the Triple Alliance, would not consider the *casus foederis* under that alliance as arising. Bearing in mind the contribution that the Italians had made, in 1891, to the making of the Franco-Russian Alliance (see Chapter 10) – their campaign to give the impression that Great Britain had, in effect, joined the Triple Alliance – there is some irony here. For Britain and France did not arrive at an understanding, never mind an alliance, in 1896. Germany and Austria-Hungary were correct to discount such fears.

Nevertheless, what the comments of Rudini and his colleagues reveal is that the Italians were coming to see themselves rather more as others saw them. By this time they were impressed, as the British Consul-General in Egypt, Lord Cromer, had been impressed in 1890 by all that he had seen and heard at a conference in Naples, with 'the weakness of Italy as a Power'. The Duc de Sermoneta put it this way, in March 1896: Italy had joined the great international combinations too early in her career; what she needed, instead of attempting to play the game of Great Power diplomacy, was forty years of *'recueillement'* to consolidate her position.

This thinking, this new cast of mind, or rather an outlook last encountered during the period of the Congress of Berlin, was reinforced by developments that occurred during the Foreign Ministry of Visconti Venosta, between July 1896 and 1898. With the demise of the Mediterranean Agreements in 1896 another link with Great Britain went by the board. And, as regards the Austro-Hungarian–Russian Agreement of May 1897, the Italians could appreciate that the Triple Alliance was seriously devalued. Not only was Italy not consulted in advance about these matters, but the *entente* between Vienna and St Petersburg raised the possibility of Italy's exclusion from a voice in any settlement of Balkan affairs. In particular, it suggested the acquisition, at some point in the future, by Austria-Hungary, of Albania. That would give Austria-Hungary the whole of the eastern seaboard of the Adriatic and pose a constant threat to the Italian coastline from Venice to Brindisi. Moreover, with Russian forces freed to concentrate more in the Far East, Austria-Hungary could more easily switch troops from Galicia to the Isonzo. From 1897 the Austro-Hungarian General Staff did in fact make contingency plans for a war against their fellow member of the Triple Alliance.

❖

The change in Italy's policy, then, was not entirely geared to her restless search for concessions commensurate with what she considered her position and status to be. It also resulted from a radical reassessment of that position and status. It represented a belated recognition of her own inherent geographical and other weaknesses, and represented a victory for the realists such as Corti, Rudini, Sermoneta, and Visconti Venosta, over the fantasists, Crispi and the Crispinis. The change, in effect, was from relying on Great Britain to relying on France; from relying on Great Britain to protect Italy from France, to reaching an accommodation with France and so removing the possibility of attack from that quarter; from hoping with British and German and Austro-Hungarian help to acquire positions in the Mediterranean which France would otherwise acquire, to agreeing with France that France should get what she wanted and Italy could have only what was left. Having, as it seemed to the Italians, been left alone by Britain to face France, the Italians realised that they could not do so. They therefore sought terms with the French, and between 1896 and 1902 – for it was a lengthy process, and Hanotaux was less keen on it than was his successor as French Foreign Minister, Delcassé – submitted to blackmail and bullying that no really great Power would have allowed itself to endure. Holstein of the German Foreign Office was right to say, as he did in 1903, that Italy's weight, thrown into whichever scale, would 'only theoretically' disturb the European balance – in other words that Italy was 'only theoretically' a Great Power.

The same conclusion, that Italy was not really a Great Power, follows from the fact that, whilst adjusting her policy, her allegiance, and her obligations, Italy remained a member of the Triple Alliance, which indeed was renewed only days before the exchange of letters between Prinetti and Barrère took place. It follows also from the Italian efforts to persuade Germany and Austria-Hungary to declare that the Triple Alliance was not directed against *France*. In themselves and in their lack of success these efforts contrast with the Italian-inspired declaration of May 1882 that the Triple Alliance could not be envisaged as being directed against Great Britain. For it must be remembered that at no stage did Italy conclude an alliance with France. To have left the Triple Alliance would have rendered Italy vulnerable, especially to pressure from Austria-Hungary. To protect herself, Italy needed to stay within the Triple Alliance, which was to be renewed once more in 1912.

❖

In 1904 something occurred which for a long time the Germans had regarded as quite impossible: France and Great Britain came to an understanding. In the years that followed there was some discussion between the British and the French as to whether or not Italy should be formally seduced out of the Triple Alliance. The French, who at one point were quite keen about this, eventually allowed themselves to be dissuaded. The following British arguments prevailed: that Italy would be rather a thorn in the side than of any assistance; that for Britain and France it was 'all to the good that Italy should remain in the Triple Alliance and be a source of weakness to the other Powers'; that the Italians would, 'owing to their inherent weakness', always be an excellent drag on the two Central Powers. On 18 May 1909 Sir Charles Hardinge, Permanent Under Secretary at the Foreign Office in London, wrote to the ambassador in Constantinople:

It is all very well to talk of detaching Italy from Germany and Austria. That is not at all our policy, since it is preferable to us that the Triple Alliance should be maintained and even renewed, because Italy is, and must always be, dependent on the goodwill of France and England in the event of a continental war. Her coastline is too long for her to defend it from attacks by these two Powers and to contribute military assistance at the same time to the other members of the Triple Alliance.

The *Italian* appreciation of these very same factors was responsible for her neutrality from August 1914 to May 1915, as well as for her joining the Entente side in the Great War, at a time when the defeat of the Central Powers appeared to be imminent.

In a very basic sense from the point of view of foreign policy – as one of what Paul Kennedy might call 'the realities behind diplomacy', Italy was in this period, as she had been in the days when Metternich first applied this description to her, 'a mere geographical expression', although some of her representatives, and especially Crispi, who preceded Mussolini in this respect, were reluctant to make the necessary adjustments.

14

LATE NINETEENTH–CENTURY IMPERIALISM: THE PROBLEM FOR BRITAIN

The imperialism of the last quarter of the nineteenth century owed much to the world commercial and financial depression which began in 1873. The *character* of this imperialism owed much to the revival of protectionist policies, initially by the French in the late 1870s, as they began their search for El Dorado in the hinterland of west Africa. The acquisition of colonies by some, the substitution of formal for informal control in other cases, however reluctantly engaged in, screened by whatever devices and agencies, was a response to the prospect of creeping protectionism. The threat of exclusion from traditional European markets and the prospect of the incorporation into the protectionist system at some point in the future of all extra-European territory not yet accounted for led to the clamour of exporters for government assistance and eventual protection by their own flag, and to the preparedness of governments to annex areas not then economically viable and in many cases completely unexplored. Following a second bout of economic depression in 1882 and its attendant social unrest, it was a fear of a French monopoly of Congolese markets that was responsible for the Anglo-Portuguese Treaty of February 1884 and for British policy at the Berlin South West Africa Conference of 1884–85. The same fear was also influential in causing Bismarck, despite an enduring interest in trade rather than territorial expansion overseas, to acquire for Germany lands in Africa and in the Pacific.

The contentions already made are suported by the following statements by Sir Harry Johnston, Eugène Etienne, Lord Rosebery, and Lord Salisbury. In a speech at the Free Trade Hall on 16 April 1884 Salisbury warned that as the markets of the civilised world were closed by tariffs, those of the uncivilised world were becoming the only fields in which traders and manufacturers might do profitable business. Following a weekend with Salisbury at Hatfield House Sir Harry Johnston, founder of the Royal Niger Company, published in *The Times* of 22 August 1888 an article entitled *Great Britain's Policy in Africa* in which he wrote:

If free trade were a universal principle, it would matter relatively little to our merchants what particular nation ruled the new markets for our commerce; but inasmuch as protectionist Powers may, and do, possess themselves of new tracts of Africa and then proceed to stifle or cramp our trade with differential duties and irritating restrictions – witness the Portuguese everywhere and the French in Senegambia and Gaboon – then it becomes a necessity for us to protect ourselves and forestall other European nations in localities we desire to honestly exploit.

Etienne, the French Under Secretary of State for Colonies in 1891, said of his country's policy: 'We do indeed believe, and assert emphatically, that since France must incur the obligations involved in a colonial domain, it is just and proper that this domain should be reserved as a market for French products.' On 1 March 1893 Lord Rosebery, then Foreign Secretary, spoke at the Colonial Institute in London in defence of his policies, which the Prime Minister, Gladstone, had condemned as 'imbued with the spirit of territorial grab'. Rosebery said:

It is said that our Empire is already large enough and does not need extension. That would be true enough if the world were elastic, but, unfortunately, it is not elastic, and we are engaged at the present moment, in the language of the mining camps, in 'pegging out claims for the future'.... We have to consider, not what we want now, but what we shall want in the future. We should, in my opinion, grossly fail in the task that has been laid upon us did we shrink from responsibilities and decline to take our share in a partition of the world which we have not forced on, but which has been forced upon us.

Finally, Lord Salisbury told the French ambassador in 1897: 'If you were not such persistent protectionists, you would not find us so greedy for territory.'

The above concerns and somewhat circular self-justifications coincided with a deepening appreciation that several large areas in Africa, Asia and the Far East were on the point of collapsing into power vacuums. This applied not only to Morocco, Persia and China, but also to the ability of Spain and Portugal to continue to be imperial powers in the Carribean, Africa and south-east Asia.

I would contend that late nineteenth century imperialism is not best seen, as it once was by D.K. Fieldhouse for example, as 'the extension into the periphery of the political struggle in Europe'. Nor is it best seen as a 'safety-valve', designed to reduce otherwise unendurable pressures and tensions between the Great Powers of Europe. As explanations, those are altogether too eurocentric, and too redolent of assumptions that something in the nature of 'a struggle for mastery' was continually taking place there. What kept Europe at peace, after 1871, was not imperialism but fear of a general war. This fear considerably ante-dated the formal groupings established by 1892. It rested on French resentment of the German Empire and the consequent dilemma posed for Germany by the incipient and then actual rivalry between Austria-Hungary and Russia resulting from nationalism in the Balkans. Salisbury put his finger on this fear in his Guildhall speech of November 1896, when he reminded his audience that 'if a war is aroused in the east of the Mediterranean, and spreads to the European empires which adjoin the Turkish Empire, vast populations will be threatened in their well-being, vast industries will be arrested, probably great territorial changes will be set on foot, and perhaps the vital existence of nations will be threatened'.

Imperialism itself did not lead to war between the Great Powers of Europe because fear of a general war was built into it and served as an inhibiting factor. Every European power appreciated that extra-European conflicts would, if allowed to get out of hand, be transferred to, and settled in, Europe itself. Early in 1898 the British Government decided not to risk what it regarded as a possible consequence of trying to prevent the Russians from taking Port Arthur from China, namely 'the whole of the civilised world in arms', 'a European war'. The Fashoda crisis in the Sudan of later that same year is another outstanding example, this time on the part of the French. The Russo-Japanese war of 1904–05 provides another example. This was a case of one Power (Russia) believing it was stronger than the other, and finding out, in Manchuria and Korea, that it was not. The thing to be noted in this context, however, is that the allies of the belligerents, France and Britain, studiously avoided becoming involved. Russia, moreover, refused to risk a conflict with Great Britain such as might have resulted had she insisted on sending her Black Sea fleet out of the Black Sea. Here again fear of a general war localised an extra-European conflict and confined it, in this case, to the Far East. In 1911, in the course of the crisis at Agadir in Morocco, the British Foreign Secretary, Sir Edward Grey, reminded the French that any action taken by them at Agadir might result in a mobilisation of the German army on the French frontier.

❖

The effects of the imperialism of the last quarter of the nineteenth century were felt most acutely by the British. Their relative monopoly in several areas was challenged both in theory (by the setting of new ground-rules in 1884 at the Berlin Conference) and in practice. In December 1886 a

Royal Commission on the Depression of Trade and Industry reported that in addition to losing her advantage in production (primarily to Germany), Great Britain was 'beginning to feel the effects of competition in quarters where her trade formerly enjoyed a practical monopoly'.

One such area was the Far East. Lord Salisbury had said in 1885 that 'the Power that can establish the best footing in China will have the best part of the trade of the world'. This deserves to be known as 'the China syndrome' and, of course, it still applies. A decade later, in November 1895, Salisbury told an audience at the Guildhall: 'In China there is room for us all.' Several Great Powers took him at his word. In July 1895 a Russian loan had been made to China. This was countered, in March 1896, by a joint Anglo-German loan. These moves, however, were mere preliminaries. Shortly after matters in the Balkans were put on ice by the agreement to maintain the status quo there arrived at by Russia and Austria-Hungary in May 1897, the Far Eastern Question proper was posed. In November 1897, with Russian connivance, Germany seized the Chinese port of Kiao-Chow. This was a distinct challenge to Britain, whose position for fifty years as the principal trading power with China rested on the presence of the British China Squadron at Hong Kong. Muraviev, the Russian Foreign Minister, wrote in a memorandum of 23 November 1897 that 'the time for maintaining the integrity of China' was over. It was in response to this possibility that Salisbury, at the beginning of the following year, approached the Russians with the offer to conclude an agreement dividing China into spheres of influence that has already been described at the end of Chapter 11. The Russian Government ignored Salisbury's overture, and in March 1898 took what they wanted – the ice-free port of Port Arthur, which because of its strategic location constituted a standing menace to the Chinese capital Peking and represented therefore a source of Russian pressure on the Chinese government. The British immediately took a lease on the less well-endowed port of Wei-Hai-Wei, in sheer self-defence.

This was still only the beginning. These early developments, however, were enought to cause some British ministers to contemplate drastic measures. Joseph Chamberlain, the Colonial Secretary, was amongst the first so to do. In December 1897 he had written to the Prime Minister: 'Talking about allies, have you considered whether we might not draw closer to Japan?' In February 1898 he wrote again, this time to A.J. Balfour, who was shortly to be deputising at the Foreign office for a convalescent Salisbury:

> If matters remain as they are our prestige will be gone and our trade will follow.... I should propose:

1. To approach the United States officially, and to ask an immediate reply from them to the question – Will you stand in with us in our Chinese policy?
2. To approach Germany at the same time with the same definite questions.

An overture to the United States for an alliance in Far Eastern matters was made in March 1898. The Americans rejected it. Chamberlain was moved to state, publicly, the following May: 'If the policy of isolation, which has hitherto been the policy of this country, is to be maintained in the future, then the fate of China will be decided without reference to our wishes and in defiance of our interests.' In 1900 the Boxer Rising, largely directed against western activities in China, took place. The Russians took advantage of it to occupy Manchuria. When the rising was put down, by an international expeditionary force, the Russians remained in Manchuria.

So much, for the moment, for the very Far East. The repercussions on the position of the British Empire were increased by the overlapping outbreak of war between Great Britain and the Boer Republics in South Africa in October 1899. In the course of this conflict Chamberlain's pre-war appreciation of the necessity for allies became much more widely held. The Secretary of State for India, Lord George Hamilton, wrote to the Viceroy, Lord Curzon, on 11 October 1900: 'Unless we are prepared to risk something ourselves or to throw in our lot with some of the great European Powers we cannot expect them to stand in with us or to assist us in protecting our own interests.' The First Lord of the Admiralty, Lord Selborne, speculated in December 1900 that 'a formal alliance with Germany' might be 'the only alternative to an ever-increasing Navy and ever-increasing Navy Estimates'. The Foreign Secretary, Lord Lansdowne, wrote in March 1901: 'our South African entanglements make it impossible for us to commit ourselves to a policy which might involve us in a war (e.g. an energetic one in the Persian Gulf) unless we can assure ourselves that any obligation which we might incur would be shared by another Power.' Hamilton wrote to Curzon again in April 1901:

I am gradually coming round to the opinion that we must alter our foreign policy, and throw our lot in, for good or bad, with some other Power.... As we now stand, we are an object of envy and greed to all the other Powers. Our interests are so vast and ramified that we touch, in some shape or other, the interests of almost every great country in every continent. Our interests being so extended makes it almost impossible for us to concentrate sufficiently, in any one direction, the pressure and power of the Empire so as to deter foreign nations from trying to encroach upon our interests in that particular quarter.

In the opinion of several senior ministers, then, Great Britain's own strength was no longer enough to sustain her position in the world. This was despite the facts that since 1895–96 the Army Estimates had risen more than those of any other Great Power, and the Navy Estimates had risen more than those of Russia, Germany and France put together. The security of the British Empire itself was perceived to rest upon a forebearance on the part of other powers which was clearly not forthcoming: the United States of America had annexed the Philippines and Cuba from Spain and become a Great Power in south-east Asia and the Caribbean; the French were advancing in Morocco; the Russians had remained in Manchuria, had in 1900 put pressure on Persia by making a loan on the condition that Persia receive no money from any other source for ten years, had also renewed her pressure on Afghanistan, and was advancing closer to the frontiers of India with the Orenburg–Tashkent railway, which she had started to build in 1899 and was expected to complete in 1904 or 1905.

The primary threat to the British Empire was clearly perceived as coming from Russia. Lord George Hamilton had written to Curzon in 1899: 'I do not believe our position in Persia or even on the Persian Gulf is such as to enable us successfully to have recourse to force to prevent the further advance of Russia.' The point of an agreement made with Germany on 17 October 1900 was to deter further Russian encroachments towards the Yangtse region of China. Salisbury had been forced by his cabinet to conclude this agreement, much against his own judgement and inclination. Indeed on the day after it was signed he wrote to Curzon: 'As to Germany I have less confidence in her than you. She is in mortal terror on account of that long undefended frontier of hers on the Russian side. She will therefore never stand by us against Russia; but is always rather inclined to curry favour with Russia by throwing us over ... my faith in her is infinitesimal.'

Appreciations of Russian strength and of British weakness mounted. Selborne wrote to Curzon in April 1901: 'Compared to our Empire, Russia's is invulnerable. We must be on the defensive in a contest because there is ... no part of her territory where we can hit her.' Salisbury, lamenting the financial impact of the Boer War, wrote in September 1901, also to Curzon:

Our main interest in the East (after China) has been the movements of the Persian Question. In the main it is a question of money. In the last generation we did much what we liked in the East by force or threats – by squadrons and tall-talk ... but the day of individual coercive action is almost passed by. For some years to come eastern advance must largely depend on payment, and I fear that in that race England will seldom win.

The Committee of Imperial Defence, which was getting into its stride at this time, reported on 30 December 1902: 'The military position of Russia grows stronger every day and the completion of the Orenburg–Tashkent railway in or about 1905 will add immensely to the danger to which India may be exposed.' The British Empire would soon be vulnerable in its greatest possession to an overland attack by a Great Power. In the following week, the first week of January 1903, Selborne followed up this Committee of Imperial Defence report with another letter to Curzon, writing:

The Middle Eastern Question is the question of the future, Persia and Afghanistan. Persia is much the more difficult. We have all the cards stacked against us there, partly owing to Beach [Sir Michael Hicks Beach, Chancellor of the Exchequer], partly to the fact that we have not the men to compete with Russia on Persian soil.

He went on:

I am sure that a day will come when a Cabinet will decide that the Army Estimates must decrease in order that the Navy Estimates may increase. All this has a very real bearing on the Middle Eastern Question. We had three exceptions to our naval and insular character – in three continents we had military frontiers with great land powers – the United States is great in every sense in America and Canada joins frontiers; the Dutch Republics were locally great and militarily powerful in South Africa; Russia is Russia in Central Asia.

Our diplomacy ought to save us from war with the United States, the Dutch Republics are eliminated, but we remain with all the difficulties and responsibilities of a military Power in Asia. That is the crux for us. It is easy with compulsory military service to be a great military Power for home defence or European warfare. It is easy to be a great Naval Power of a natural and continuous growth such as ours. It is a terrific task to remain the greatest Naval Power when Naval Powers are year by year increasing in numbers and in naval strength, and at the same time to be a military Power strong enough to meet the greatest Military Power in Asia.

In the following month the Chancellor of the Exchequer, now C.T. Richie, reported to the Cabinet that since 1899 expenditure had gone up by £30 million and revenue by £42 million, but that 34 of that 42 had been raised by special war taxes. Such levels of expenditure and of taxation could not be continued, in his view, without risking severe social unrest.

❖

In these circumstances, circumstances which accelerated from the mid-1890s and which grew worse through the period of the Boer War, the question for the British Government was twofold: should Great Britain abandon what some described as 'isolation', and, if so, to whom should she turn for help in the maintenance of the British Empire and of her world position? With considerable reluctance Salisbury had allowed Balfour to approach the United States in the first months of 1898. He could not prevent Chamberlain, and others, from considering the merits of a connection with the German Empire. He allowed himself to be pushed into making an agreement with Germany in October 1900 as far as a particular part of the Far East was concerned, with, as already remarked, no great enthusiasm. Salisbury's phlegmatism, his apparent disposition to try to ride out the storm of the Boer War, proved too much for his cabinet colleagues. In November 1900 enough of them insisted that he hand over the Foreign Office and the conduct of foreign policy to Lord Lansdowne. As a result, Lansdowne as Foreign Secretary had something in the nature of a mandate to end the recent policy, which if not regarded as one of 'isolation' was certainly regarded as one of 'drift'.

This proved easier said than done, but from the commencement of his Foreign Secretaryship Lansdowne was on the look-out for agreements with other powers in order to ease Britain's position and reduce the burden carried by the British Empire. Behind everything he considered was the ultimate objective of reaching an accommodation with the chief threat to the British Empire, Russia.

Although no longer Foreign Secretary, Salisbury was still Prime Minister, and throughout 1901 fought a strong rearguard action which represented, in effect, one side to an ongoing debate as to the merits of a policy of 'isolation'. This debate, and its outcome, reveal that the disposition to change was rather more transient than many commentators and historians have maintained. They also reveal that 'isolation' was understood as consisting of no solid commitments on the part of Great Britain to *European* Powers. The debate may be illustrated by two sets of remarks, both made in connection with the proposition of joining the

Triple Alliance, an invitation renewed by the Germans early in 1901. In May 1901 Salisbury maintained that isolation was 'a danger in whose existence we have no historical reason for believing'. In the following November Lansdowne stated that 'We may push too far the argument that, because we have in the past survived in spite of our isolation, we need have no misgivings as to the effect of that isolation in the future'.

In logic, Lansdowne clearly won that particular point. It was Salisbury, however, who was amongst the majority at the end of the debate as a whole. By November 1901 Lansdowne had decided against a full-blown defensive alliance of the kind the Germans were insisting upon. He preferred 'a much more limited understanding as to policy in regard to certain matters of interest to both Powers'. Of course, by November the war in South Africa had been won, and the pressure had eased to that extent. There was, however, no escaping the force of the case put forward by Salisbury in May: 'The liability of having to defend the German and Austrian frontiers against Russia is heavier than that of having to defend the British Isles against France.' In other words, if the main objective of British policy was the reduction of obligations as well as of the number of disputes with Russia, an alliance with Germany and her allies would be counterproductive, for it would increase both. As Francis Bertie, Assistant Under Secretary at the Foreign Office and an advocate of an arrangement with Japan, regarding which Lansdowne had opened negotiations in July 1901, expressed it:

If once we bind ourselves by a formal defensive alliance and practically join the Triplice we shall never be on decent terms with France our neighbour in Europe and in many parts of the world, or with Russia whose frontiers are coterminous with ours or nearly so over a large portion of Asia.

Lansdowne came to agree with this. In November 1901 one of the objections he lodged to an alliance with Germany was 'the certainty of alienating France and Russia'.

By this time the Germans had fully justified Salisbury's lack of confidence in them of October 1900, a lack of confidence which went back as far as the overtures he had made in 1885 (see Chapter 11), by refusing to interpret the agreement of that date in the sense that would have suited the British. Moreover, by the autumn of 1901 the press of both Britain and Germany was full of articles which seemed to suggest that the populace of the two countries were on the worst possible terms. Lord George Hamilton revealed that he was more and more impressed with revelations of German antipathy to Britain. Public opinion, not hitherto a force greatly to be reckoned with, was now beginning to penetrate the corridors of power.

Lansdowne made clear how close he was, at heart, to Salisbury's position, and how much of an isolationist he remained, when he concluded the specific, localised alliance with Japan instead of a general one with Germany. Sir F. Bertie had written on 9 November 1901 that the result of a formal defensive alliance with the German Empire would be 'the sacrifice of our liberty to pursue a British world policy'. On 12 December Lansdowne defended his decision to ally with Japan rather than persevere with Germany in a letter to Balfour, writing: 'the chances of the *casus foederis* arising are much fewer in the case of the Anglo-Japanese agreement than they would be in that of an Anglo-German agreement. The area of entanglement seems to me much more restricted under the former.'

As a postscript to this debate, how easy it was for isolationists to revert to type may be illustrated by the fact that the man originally responsible for diagnosing 'the British condition', Joseph Chamberlain, extolled the virtues of 'splendid isolation' in a speech at Birmingham on 6 January 1902. In September of that year he wrote: 'If the worst comes to the worst we could hold out, as our ancestors did, against the whole of them.' By then, Chamberlain had discovered his remedy for the malaise, and his answer to protectionism, in a scheme for Imperial Federation and Tariff Reform. Others moved in the same direction. Selborne, who in April 1903 was still prepared to keep open the option of a German alliance – 'it cannot in any way serve our interests to make the cleavage between England and Germany greater', he told Curzon – was in October writing that whilst 'in the years to come the UK by itself will not be strong enough to hold its proper place alongside the United States, or Russia, and probably not Germany ... the British Empire could hold its own on terms of more than equality', and 'from UK to Empire can only be done through the tariff'.

❖

The Anglo-Japanese Alliance of February 1902 appeared to solve, or at least to reduce temporarily, Great Britain's problem in the Far East. In Japan the British had found, as the French put it, their 'soldier' in the Far East – although, given the influence of the Admiralty on this matter, 'sailor' might have been more appropriate nomenclature. The Anglo-Japanese Alliance, however, did not mark a distinct and categorical change in British policy. It was merely a tactical device designed to enable Great Britain to continue to function as a world power. In this respect her main opponents remained Russia, and to a lesser extent, France. These were the powers against which, from 1901, the Two-Power Standard of naval building was directed, instead of against the combined battle-fleets of whichever two powers possessed at any one time the largest fleets. Despite overtures to the French early in 1902, overtures which included the idea of deploying the new King, Edward VII, on a state visit, the French Foreign Minister, Delcassé, remained adamantly opposed to any agreement with Great Britain which did not include the British evacuation of Egypt. Delcassé remained of this persuasion until after November 1902, when the internal collapse of Morocco concentrated the French mind on the support that Britain might afford in helping the French to achieve their own selfish objectives there. The main goal of British policy, namely an understanding with Russia, was secured only after Russia had been brought round, and to the negotiating table, by her defeat in the Far East at the hands of Japan and by the internal disorders that ensued. All the tactical devices that Lansdowne had resorted to – including the alliances with Japan of 1901 and 1905, the commitment to Afghanistan of March 1905, and the declarations that Britain would consider the establishment of another power within the Persian Gulf as an unfriendly act – were intended to help secure this end. It was thanks to the Moroccans and the Japanese that the British were able to escape the calling of their imperial bluff.

15

THE ERA OF WORLD POLICIES, 1898–1912: GERMANY, BRITAIN AND RUSSIA

Many historians would maintain that, from the moment that the Franco-Russian Alliance became a feature of the diplomatic landscape in the early 1890s, the mechanism that kept the Great Powers of Europe at peace with one another was the balance of power. The same historians would maintain that the emergence of Great Britain from isolation, which is how they interpret the Anglo-French Agreement of April 1904 and the Anglo-Russian Conventions of September 1907, enhanced this mechanism. In their view, the Triple Alliance of Germany, Austria-Hungary and Italy was counterbalanced by the Triple Entente of Russia, France, and Britain, and a system of mutual deterrence operated to keep the peace of Europe.

For at least half of the period in question, however, there was a demonstrable *imbalance* of power. This imbalance lasted from the beginning of the Russo-Japanese War in February 1904 until the spring of 1912, by which time Russia's recovery from her exertions, her defeat, and the internal problems that followed, was perceived, by contemporary observers, to be well advanced. During this phase of imbalance war in Europe was in sight on a number of occasions. It was in sight between the visit of Kaiser Wilhelm II to Tangier in March 1905 and the Algeciras Conference of January to March 1906; it was in sight in November 1908, when Imperial Germany made an issue of another Moroccan matter; it was in sight between the Austro-Hungarian annexation of Bosnia and Hercegovina in October 1908 and the Russian and Serbian climb-down over compensation of the following spring; it was in sight in the course of the Agadir crisis of July to September 1911. That none of these crises led to war rather discredits the balance of power as a peace-keeping mechanism. For the absence of a balance of power did not have the devastating consequences which, in theory, it was supposed to have – war did not ensue. A large part of the explanation for this is to be found in the extra-European, or *Weltpolitikal*, priorities of the Great Powers of Europe.

❖

The interest of the German Empire in extra-European affairs followed naturally and directly from the growth of the German population, the development of German industrial capacity, and the expansion of German commercial activities. In the early 1890s, even as Chancellor Caprivi was contemplating the construction of an economic bloc of Germany and Austria-Hungary in Europe, to be known as *Mitteleuropa*, the German government was envisaging expanding the colonial legacy of Bismarck by making agreements with Great Britain in 1893 and with France in 1894 delimiting spheres of influence in parts of Africa, and taking the first steps, through agreements with the Ottoman Empire, towards a railway from Berlin to Baghdad, which when completed would extend German influence, economic and commercial, through Asia Minor and Mesopotamia to the head of the Persian Gulf and on into the Indian Ocean. In 1895 the German government joined with those of other European powers, with the notable exception of Great Britain, in order to prevent the Japanese from reaping the full rewards of their recent victory over the Chinese Empire.

German *Weltpolitik*, then, clearly pre-dated the birth of the German Navy. The German Navy is perfectly understandable as a bid to remedy a particular deficiency, a deficiency which the events of the mid-1890s made increasingly clear to German governments. The German Navy was the means whereby to increase German leverage and ability to participate in extra-European affairs and opportunities. It was the instrument which would make the pursuit of *Weltpolitik* both possible and profitable. In October 1894 Lord Kimberley, the British Foreign Secretary, had called for a demonstration of force to meet what he called 'the arrogant attitude of Germany' over Delagoa Bay on the coast of south-east Africa. He said:

> We shall have to make the Germans clearly understand that we intend to maintain our supremacy in that Question, and that we are too strong to be meddled with by any other Power especially one whose naval force is so palpably inferior to ours. The Germans must learn that though they have a large army, we are supreme at sea.

Immediately after Wilhelm II's telegram of January 1896 to Kruger, President of one of the independent Dutch Republics in South Africa, congratulating him on beating off an armed incursion into the Transvaal (an action which earned the Kaiser the title of His Impulsive Majesty William the Sudden) the formation of a flying squadron was announced by the British Admiralty. The Germans felt compelled to beat a hasty retreat, and immediately recalled their two battleships from the Indian Ocean. In connection with reinforcing the German naval presence there with a ship from the Far East, Chancellor Hohenlohe remarked that Germany's position in the Far East depended on 'the development of a strong maritime force': 'Only if we display our power continually before their eyes can we arrive at a realisation of our wish to acquire a naval station in China.' In March 1897 Wilhelm II commented, in regard to recent movements in the Near Eastern Question and the lead taken by Great Britain in the affairs of Crete: 'This again makes it clear how painfully Germany suffers from the lack of a strong navy, since she cannot make herself effectively felt in the Concert.... England has paralysed all action. And why? Because she has the strongest fleet!'

Historians of Germany who have accounted for the German Navy primarily in terms of its being regarded as the solution to the problems of German domestic politics have, in my opinion, emphasised the wrong motive. In 1895, before he became State Secretary of the Reich Naval Office, Admiral von Tirpitz wrote:

> In my view Germany will, in the coming century, rapidly drop from her position as a Great Power unless we begin to develop our maritime interests energetically, systematically, and without delay. Such an expansion has become necessary also because the great patriotic task and the economic benefits to be derived from it will offer a strong palliative against educated and uneducated Social Democrats.

I take it from this that the domestic benefits were regarded by Tirpitz as essentially *secondary* considerations. Moreover, from the Far East, where Tirpitz spent the next two years, he wrote in January 1897 about the setting up of a base there: 'The question is entirely different for a state which does not possess the necessary measure of sea power and out here Germany will fall into that class for a long time to come.' In September 1899 he made it clear to the Kaiser that the purpose of the fleet he was then planning was to achieve 'such a measure of maritime influence as will make it possible for Your Majesty to conduct a great overseas policy'.

One of the first naval war plans devised by the Reich Naval Office, on the Kaiser's instructions and before the turn of the century, was for a naval war with the United States of America. Planning for this particular contingency, in itself testimony as eloquent as the Kaiser's simultaneous concern about the 'Yellow Peril' to the prevalence of an outlook on the affairs of the world as a whole as opposed to an outlook that took into consideration only the affairs of the European continent, was halted when the planners realised that the German fleet would only have such a range as would enable it to reach precisely the middle of the Atlantic, whence it would be unable to return.

Despite this German projection into the future of rivalry with the United States, the German Navy's principal, and much more immediate problem, was the superiority of British over German naval power which currently existed. The Austro-Hungarian ambassador in Berlin, Szogyeny, analysed in February 1900 for the benefit of the decision-makers in Vienna the aims of the German Government's *Flottenpolitik*, and forecast some of the problems, and some ways of dealing with some of the problems, that would accompany it:

> The leading German statesmen, and above all Kaiser Wilhelm, have looked into the distant future and are striving to make Germany's already swiftly growing position as a world power into a dominating one, reckoning hereby upon becoming the successor to England in this respect. People in Berlin are, however, well aware that Germany would not be in the position today or for a long time to assume this succession, and for this reason a speedy collapse of English world power is not desired since it is fully recognised that Germany's far-reaching plans are at present only castles in the air. Notwithstanding this, Germany is already preparing with speed and vigour for her self-appointed future mission. In this connection I may permit myself to refer to the constant concern for the growth of German naval forces.... England is now regarded as the most dangerous enemy which, at least as long as Germany is not sufficiently armed at sea, must be treated with consideration in all ways ... yet if the German Reich regards itself as the heir to a possible disintegration of the British colonial empire, people here carry on sufficiently practical policies to know well that the assumption of this so hotly desired, possible succession can only be feasible in the very distant future. On the length of time which will elapse until then, Kaiser Wilhelm himself nourishes the smallest illusions of all, for he has repeatedly hinted that he personally will not survive to see the realisation of these ambitious plans, although he regards it as his duty to prepare his country in the best way for these expected events.

As Szogyeny pointed out, only in the 'very distant future' would the naval power at the disposal of the German Empire be formidable enough to enable her to challenge Great Britain for the position of the dominating world power or to inherit the British colonial empire. So far as Britain, and British naval supremacy, was concerned, what was required of the German Empire was that most elusive of qualities – patience. With regard to other powers, both great and small, this was not necessarily the case. Great Britain might have to be treated with 'consideration in all ways'; on other states pressure of one kind or another could more easily be brought to bear, and might produce the results that were desired. Hence whilst waiting for the arrival of what Tirpitz called the 'power political factor' against the British Empire that the German Navy would eventually be, German governments tried to seize whatever opportunities presented themselves to expand Germany's influence throughout the world, to increase her trade and her penetration of extra-European markets. They pressed on with the Baghdad Railway project. They hoped that the Portuguese would dispose of some of their colonies, and enable Germany as a result to have a band of possessions running from the west coast to the east coast of southern Africa. They did not entirely lose sight of the idea of making Venezuela into a German colony in South America. They maintained an interest in parts of north Africa, parts of central Africa, and parts of the Far East. They did all this because of the importance to them of participating in the redistribution of the globe which they, like others, were convinced that the twentieth century would see.

❖

The necessity of not allowing a world position to go by default can be further illustrated. In March 1904, on the outbreak of the Russo-Japanese War, Friedrich von Holstein, who from within the German Foreign Office was one of the architects of German policy, noted: 'What is at stake is the China market.' In June 1904 he wrote: 'France is preparing to annex Morocco while completely ignoring the legitimate interests of third parties.... Morocco is today one of the few countries where German trade can still compete freely; the damage that Germany would suffer as the result of a French monopoly would be very significant.' In the course of the Russo-Japanese War the Germans made two attempts to break up the Franco-Russian Alliance. They also made a bid for the recognition of their interests in any future settlement of Morocco, which they maintained it was not for Great Britain and France to dispose of, given that Germany was a signatory of the Madrid Convention of 1880 which had governed the situation there, and, in Germany's view, still did.

The two attempts to detach Russia from France, and the Kaiser's visit to Tangier and consequent reopening of the Morocco question, are all closely connected with possible outcomes of the war in the Far East, and with the mediation efforts of France, Britain and the United States. What the Germans feared was a Far Eastern settlement between Russia and Japan at the expense of China. They feared that such a settlement would produce a Quadruple Alliance which would embrace the Anglo-Japanese and Franco-Russian Alliances – a possibility increased as a result of the

Anglo-French Agreement of April 1904. In October and November 1904, believing that France was 'working with some chance of success at a friendly rapprochement between England and Russia and that this entente between the three Powers might be facilitated by a partition of Chinese territory', Chancellor von Bülow forwarded to the Kaiser the draft of a treaty of alliance between Germany and Russia. The object of this alliance, he said, was 'to thwart the possibility of a Russo-French–English alliance'. This was the project ressurrected at Bjorko in July 1905; the argument then was that 'there would be an advantage in engaging the Tsar in such a way that, the peace once concluded, Witte and Lamsdorff [the Russian Finance and Foreign Ministers respectively] could not prepare forthwith a Russo-French–English entente'. England, according to Bülow, was insisting on an Anglo-French–Japanese–Russian alliance.

Midway between these efforts, in March 1905, the German Foreign Office decided that the Kaiser should visit Tangier. This was to avert what Wilhelm II called the 'dangerous consequences' of United States President Theodore Roosevelt and French Foreign Minister Théophile Delcassé's mediation attempts in the Russo-Japanese War. The Germans believed that Delcassé was planning a peace conference at Paris where a secret alignment would be formed and the partition of China worked out between the two former belligerents and their respective ally and friend. The first of the three crises provoked by the Germans over Morocco, then, might best be interpreted as primarily the product of German fears of a Far Eastern settlement that would damage German prospects in the Far East.

Given that it is at this time, in connection with the possibility of an alliance between Britain, France, Japan and Russia, that the Germans talk so much about the 'encirclement' of Germany, it is most probable that what they mean by 'encirclement' is 'exclusion'; that what they fear is that other powers will divide up the world between them, and without reference to them. At one point Holstein did describe his Moroccan policy as follows: 'When I became fully aware of the danger that England would join the Franco-Russian Alliance I was convinced that, before the ring of these other Great Powers had been closed, we should have to endeavour with all our might to break this ring, and not recoil even before the ultimate decision. Hence the Kaiser's Tangier landing.' Testing the Anglo-French *entente*, however, and the degree of British support for France, whilst at the same time trying to break up the Franco-Russian Alliance, was simply a complicated way of trying to kill several birds with one stone: had the Germans been successful, they would have found it easier to make headway with *Weltpolitik*, for instead of facing combinations, or groupings, of powers, they would have faced individual, isolated powers on a one-to-one basis, and would have had a much better chance of participating in the global opportunities for the redistribution of territory.

War, the 'ultimate decision', might have been on Holstein's personal agenda in 1905. It was not on the agenda of his political superiors. Indeed, at the close of that year, Wilhelm II ordered Bülow to preserve the peace. Germany, he said, must first conclude a firm alliance with the Ottoman Empire, and then she must be given a chance to equip her troops with new armaments. The Social Democrats had also to be neutralised: 'First cow the Socialists, cut off their heads and make them harmless, if necessary by a bloodbath, and then a foreign war. But not before and not *a tempo*'; German foreign policy should be conducted in such a way as to avoid war 'so far as at all possible, and certainly for the present'. Similar instructions were issued to Kiderlen-Wachter, the German Foreign Minister at the time of the Agadir crisis of 1911.

Had the German Empire had any designs on Europe during these years, it is almost inconceivable that they would not have taken advantage of the imbalance of power produced by Russia's involvement in the Far East and her defeat there in order to implement them. As it was, the Germans did not believe that they had a European problem. The European situation seemed, to them, perfectly satisfactory until the result of the Balkan war of November 1912. The size of the German Army did not increase by a single man between 1894 and 1912. On the contrary, it is as if the Germans were so dazzled by extra-European prospects that they concentrated upon those prospects to the exclusion of all others. This is why they so lost touch with the foreign policy of Austria-Hungary that Aehrenthal, the Austro-Hungarian Foreign Minister, did not bother even to inform them of his plans to annex Bosnia and Hercegovina in 1908. The entirely gratuitous German ultimatum to Russia in the spring of 1909 was primarily designed to reassert German control over Austro-Hungarian policy, which if not supervised might have unwanted European effects. The German bids to secure British neutrality in the event of a war between Germany and France or between Germany and Austria-Hungary on one side and France and Russia on the other, attempts which began in April 1909, which were resumed by Chancellor Bethmann-Hollweg in August 1909, and which persisted off and on until April 1912, were taken literally by the British Foreign Office as revealing that Germany really did seek to dominate Europe in the same fashion, and to the same extent, as the first Napoleon; but they were not intended by the Germans to be so taken. From the German point of view the objective was, as it had been in 1905–06, to split Britain away from France and Russia, and to render the pursuit of *Weltpolitik*, either with Great Britain or against her, more effective and productive.

There remains one peculiarity to be accounted for. It is this: had the Germans pressed the French harder, in 1905–06 or in 1911; had they insisted, for instance, on having a port on the Atlantic coast of Morocco (something which, in 1911, the British were not prepared to oppose) or had they maintained their initial demands of July 1911 for the whole of the French Congo, a vast area in the fate of which neither Great Britain nor Russia had the faintest interest, then the Germans might well have advanced spectacularly the cause of their *Weltpolitik*. Insofar as there is a rational explanation for their failure to do so, it may be found in the idea that those who ran the German Empire were incapable of making a necessary conceptual leap: they could not but reject the idea of disturbing a European status quo with which, from their point of view, there was nothing wrong, for the sake of gains outside Europe; they were reluctant to bring their Army to bear on the Franco-German frontier for this purpose, because, in their collective mind, it was the German Navy that was regarded as the lever to a dominant position in the world, and because that dominant position in the world was supposed to be acquired at the expense of Great Britain rather than at the expense of France.

❖

Great Britain, unlike the German Empire, was already a world power, with a world position to defend, rather than to acquire or inherit. Late in 1902 the Balfour administration came to the conclusion that the best, indeed only, solution to the problem of the defence of the British Empire, and in particular of the defence of India, which was particularly vulnerable to the Russian threat, was an agreement with Russia. It was decided that the route to a general settlement of differences with St Petersburg went through Paris. As Lord George Hamilton, the Secretary of State for India, put it in July 1903 at the beginning of the negotiations with France, it was the prospect of France helping to bring about an Anglo-Russian agreement that was 'the tendency of the negotiation, and the expectation ... of those who are behind the scenes'. 'Those behind the scenes' included Lord Selborne, the First Lord of the Admiralty, who in April 1903 had insisted in a letter to the Viceroy of India that 'it would indeed be an immediate advantage to us to have a real equable final all-round settlement with Russia'. They included the Prime Minister, Balfour, who typically added a twist not voiced openly by any of his colleagues: in a memorandum for the Committee of Imperial Defence he wrote, on 30 April 1903: 'There is a third peculiarity of the Indian problem ... namely, that if Russia had as her ally a great sea power like

France, safe military communication between Great Britain and the theatre of warlike operations would, in the earlier stages of the war, be greatly hampered.' They included Lord Lansdowne, the Foreign Secretary, who in September 1903 stated in a memorandum for his Cabinet colleagues: 'A good understanding with France would not improbably be the precursor of a better understanding with Russia.' They included the Earl of Cromer, Consul-General in Egypt, who in October 1903, in a letter to Balfour, looked far beyond the immediate benefits that a resolution of Anglo-French friction over Egypt itself would bring: 'I cannot help regarding an understanding upon all pending questions with France as possibly a stepping-stone to a general understanding with Russia and that this, possibly again, may prepare the ground for some reduction in our enormous military and naval expenditure.' There was a somewhat belated recognition of what was 'behind the scenes' on the part of Cecil Spring-Rice, of the British Embassy in St Petersburg, when he wrote to Lansdowne's Private Secretary on 13 April 1904, concerning the Anglo-French Agreement signed five days earlier: 'This agreement with France is a finger-post pointing to Russia. The next step should be to use the French arrangement as a stepping-stone to some sort of improvement in our relations with Russia.' Lansdowne made no comment on this letter when it was passed to him. He had already written, on 23 March 1904, to his ambassador in Berlin: 'I believe that, if anything, France will endeavour as time goes on to bring us and Russia together.'

Insofar as Great Britain had a European policy at all, it must be seen against the above background of imperial priorities and in this wider, and world, context. It would not be going too far, indeed, to say that any British European policy was a function of her world policy. British support for France over Morocco in mid-1905 and at the Algeciras Conference early in 1906 was necessary in order to keep alive the prospect of an agreement with Russia. It may seem strange that British ministers, and especially those in the Liberal administration which took over in December 1905, should apparently risk British involvement in a Franco-German war for the sake of an agreement with a power which by the end of 1905 had been defeated by Japan, a power whose navy was at the bottom of the China Sea, a power in the throes of revolution. A number of considerations, however, have to be borne in mind. It was presumed, for one thing, that Russia would immediately set about re-establishing herself as a naval power, and utilise the latest technology in so doing. It was also presumed that, as the Secretary of State for India, Brodrick, put it to the Secretary of State for War, Arnold-Foster, on 1 December 1905, in connection with the possible demands of a war with

Russia, 'it is by no means improbable that the Russians may endeavour to regain either in Persia or on the frontier of Afghanistan, by a war in which their liability is strictly limited, some of the reputation which they have lost in the last two years'. In the course of the negotiation of the renewal of the Anglo-Japanese Alliance in the summer of 1905, the Japanese had refused to commit themselves to participating in military operations on the actual frontiers of British India and its buffer states. Despite her internal difficulties, Russia was still capable of maintaining an army of 250,000 men 3,000 miles from Russia proper. It could not be guaranteed that the building of railways which already brought Russian armies within striking distance of Kandahar and Kabul would not be resumed, or that the Russian Imperial General Staff would not dominate and determine Russian policy.

A sub-committee of the Committee of Imperial Defence set up in January 1907 to examine the demand that would be made upon the military resources of the British Empire in case of war on the land frontier of north-western India reported in May 1907 and confirmed those who had commenced negotiations with Russia in the rightness of their approach. The sub-committee was in favour of 'the school who look to diplomacy rather than to arms', and pronounced that 'In default of an understanding with Russia the process of insidious advance and slow absorption on Russia's part would have to be reckoned with'. Amongst the points made were these: that the mere rumour of a Russian seizure of Herat, in western Afghanistan, would cause a great stir amongst the population of India; that the permanent occupation of Kabul by Russia, and the establishment there of a military base, would make it necessary for Britain to keep up in India a force far exceeding in size the present British garrison, and perhaps exceeding the capacity of the British Empire as a whole; and that to retain a great force of native soldiers far from their homes for year after year, waiting on Russia's processes, would be to ask more of the native soldiery than it had shown itself ready to provide. The Indian Mutiny cast a long shadow.

The British policy of making agreements that settled outstanding differences, and reduced especially the financial burdens of empire, with France in 1904 and with Russia in 1907, was pure *Weltpolitik* on the British part. European matters did not figure at all in these calculations. Once the great goal of British *weltpolitik*, an agreement with Russia, had been secured, and 'repose' obtained upon the North-west Frontier, it remained the first priority of British policy to maintain it. The British could not deviate from this position without ceasing to be a great imperial power, or in Lord Curzon's words 'the greatest power in the world' ('as long as we rule India'), something which had long since

PERSIA
as divided by the
Anglo-Russian Convention
of 1907

Caspian
Sea

AZERBAIJAN

GILAN

•Tabriz

•Resht

•Asterabad

•Kuchan

Merv•

Northern boundary
of Afghanistan

ARDALAN

•Kazvin

•Tehran

Meshed•

Sarakhs•

Zulficar•

RUSSIAN SPHERE OF INFLUENCE

Kasr-el-Sherin

Anikin•

•Hamadan

•Kermanshah

IRAK-I-AJAM

•Kum

KHORASSAN

Turbat-i-Haidari•

Karez•

Kuhsan•

LURISTAN

Sultanabad
(Irak)•

•Kashan

Rui Khaf•

Kakh•

•Tun

Herat•

•Isfahan

Tabas•

•Kain

•Nain

Gazik•

•Dizful

Shushtar•

DASHT-I-LUT

Birjand•

Tabbas•

•Ahwaz

•Yezd

Basra

Mohammerah•

KHUZISTAN
(ARABISTAN)

NEUTRAL SPHERE

Nasretabad•

SEISTAN

Fao•

Shahr-i-Babak•

•Kerman

Mt Kuk Malik Siah

Robat•

Kuwait•

KERMAN

•Shiraz

•Bam

Bushire•

FARS

•Jahrum

BRITISH

SPHERE OF

LARISTAN

INFLUENCE

Bahrain•

Persian Gulf

Lingah•

Bunder Abbas•

•Kishm Is.

•Jask

Charbar•

Gulf of Oman

Gwaddar•

SCALE OF MILES

10 40 60 80 100 120 140 160 180 200

become, so far as the British ruling classes of whatever political persuasion were concerned, an integral part of their identity. As Sir Edward Grey put it to the Prime Minister of Canada, MacKenzie King, on 28 December 1908, 'The pride of Engand would be broken if India were lost'.

❖

Like Great Britain, Russia was already a world power. Her extra-European interests stretched from the Caucasus, across Central Asia, to Manchuria and the very Far East. Unlike Great Britain, Russia also had interests on the European continent, primarily in the Balkans but also in her Polish provinces. It is obvious that, from the turn of the century until the end of the Russo-Japanese War in September 1905, Russia was according a higher value to her *Weltpolitik* than to Europe. She was able to do this as a result of the agreement of May 1897 with Austria-Hungary to uphold the status quo in the Balkans. She was all the more able to do so following her conclusion in October 1904 of an agreement with Austria-Hungary binding both parties to observe benevolent neutrality in case of a war with a third power. At the end of 1904 Russian intelligence supplied St Petersburg with Austro-Hungarian military staff documents which confirmed that the Habsburg Monarchy viewed the current international situation as propitious, if anything, for an attack upon Italy, not Russia. The Chief of the Austro-Hungarian General Staff, Conrad von Hotzendorff, was calling for the diversion of his armies away from the north-eastern frontier to the southern frontier. In her Far Eastern adventures, Russia also had the encouragement of the German government, and of Wilhelm II in particular.

Isvolsky, who replaced Lamsdorff as Russian Foreign Minister in May 1906, found, on taking up his duties, 'certain plans, the breadth of whose designs produced upon me an impression of something fantastical. Such were the plans for the subordination of Tibet, for the construction of a military port on the Persian Gulf, the extension of a railway to the latter, and so forth'. Such schemes for imperial expansion, said Isvolsky, had to be renounced, or at the very least postponed. Stolypin, the new Chairman of the Council of Ministers, agreed: 'Our internal situation does not permit us to conduct an aggressive foreign policy.' In these circumstances, the active rivalry with Great Britain was put on hold, to the chagrin of some elements in Russia, notably the General Staff, through the Conventions of September 1907 relating to Persia and Tibet, until such time as Russia was sufficiently recovered to resume it. An early indication that this would be the case came in April 1908, when the Russians resumed railway construction in the Far East, to the chagrin of the French. Later that year Russia took advantage of the deteriorating situation in Persia, where a constitutional struggle was raging, to intervene there. This was done despite the breakdown of the entente with Austria-Hungary over the Balkans, with the annexation by the latter of Bosnia and Hercegovina without the compensation Russia was seeking in the shape of a change in the rules governing the Straits of the Bosporus and the Dardanelles – a change which, by giving Russia free access to the Mediterranean in the first instance, would have made easier her resumption of her policy of *Weltpolitik*. At the end of 1909 Russia suggested a Trans-Persian railway, something which the British regarded as meaning, in political terms, 'the disappearance of British influence in Persia'. In November 1910 the Russians contacted Germany and offered to connect their Caucasus to Tehran railway with the Berlin to Baghdad line. By 1912 the Russians were again penetrating Mongolia, Tibet, and Chinese Turkestan, and consolidating a position only 150 miles from Srinagar and 200 miles from Simla, the summer residence of the Viceroy of India.

Putting the rivalry with Great Britain on hold was one thing. Dealing with their fears of continuing rivalry with Japan was quite another. The military deployment plan of December 1909, approved by the Tsar in 1910, introduced a new system of territorial recruitment and transferred a large proportion of Russia's forces from the western borders to the heartland. According to the Chief of the Russian General Staff, Sukhomlinov, the strength and ambition of Japan and the weakness of China meant that 'we cannot concentrate our exclusive attention on the West any longer; we also have to ready ourselves for a serious struggle on our far-flung eastern borders'. The priorities of Sukhomlinov, who held that another Russo-Japanese war, on the shores of the Pacific, was more likely than a war with the Central Powers on the banks of the Vistula, were clearly biased towards the east. A full and sustained implementation of this plan would have made it impossible for the Russian Empire to fulfill its military obligations to France under the Franco-Russian Alliance. Baron R.R. Rosen, who was appointed to the State Council in 1911, almost immediately delivered the following views on foreign policy to Nicholas II:

> Russia's cultural mission lies exclusively in Asia, in the development of her gigantic Siberian Empire and in the spread of her culture which is inferior to Western European culture but vastly superior to that of her Central Asian neighbours, to whom Russian domination has been of unquestionable benefit.

16

BRITISH IMPERIAL POLICY, 1906–14: RUSSIA AND THE BALANCING OF POWER IN EUROPE

The Conservative government of A.J. Balfour which left office in December 1905 was much more unanimous in its approach to British foreign/imperial policy than the Liberal administrations of Sir Henry Campbell-Bannerman and Henry Herbert Asquith were to be. There was, however, little to distinguish Sir Edward Grey, who took over the Foreign Office, from his predecessor Lord Lansdowne. Since at least the turn of the century Grey had been keen to see the making of an Anglo-Russian agreement. In March 1899 he had written to Brodrick, who was then Under Secretary of State for Foreign Affairs: 'I shall press to be told what efforts have been made to get an understanding with Russia. After all that has passed in the last year I shall never believe that a Russian understanding about the Far East is impossible, till I see it proved in black and white.' In October 1901, commenting on the draft of an article which the journalist Leo Maxse was preparing for publication in his fortnightly *National Review*, Grey indulged in the following strategic thinking: 'If our diplomacy is wise, it is just the fear of having Russia on her back that will prevent Germany from quarrelling with us. If Russia is bound to be *neutral* in a war between us and Germany, you remove this fear from Germany.' He went on:

> I long to see an effort made to lift the cloud of suspicion which hangs over us and Russia, and defeat the German policy of keeping her opposed to us. There are difficulties, but it is *the* thing to be striven for and I do not believe a real effort has yet been made on our part. Salisbury's *obiter dicta* and tentative and intermittent diplomacy hardly count. We get precious little except armed neutrality from Germany anyhow, and it is an axiom of the European situation that in a row between us and Russia we should get nothing from Germany. The idea, in face of the Franco-Russian Alliance, of supporting ourselves against either Russia or France by an alliance with Germany is rotten but the German Emperor is very clever and got Chamberlain to entertain it apparently.

Following the publication of Maxse's article, in November 1901, Grey wrote again:

> The first practical point is to establish confidence and direct relations with Russia and to eliminate in that quarter the German broker, who keeps England and Russia apart and levies a constant commission upon us, while preventing us from doing any business with Russia ... the business of the British Government is to bring about a better [position] and the first step is an understanding with Russia.

In the House of Commons in January 1902 Grey described as 'undesirable' a policy of perpetual resistance to Russian expansion everywhere in Asia, and as 'intolerable' a policy of drift. The policy he recommended as being both desirable and practical was 'that of an understanding between the two Governments which would result in a fair and frank interchange of views and adjustment of interests in Asia'.

Only regarding one issue was Grey not at one with Lansdowne. Whereas the latter in October 1903 had not been afraid to guarantee a loan to Japan, hoping that such evidence of British firmness and support might bring about 'what I have always hoped to see, a frank understanding between [Britain and Russia] as to Manchuria, Tibet, Afghanistan, Persia etc.', and whereas Lansdowne maintained of the second Anglo-Japanese Alliance of August 1905 that 'it by no means excludes the idea of a friendly arrangement with Russia about our future policy in areas where the interests of the two Powers come in contact', Grey tended to view the Anglo-Japanese Alliance as something that would obstruct rather than facilitate a settlement of outstanding affairs with Russia.

❖

On 10 January 1906, one month and two days into his Foreign Secretaryship, less than a week before the first meeting at Algeciras of an international conference about Morocco, and with the British general election, which would take the rest of the month to complete, already begun, Grey received an enquiry which successive French governments were to make over the next eight years, in one guise or another, as to whether France could rely on British armed support if attacked by Germany. In the domestic political circumstances Grey had to tell the French to wait, at least until the end of the month, for an answer. Three days later, he conferred with his closest colleague and great personal friend R.B. Haldane, the new Secretary of State for War; they agreed that conversations referred to by the French Ambassador between representatives of the British and French Admiralties and War Offices should continue, albeit on a 'solely provisional and non-committal' basis.

When telling Grey on 19 January that he had instructed the Director of Military Operations, General Grierson, to communicate with the French Military Attaché, Haldane went on: 'We shall be able to despatch two Army Corps, four cavalry brigades and six battalions of infantry – we should be able to begin at once, and complete the landing of the entirety within the year – most of it much earlier. The entirety would amount to about 105,000 men and 336 guns.' He concluded, with some nonchalance, 'This is satisfactory.' The amount, and especially the time-scale envisaged, both suggest a certain lack of seriousness and of urgency. When Grey wrote to Sir F. Bertie, now British ambassador in Paris, at this time, 'All this is sheer precaution', it cannot be said that his 'All this' amounted to very much. As he more rightly said, 'I am told that 80,000 men with good guns is all we can put into the field in Europe to meet first-class troops; that won't save France unless she can save herself'. Haldane's and Grey's ideas of what was 'satisfactory', their interpretation of 'precaution', suggest that both their spirit and their flesh were weak. Those of their colleagues, with the possible exception of Asquith, were, as they well knew, weaker still.

The attitude adopted by Grey and Haldane was the more easily embraced by them as a result of their appreciation that it was really for Russia, France's ally, to save France. Having at the end of January delivered a negative answer to the enquiry made by the French on the 10th, Grey noted on 12 February that it was *time* that was on the side of France, in the form of the recovery of Russia from her defeat by Japan in the Far East and from revolution: 'the recovery of Russia will change the situation in Europe to the advantage of France, and it is the situation in Europe that will in the long run decide the position of France and Germany respectively in Morocco.' This appreciation was shared and sustained by the new Permanent Under Secretary at the Foreign Office, Sir Charles Hardinge, formerly ambassador at St Petersburg, amongst whose initial contributions was the following minute: 'If France takes action in Morocco to protect herself which Germany might resent it is *not* certain that Germany would declare war and attack France in Europe *since such action would at once present a* casus foederis *and bring Russia into line with France.*' (author's italics)

Grey's determination to afford France diplomatic support at Algeciras, and his personal determination to go beyond this if necessary and to afford military support (although it was in the highest degree unlikely that such a course would have been adopted by Campbell-Bannerman – the Foreign Secretary's resignation would have been accepted instead, just as that of Delcassé had been accepted by the French Premier Rouvier on 6 June 1905) were both geared to the advancement of a cause to which, as already noted, he had long been deeply committed, and which he had inherited from Lansdowne, namely the securing of an agreement with Russia. As he put it in a memorandum of 20 February 1906, if war broke out between France and Germany, and Great Britain kept out of it, there would be a general feeling in every country 'that we had behaved meanly and left France in the lurch'. In these circumstances, 'The United States would despise us, Russia would not think it worth while to make a friendly arrangement with us about Asia, Japan would prepare to re-insure herself elsewhere, we should be left without a friend and without the power of making a friend.' Haldane put it more cynically, as follows: 'The Expeditionary Force had a double purpose from the first. It was intended as a possible help to France if we made an agreement with Russia. But that was a state secret. The Cabinet hardly knew.' In other words, if no agreement with Russia was made the Expeditionary Force would be reserved for the protection of the British Empire, primarily against Russia; but, even if an agreement with Russia was made, this did not automatically release the Expeditionary Force to help save France. That was only 'possible'; it was by no means certain. How could it be, when the 'state secret' was never known by more than four ministers at any one time before the autumn of 1911, and never espoused by more than five ministers (out of twenty) at any one time thereafter?

In the spring of 1908 Grey recorded telling the French Premier Clemenceau that he considered 'that Russia ought to be looked to as a great counterpoise to Germany on land'. Grey's thinking on this matter had not changed since at least June 1904, when he had written:

> We ought to be able to pursue a European policy without keeping up a great Army. The friendship of the Power with the biggest navy in the world ought to be worth enough to France, Italy and Russia to make them our friends. And the more Germany increases her Navy the more value will our Navy have in the eyes of France.

Asquith, now Prime Minister, took the same line in September 1908, having seen a report of an interview between Clemenceau and King Edward VII in which the former had once again argued that Britain should adopt conscription and remember, so far as the domination of the Continent by any one power was concerned, that Napoleon had been finally defeated at Waterloo, not at Trafalgar. Asquith wrote to Grey that Clemenceau was 'ignorant, if he imagines we are going to keep here a standing army of one half to two-thirds of a million men, ready to meet the Germans in Belgium if and when they are minded to adopt that route for the invasion of France. As you point out, he completely ignores the existence – from a military point of view – of his Russian ally.' The British ambassador in Berlin made the same point:

> Of course the danger to France, if we and Germany were to come to real loggerheads is very patent and real: and M. Clemenceau says what a great many people in France only think now, but will also say very loudly if things should come to the worst: but in his anxiety that we should be in a position to give France military assistance if necessary, he omits, or at all events he omitted in his conversation with me, all thought of Russia, who would at least require a large containing force on her frontier.

During the Casablanca incident of November 1908 between France and Germany the Russian ambassador in London, Benckendorff, asked Grey what England would do if Germany took the part of Austria-Hungary over the annexation of Bosnia and Hercegovina, which had coincidentally with the Casablanca affair put an end to good relations between Russia and Austria-Hungary. Grey, who had already reminded Benckendorff that France and Russia had an ally each, 'namely, each other', countered by asking what Russia would have done had Casablanca produced a Franco–German war. Benckendorff replied to what was, from Grey's point of view, the reassuring effect that he knew the terms of the Franco-Russian Alliance to be 'very wide'. On the very next day, Hardinge wrote a memorandum in which he 'presumed that France would be able to count on the armed support of her ally Russia'.

So it went on. Here is the significance of the interest taken by Haldane in the military progress of Russia in subsequent years. The next 'war-in-sight' crisis, of July to September 1911, also over Morocco, was characterised by Grey's systematic urging upon France of a policy of making concessions to Germany. It was also characterised by Grey's by now habitual reliance on the role of Russia. At lunch on 9 August 1911 with Haldane and the Director of Military Operations, General Henry Wilson, Grey, according to Wilson's diary, 'advanced the theory that Russia was a governing factor'. Wilson believed that he 'shattered rather rudely' this theory, by telling Grey that the divisions Russia could produce in twenty-eight days would be outnumbered by those of Germany and Austria-Hungary, and that Russia could not therefore relieve the pressure on the French. Grey's conviction, however, survived Wilson's assault. Grey asked Benckendorff that very day what Russia would do if the Germans gave 'a brusque and unfavourable turn to the situation'. Benckendorff replied that owing to the terms of the Russian alliance with France, he thought it was clear what Russia would do; that, moreover, in one of the first conversations between Neratoff, the Acting Minister for Foreign Affairs, and the German ambassador in St Petersburg, the former had told the latter that Germany must remember that France and Russia were allies. This information and assurance made Grey's lunch with General Wilson digestible. On 16 August Grey again asked Benckendorff what the Russians would do 'in case of complications'. This time, as Benckendorff reported to Neratoff, 'I told Sir Edward that I had not the right to give an official answer; the Treaty Alliance between France and Russia existed in its full compass; war would certainly be a great misfortune for Russia; personally, however, I had not the slightest doubt but that the terms of the Treaty would be strictly carried out'. An official view, to the same effect, was delivered by the French ambassador on the same day. The ambassador's information was that Isvolsky, now Russian ambassador in Paris, had been instructed to say officially 'that if owing to a check on the negotiations between France and Germany there was a conflict, Russia would give not only diplomatic but military support against Germany'. Grey attempted to make it quite clear to the French ambassador on this occasion that, as a British disembarkation at Agadir might lead to a German mobilisation on the French frontier, no such move would be made in advance of deliberation between the governments of Russia, France, and Britain. From Paris, Bertie confirmed Cambon's information about Isvolsky's instructions.

Thus when Grey attended the Committee of Imperial Defence on 23 August 1911, when General Wilson elaborated the line dismissive of Russia that he had taken in private on the 9th, Grey faced it with equanimity. Whereas Wilson thought that Russia would not fight or make a crucial contribution, Grey was sure that she would. Grey's conviction would not have been diminished by Buchanan's telegram from St Petersburg of 24 August to the same effect as the information already received from Cambon and Bertie. Nevertheless, to such an extent did Grey rely upon Russian assistance for France that he lost no opportunity to remind the Russians of their alliance obligations. Hearing that Buchanan was due to see the Tsar at the end of August, Grey telegraphed that Nicholas II should be told 'that we are very anxious to see the Franco-German negotiations succeed and think the possible consequences of their failure may be very serious'. Buchanan reported that Russia would do her duty as France's ally if there was a rupture between France and Germany, and that the French and Russian Chiefs of Staff had been engaged in a consultation as to a plan of campaign in case of war. As a result, Grey again ignored General Wilson's opinion, repeated early in September, that the Russian army was not yet able to render much help to France, and maintained his pressure on Russia to fulfil the role assigned to her by himself and Haldane. He was rewarded when Benckendorff told the King, in the presence of the Chancellor of the Exchequer, Lloyd George, on 15 September, that if Germany attacked France 'Russia would certainly throw herself into the conflict. Of that he had no doubt'. A report from the military attaché in Russia, Colonel Knox, sent in October, was to support Grey's line rather than that of the Director of Military Operations.

Two years later, at the 16th meeting of a Committee of Imperial Defence sub-committee on attack on the British Isles from overseas, Haldane declared that Russia was 'the crux' in relation to the scenario of a war between the Triple Alliance and the Triple Entente. Winston Churchill, whom Asquith appointed First Lord of the Admiralty in October 1911, and who throughout the Agadir crisis had worked closely with Grey and Haldane, was to remind the Committee of Imperial Defence in 1925 that, when dealing with the problem of Franco-German relations, 'We haven't got the Russians now as we had before the war'.

❖

On 19 August 1908, in an interview at Karlsbad with the Vienna correspondent of *The Times*, Henry Wickham Steed, Clemenceau rehearsed arguments which he would put directly to King Edward VII a few days later. One statement he made was, 'it is hard to get Englishmen to look at things from our point of view'. The most poignant example given in the above of the accuracy of this remark is, perhaps, Grey's persistence in believing that the French should value the British Navy for, as he put it to them, the deterrent effect that it would have. Another statement made by Clemenceau on this occasion was:

> I know you Englishmen do not want to be entangled in a Continental war, but I ask you, as I have asked Campbell-Bannerman, Haldane and Grey, whether your policy is today what it was a century ago – to prevent the domination of Europe by any one Power? If it is, then you ought to look things in the face.

When Lansdowne and Grey looked things in the face what they saw, above all, was Russia. And they saw Russia both as their own main imperial opponent *and* as the ally of France. In June 1914, in the course of exchanges with Russia concerning the working in Persia of the

Anglo-Russian Convention of 1907, Grey revealed to Sazonov, the Russian Foreign Minister, even though to do so was to acknowledge the leverage the Russians possessed, that the policy of Anglo-Russian friendship was 'the corner-stone' of the foreign relations of the British government. In a memorandum commissioned by Grey at that point and finished on 21 July 1914, G.R. Clerk, who was responsible for the Russia desk in the Foreign Office, described Russia as 'the one Power with whom it is our paramount duty to cultivate the most cordial relations'. Clerk was prepared, as were his superiors Sir Eyre Crowe and the Permanent Under Secretary Sir Arthur Nicolson, to offer Russia a revised convention 'deliberately based on this assumption that the first principle of our foreign policy must be genuinely good relations with Russia', and on the belief that if concessions to Russia were not made, the British would be faced 'with a situation where our very existence as an Empire will be at stake'. Early in August 1914 Nicolson was to describe India, the part of the British Empire most at risk and least capable of being protected, should Russia be alienated, as 'our chief concern'. (In this, the Permanent Under Secretary was at one with Earl Roberts of Kandahar, former Commander-in-Chief of the Indian Army, who in May 1913 had written to J.L. Garvin, editor of *The Observer*: 'I rejoice to see you keep pointing out the necessity for maintaining the Entente Cordiale and keeping friends with Russia. Now that railways are approaching nearer to India, it is more than ever necessary we should not break with Russia.') Nicolson's son, Harold, who had already joined the staff of the Foreign Office, was in July 1920 to write a paper for the Committee of Imperial Defence in which he was just as explicit:

> For the last century the policy of His Majesty's Government has been inductive, intuitive and quite deliberately opportunistic, but through it all has run the dominant impulse of the defence of India.

Because Russia was the ally of France, and because Great Britain needed to be on the best possible terms with Russia for her own selfish imperial reasons, the British took advantage of the French connection with Russia to establish a purely imperial one of their own. But the British connection with France was never intended to develop, nor did it develop, in these years, except in the personal and private dispositions and inclinations of Sir Edward Grey and of two of his Cabinet colleagues, Asquith and Churchill, into a continental commitment. The titles of such works as Samuel J. Williamson's *The Politics of Grand Strategy: Britain and France prepare for war 1904–1914* (1969) and Michael Howard's *The Continental Commitment* (1972) should not be allowed to obscure this fact.

17

RESPONSIBILITIES: 1914

What followed from, and developed out of, the diplomatic crisis of July–August 1914 was described, initially, as the Great War; since 1939 the phrase 'First World War' has been substituted. It is my contention here that this was and is a misleading term. However great, in terms of their scale and consequences, were the events that took place between 1914 and 1918; however extensive, in terms of both time and geographical area, were these hostilities; however large the casualty toll and the number of states involved, it is fundamentally misleading to refer to them in such a way as to give the impression that all these things were manifestations and ramifications of one conflict. The terms 'Great War' and 'First World War' ought rather to be regarded as collective terms. For what really happened in mid-1914 is that several wars broke out simultaneously.

The Austro-Serbian War

The first war to be dealt with here was the first war to be declared in 1914, by Austria-Hungary on Serbia on 28 July, and later joined by Bulgaria on the Austro-Hungarian side and by Romania and Greece on the Serbian side. This was the third Balkan War, and is fittingly so commemorated by the monument erected in Belgrade in 1919 to the Unknown Soldier, into the floor of which is set the unaccompanied inscription '1912 – 1918'.

This particular ball was set rolling by Italy who, in September 1911, with a view to acquiring the north African province of Libya, attacked the Ottoman Empire. For it was the weakness of the Ottoman Empire that was exposed by the Italo-Turkish war that inspired Bulgaria, Serbia, and Greece to combine as they did in 1912 to make gains for themselves at its expense. In October and November 1912 their armies overwhelmed those of the Ottoman Empire. All three Balkan allies, together with Montenegro, made extensive territorial gains at the expense of the Ottoman Empire, whose European frontier was pushed eastwards to within three hundred miles of Constantinople.

THE BALKANS
1912-1914

Vienna

AUSTRIA - HUNGARY

Budapest

RUSSIA

R Dniester

R Prut

Transylvania

R Save

R Danube

ROMANIA

Belgrade

Bucharest

Constanţa

Bosnia

SERBIA

Silistria

MONTE-
NEGRO

Djakova

BULGARIA

Sofia

Varna

BLACK
SEA

ADRIATIC
SEA

Scutari

Dibra

Adrianople

ALBANIA

Durazzo

Kavalla

Constantinople

Salonika

OTTOMAN EMPIRE

Janina

AEGEAN
SEA

GREECE

Athens

——————— Frontiers in 1913
- - - - - - - Frontiers in 1912

0   Miles   150

0   Km   150

Crete

In June 1913 the second Balkan War occurred, between Serbia, Greece, and Romania on the one hand, and Bulgaria on the other. Bulgaria, defeated, was forced to sign the Treaty of Bucharest in August 1913. After the Treaty of Bucharest the situation was as follows: the Ottoman Empire, by virtue of her defeat in 1912, and Bulgaria by virtue of hers in 1913, were both disaffected, revisionist states. Both were in dispute with Greece – the former over Greek possession of the Aegean Islands, over Greek control of Crete and over Greek aspirations in Asia Minor – the latter because Bulgaria wanted a considerable part of Macedonia for herself. In addition, Greece was in dispute with Austria-Hungary over southern Albania, which to the Greeks was northern Epirus, and which was in a position to control the entrance to the Adriatic; there was complete antipathy between Bulgaria and Romania; there was much resentment in Romania of Austria-Hungary, for sympathising with the Bulgarian attack on her of July 1913, and for appearing to favour Bulgarian claims subsequently, and because 55 per cent of the population of Transylvania was Romanian, under Magyar rule within the Austro-Hungarian Empire.

In September 1913 Bulgaria and the Ottoman Empire drafted, but did not sign or ratify, a military convention. They too were in dispute over the fate of certain ethnic groups, and over the future of Thrace and Macedonia. The Bulgarians feared that the Turks would immediately attack Greece, and leave them to face a Romanian-Serb combination which would go to the rescue of Greece, Serbia's ally. This Bulgarian fear was not unfounded. For in March 1914 the Ottoman Empire announced that it would make good its claims to the islands disputed with Greece within three or four months, and began taking steps to achieve local naval superiority over Greece by attempting to purchase warships from Germany, France, Italy and Argentina. These powers refused to sell. British shipyards, however, were fast nearing completion of two battlecruisers for the Ottoman Empire. One of these, the *Sultan Osman*, would be at least equal to any dreadnought afloat, and would swing the balance of naval power in the Aegean and Black Seas in favour of the Turks. The Greeks responded by buying the *Idaho* and the *Mississippi* from the United States in June 1914. Since May, the Greeks and the Turks had been committing atrocities against one another's nationals in Smyrna, Thrace, Crete and Macedonia, under the guise of transfers of populations. On 12 June 1914 Greece delivered an ultimatum to the Ottoman Empire, demanding an end to these persecutions, together with compensation for damages and a guarantee for the future of the lives and property of Greeks in Asia Minor. The Greek representative at Constantinople was told to break off diplomatic relations if not given a satisfactory reply.

The point is that between several Balkan states there were disputes which looked as if they could be resolved only by resort to war; that there was a strong likelihood that any such war would involve most, if not indeed all, the Balkan states; and that at least one Great Power, Austria-Hungary, might decide to take advantage of any such war in order to recover its own position in that region. On the occasion of the Greek ultimatum of June 1914, Kaiser Wilhelm II remarked, 'We shall shortly see the third chapter of the Balkan Wars in which we shall all be involved'.

Although as a result of the first Balkan War it was the Ottoman Empire that had lost the most territory, it was the Austro-Hungarian Empire that had lost most in terms of position, prestige, and potential. For, in November 1912, Serbia had doubled in size, had many times multiplied the threat that its existence posed to the integrity of Austria-Hungary, and had placed itself in a position both to dominate the eastern Adriatic and to exclude Austria-Hungary from Asia Minor, a 'place in the sun' that the Dual Monarchy still nurtured hopes of reaching, however slowly. Since November 1912 Austria-Hungary had tried, and failed, to improve its position diplomatically. Its only success had been the creation of Albania, with a view to keeping Serbia landlocked. Austria-Hungary had failed to gain Bulgaria as an ally. Most seriously of all, by the spring of 1914, Austria-Hungary appeared to have lost its ally since 1883, Romania – the Balkan state upon whose allegiance and loyalty Austria-Hungary's existence as an empire primarily depended. Although from October 1913 successive Austrian Crown Council meetings had discussed 'the Serbian threat', that threat had never reached the head of the agenda, and at the time of the assassination of the Archduke Franz Ferdinand it was upon retrieving Romania that Austro-Hungarian diplomatic efforts were concentrated. The outbreak of the Austro-Serbian, or third Balkan, War should be viewed in this context. In December 1913 King Carol of Romania, who was a member of the House of Hohenzollern, confided to the Austro-Hungarian military attaché that he was not in a position to guarantee the fulfilment of the secret treaty that existed between Romania and the Dual Monarchy. In January 1914 the Chief of the Austro-Hungarian General Staff wrote in a memorandum reviewing the year 1913 that Romania, by intervening against Bulgaria in July, had thereby 'appropriated the role of the most influential state in the Balkans'. He went on:

> It can be said in advance that with a constellation such as France, Russia, Romania, Serbia, and Montenegro on the one hand and Austria-Hungary, Germany, Italy on the other, the military preponderance not

only in relative figures, but also in respect of geography lies on the side of the Triple Entente and that it is especially Austria-Hungary which at the beginning of a war against such a constellation will have to bear the heaviest burden. This will be the case even if Romania merely remains neutral, while military intervention on her part against the Monarchy would create a highly dangerous preponderance on the enemy side.

On 14 June 1914 Tsar Nicholas II paid an official visit to Constanţa, on the Romanian Black Sea coast. A week later Count Czernin, who had been sent by the Austro-Hungarian Foreign Minister Count Berchtold to Bucharest on a special mission to bring Romania back into the Austro-Hungarian fold, reported that the Tsar's visit constituted 'a milestone in the career of the Romanian State and perhaps also in that of the (Dual) Monarchy.... Romania's swing over to the Triple Entente, which has been expected for a year, took place before the public eye on the day of Constanţa'. Emperor Franz Josef's argument for action against Serbia, an argument which he took from a long memorandum on future policy which had been written in the Ballhausplatz and which he embodied in a letter to Wilhelm II at the beginning of July, was that only the employment of force against Serbia would cause Romania to reverse her recent swing to the Triple Entente. An attack upon Serbia, despite the assassination of the heir to the throne of the Dual Monarchy, was not the main thing. Such an attack, if successful, would kill at least two birds with one stone. It would dispose of 'the Serbian threat'; but the more important objective was the re-establishment of the thirty-year-old connection with Romania, which alone would give Austria-Hungary a chance to dominate the Balkan region.

The German-Russian War

A resolution of Austria-Hungary's problems with Serbia had been pressed upon the Dual Monarchy by the German Empire since March 1913, rather to the discomfort, and mystification, of the authorities in Vienna, whose view was that the Germans did not understand the Balkans and did not know what was possible and what was not possible there. Here, however, we come to the second of the wars that broke out in July–August 1914: the German-Russian War.

Both Wilhelm II and Chancellor Bethmann-Hollweg regarded the outcome of the first Balkan War as having altered in favour of the Slavonic peoples and against the Germanic powers the balance of power in the Balkans, and, therefore, the balance of power in Europe as a whole. At this point Wilhelm II began to use a particular vocabulary. In December 1912 he referred to 'the final struggle between the Slavs and the Teutons', to 'the struggle of the Teutons against the Slav flood'. He went on to write:

> If we are to take up arms it will be to help Austria, not only to defend ourselves against Russia but against the Slavs in general and to remain *Germans*. *Id est* there is *about to be* a racial struggle between the Teutons and the Slavs who have become uppish.... It is a question of the existence of the Teutons on the European Continent.... The question for Germany is to be or not to be.

This language and these concepts, which were immediately taken up by the Kaiser's civilian and military entourage, recurred following the Serbian defeat of Bulgaria in the second Balkan War. In October 1913 Wilhelm II described the Balkan Wars as 'not passing phenomena created by diplomatic activity but a World Historical Process of the same order as the migrations of nations which in this case took the form of a strong Slav advance'. His mind had clearly leapt back in time to the early centuries of the Christian era, or to the Dark Ages, when Franks, Gauls, Goths, Vikings and others took up in western Europe the positions they developed subsequently. Something equivalent, in his view, was taking place, this time at the expense of the Teutons. These same sentiments made another spectacular appearance in July 1914, shortly after the publication of the Austro-Hungarian ultimatum to Serbia.

In December 1912, following a special council convened by Wilhelm II, the German decision-making hierarchy began to prepare the German public, through the press, for the German-Russian war which they now believed to be inevitable, and which they believed their only chance of winning lay in fighting before the Russian military improvements and increases begun in 1912 were completed, as they would be by 1918. The Germans had, as they saw it, some six years' grace. An Army Bill, which had been considered unnecessary by the General Staff on 13 October 1912, four days before the outbreak of the first Balkan War, was now drafted, and passed into law in April 1913. The Germans also commenced to lay the diplomatic framework for their war with Russia. One element in this framework was the freeing of their ally Austria-Hungary from concern about Serbia, so that the whole of the Austro-Hungarian war effort could be concentrated against Russia. As Wilhelm II put it to Conrad at manoeuvres in Silesia between 17 and 19 September 1913, 'it would be better to see Serbia united with Austria than for Austria to have as its neighbour a south Slav state which would at all times stab it in the back'. Unity between Serbia and Austria-Hungary was a strand of German, and particularly of the Kaiser's, foreign policy that was assiduously pursued for the last eighteen months of peace between the Great Powers. This unity could be achieved, and the problem of Serbia solved, in one of two ways, according to the Germans. If the carrot failed, there was always the stick.

In March 1913 the Kaiser made it clear that he considered a combination of Serbia, Romania and Greece under Austrian leadership a natural and good one. In April, War Minister von Heeringen told the Budget Commission of the Reichstag that the enlarged Serbia would tie down Austro-Hungarian forces which would therefore be absent from the Galician front in a war with Russia. After speaking to Conrad in September 1913 Wilhelm II took up the matter again with Berchtold in October, saying:

> The war between east and west is in the long run inevitable, and if Austria was then exposed on its flank to the invasion of a respectable military power it could be fatal to the outcome of the great struggle. With Serbia there could be no other relationship for Austria than that of the dependence of the small power on the big one. Austria must attract Serbia by providing money, military training, trade preferences. In return for the protection which the Austrian army could offer Serbia against foreign intervention she would place her army at Austria's disposal. If Serbia refused to do this force must be used – if Franz Josef makes a demand the Serbian government must comply and if it refuses to do so Belgrade will be shelled and occupied till Franz Josef's will has been done – and you can be sure that I shall stand behind you ready to draw my sword whenever your action requires it.

The German ambassador in Vienna reported this conversation to Bethmann-Hollweg in the following terms:

> The Emperor [Wilhelm II] remarked that Austria-Hungary must do everything to establish, if at all possible à l'aimable, an economic and political understanding with Serbia, but if that could not be achieved by peaceful means more energetic methods must be employed. Somehow or other Serbia must in all circumstances be made to join forces with Austria-Hungary, particularly in the military sphere; so that in case of a conflict with Russia Austria-Hungary will not have the Serbian army against it but on its side. He added that it could be assumed with certainty that for the next six years Russia would be incapable of taking military action.

Wilhelm II further elaborated his policy in a conversation with the Austro-Hungarian military attaché in Berlin in December 1913. Taking into account what Conrad had told him in September to the effect that Serbia would shortly have twenty divisions at her disposal, he said: 'The Serbs must be harnessed before the car of the Austro-Hungarian Monarchy – in one way or another. The final decision in south-east Europe may involve sooner or later a serious armed conflict, and we Germans then stand with you and behind you, but it can in no case be a matter of indifference to us whether twenty divisions of your army are earmarked for operations against the southern Slavs, or not.' In March 1914, at a meeting in Berlin which included Foreign Minister von Jagow, Colonial Minister Solf, and Zimmerman and Koerner of the German Foreign Office, the Kaiser advised the former Austro-Hungarian Minister of Trade, Baernreither, 'to conclude a customs alliance with Serbia and in the end a military convention'. On 16 and 17 June, in conversation with the Archduke Franz Ferdinand, Wilhelm II maintained that it was vital for Austria-Hungary to take energetic steps against Serbia, arguing once more that Russia was by no means ready for war and that she would probably not oppose such an action.

German support and encouragement for Austro-Hungarian action against Serbia at the beginning of July 1914, then, is best seen as a continuation of a policy consistently pursued and pressed upon Austria-Hungary for at least the previous eighteen months. Even before the assassination of the Archduke the Kaiser's patience was wearing thin. The assassination itself merely confirmed what the Austrians had always maintained, that the Serbs were irreconcilable, and would never be won over by the peaceful means suggested, in the interests of Germany in having the whole of the Austro-Hungarian forces committed against Russia, by the Kaiser in particular – a typical manifestation on his part of an inability to see the trees for the wood.

❖

Thus far, it has been suggested that there was an extreme likelihood of a third Balkan war breaking out at some point in 1914; and it has been maintained that this third Balkan war took the form of an attack by Austria-Hungary on Serbia, a move that, from the German point of view, was seen as a clearing of the decks, a freeing of Austria-Hungary's back as a move to improve the position of the German powers for a war at some unspecified point before 1918 against Russia, the greatest of the Slavonic powers. What happened in July 1914 was that the German calculation that Russia was not ready for war and would not oppose an action of Austria-Hungary against Serbia proved to be mistaken. When, in the last week of July, the Germans realised that they had miscalculated about Russia, they made last-minute attempts to make the rulers of

Austria-Hungary see the situation in a European or German, as opposed to a Balkan, perspective. It was too little and too late. When the Austro-Hungarians deliberately ignored the Germans at this juncture the latter, fearful of what would otherwise happen to Austria-Hungary, in turn deliberately misinterpreted the Russian mobilisation, which all of them knew would take at least six weeks to complete, as an act of war, instead of as the diplomatic move to buy time for negotiations which it really was. The German-Russian war, planned but not fixed for the future, was thereby brought forward. It followed by four days, instead of by four months, or by four years, the Austro-Serbian war which was, in German thinking, supposed to increase in it the chances of Teutonic success.

The German-English War

Another war was brought forward in 1914. This was the third of the wars that broke out at this time – the German-English war. War against Great Britain had been contemplated by the German Empire since at least the turn of the century. As in the case of the German-Russian war, no precise date had been fixed; but the idea was implicit in the reasons given by Admiral von Tirpitz to Wilhelm II for the adoption of *Flottenpolitik*: the possession of a great navy by Germany would compel the British to make colonial concessions to the German Empire. As a result the latter would become a world power, like Great Britain. Chancellor von Bülow admitted in a memorandum of 29 March 1900 for the Bavarian representative in Berlin Count von Lerchenfeld that the Imperial Government was basing its naval calculations upon a probable war with England. In 1903 Bethmann-Hollweg, then Oberpräsident of Brandenburg, the highest administrative office in Prussia, described the Kaiser's intentions to Baroness von Spitzemberg as follows: 'His basic and primary idea is to destroy England's position in the world to the advantage of Germany; therefore – it is the Kaiser's firm conviction – we need a navy and, to build it, a great deal of money.' If the British refused to make the sort of accommodation that was envisaged, if they resisted German demands and insisted on continuing to occupy their position in the world, Germany would have to resort to force. The Germans well knew that not until 1918/1920 would they have enough naval power to risk a contest. By that time, however, events would have demonstrated whether the British were disposed to resist or to yield.

This German outlook was heavily conditioned by the animosity of France and Russia towards the British Empire which was such a feature of the international scene at the turn of the century. Whilst that animosity ceased to be such a feature, Germany's long-term aims remained the same. Instead of altering or adjusting them, they tried instead to spoil Franco-Russian-British relations in a bid to return themselves to the relatively advantageous diplomatic position that they had formerly enjoyed, in addition to being the strongest single power on the European continent.

Germany's relatively untroubled, and unchallenged, position on the continent of Europe ended, precisely, so far as they perceived the matter, in October–November 1912. The recovery of Russia from the defeats and disturbances of 1904–07, together with the 'Slav threat' given substance by the victories of the Balkan states, presented to the German mind an unexpected and unwelcome European problem, the solution of which they sought in a deviation from, or interruption of, *Weltpolitik*. The Germans convinced themselves that they had to deal with the 'Slav threat', had to secure their European position, had to readjust in their favour the balance of power which, as they saw it, had suddenly changed against them. Only when this had been accomplished would they be able to concentrate on *Weltpolitik* again. Hence the necessity for the German-Russian war. Essentially, this was a nuisance, something to be got out of the way quickly in order to return to the long-term business of acquiring an extra-European empire at Britain's expense.

In July–August 1914 the German government made only the most half-hearted of efforts to secure British neutrality. They were half-hearted in this respect for two reasons. In the first place, they did not regard British military and naval power as sufficient to deter them from their war with Russia, even though this entailed that they should invade and defeat France, Russia's ally, first. Such power as Britain possessed could not, in their view, be brought to bear quickly enough to affect the outcome of either campaign. The Germans had a deterrent of their own: as von Jagow told his ambassador in London in February 1914, 'We have not built our fleet in vain, and in my opinion people in England will seriously ask themselves whether it will be just that simple and without danger to play the role of France's guardian angel against us'. To this should be added, by July 1914, the German appreciation of the likelihood of civil war in Ireland. In the second place, the British had recently demonstrated their recalcitrance, their indisposition to make concessions, by refusing at French insistence to ratify agreements with Germany on the future of Portuguese colonies and on the Baghdad Railway, and by commencing negotiations with Russia for a naval convention. Bethmann-Hollweg described this last development, all details of which reached him through a German spy in the Russian Embassy in London, as 'the last link in the chain' of British 'encirclement' of the German Empire.

In these circumstances, or interpretations of circumstances, it seemed to the German government that they might as well have their war with

Britain at the same time as their war with Russia. At the very least, with the help they fully but misguidedly expected from both Austria-Hungary and Italy, they expected to defeat Britain's two friends, France and Russia, and to re-establish a British isolation of which they hoped to take advantage later.

The English-German War

The obverse of the German-English war is, of course, the English-German war. In the face of German naval building and commercial competition, many within the British establishment did Tirpitz's calculations for themselves, and reached the same conclusions. They too forecast a war between England and Germany at some point in the future. Their estimates of this point tended to change as the German naval programme developed, but the majority of these estimates predicted either 1913–14 or 1917–18. There was also a parallel with the idea held in some high German circles, that if a war came, or developed out of, a situation in which Austria-Hungary was already involved, then the German powers could operate as a unit in a way that might not be possible if the war developed out of any other situation or region. In the circumstances of July–August 1914, Britain would have France and Russia as allies; this would not necessarily be so in other cases, or at a time selected by Germany to act against Great Britain.

The elements within British political life which regarded war with Germany in either a deterministic or a positive way broke the surface many times before the final crisis. A lasting impression was made upon the Germans by a speech at Eastleigh on 2 February 1905 in which Arthur Lee, the Civil Lord of the Admiralty, perhaps inspired by the success of the Japanese attack on Russia in the previous year, reminded his listeners that 'Thrice blest is he who hath his quarrel just, but four times he who gets his blow in *fust*'. Two months later, in April 1905, the First Sea Lord, Sir John Fisher, wrote to the Foreign Secretary, Lansdowne, that the German interest in acquiring a port on the coast of Morocco – an interest which was entirely a product of Fisher's imagination – provided 'a golden opportunity for fighting the Germans in alliance with the French, so I earnestly hope you may be able to bring this about'. Despite the jocular tone, Fisher was not joking. As Louis Mallet, Lansdowne's Private Secretary, found out, Fisher 'simply longs to have a go at Germany'. What is more, Mallet admitted that he himself 'abound[ed] in [Fisher's] sense', and told Fisher that he would do all he could to prevail upon Lansdowne. To Sir F. Bertie, a fellow spirit and British ambassador in Paris, Mallet expressed his dismay that Germany might not, on this occasion, resort to force: 'But of course she won't, unluckily for us. She will wait til her fleet is twice as strong as it is.' In October of that year Sir George Clarke, the Secretary of the Committee of Imperial Defence, reminded John Walter, the owner of *The Times*, of articles in the *Army and Navy Gazette* advocating an attack upon Germany. Walter sent Clarke's letter to George Saunders, *The Times'* correspondent in Berlin, whose reply contained the information that Whitehead, the Counsellor of Embassy at Berlin 1904–06, 'thinks that England may lose patience and may consider that it is better to have it out with Germany – in a word to come to blows now rather than ten years hence, when the German Navy will be really formidable'. At the very end of 1905 Colonel Repington, the influential military correspondent of *The Times*, told the French Military Attaché that if a Franco-German war broke out, England would never find a better opportunity and would certainly take advantage of it.

In September 1906 Lord Esher, a permanent member of the Committee of Imperial Defence, wrote three letters in quick succession. To his son, on 4 September, he said:

> There is no doubt that within measurable distance there looms a titanic struggle between Germany and Europe for mastery. The years 1793–1815 will be repeated, only Germany, not France, will be trying for European domination. She has 70 million people and is determined to have commercial pre-eminence. To do this *England* has got to be crippled and the Low Countries added to the German Empire.

Two days later, that message was reinforced: *'L'Allemagne c'est l'Ennemi –* and there is no doubt on the subject. They mean to have a powerful fleet, and commercially to beat us out of the field, before ten years are over our heads.' On 7 September Esher wrote to the Duchess of Sutherland: 'There is a very bad time coming for soldiers; for the laws of historical and ethnographical evolution ... require that we shall fight one of the most powerful military empires that has ever existed. This is certain.' The element of commerical competition with Germany was picked up by the journalist and political commentator W.S. Blunt in a postscript to the diaries he kept during these years: 'The real cause of the quarrel with Germany', he wrote, was 'our dread of a too powerful commercial rival and the fear of Kaiser Wilhelm's forcing France, if we stood aside, into commercial alliance with him against us in the markets of the world.'

In January 1907 Lord Rosebery told the editor of the *Westminster Gazette*, J.A. Spender, of the declaration by Clemenceau that he would not be hurried into war with Germany by English Teutophobes. In April 1908 Algernon Law of the Foreign Office wrote to Bertie in Paris: 'I should like to go for the Germans at once before they have built up a formidable navy, and put a stop once and for ever to their competition which is so serious to us.' On 29 March 1909 Arthur Lee made another contribution: from the Opposition benches he introduced the following censure motion: 'That in the opinion of this House, the declared policy of His Majesty's Government respecting the immediate provision of Battleships of the newest type does not sufficiently secure the safety of the Empire.' At the height of this naval building scare Spencer Wilkinson, defence correspondent of the *Morning Post*, pounced upon a remark of Fabian Ware, the editor, concerning the time when Delcassé resigned as French Foreign Minister in June 1905: 'You [Ware] now think we ought to have fought Germany then. You thought so if I remember right at the time.' Wilkinson followed this up on 3 April 1909 with another warning: 'You, as I understand, want to hasten a war with Germany while I hope it may be averted by proper attention to navy and army and by a sound foreign policy.' On this occasion the editor of *The English Review* (later better known as the novelist Ford Madox Ford) demanded that an ultimatum be sent to Germany, threatening war if she laid down another battleship.

To Winston Churchill in November 1909, whose ministry the Board of Trade had recently conducted an enquiry into the internal financial constraints on German shipbuilding, the following questions were still open: 'Will the tension be relieved by moderation or snapped by calculated violence? Will the policy of the German government be to smoothe the internal situation or to find an escape from it in external adventure?'; within a year, Churchill's mind was made up, and the questions closed: in October 1910 he stated, 'The fate of Egypt would be decided by the issue of the coming war with Germany'; in October 1912, one year after he became First Lord of the Admiralty, he said that he believed 'in the coming of a war in which we shall be involved in order to prevent France being overpowered by Germany, and forced into alliance against us'. In August 1911, at the height of the Agadir crisis, the Director of Military Operations, General Sir Henry Wilson, urged the government to commit the British Expeditionary Force to France, should Franco-German negotiations break down, even though he knew full well that that force lacked vital equipment. At the Foreign Office Sir William Tyrrell, Grey's Private Secretary, said in September 1911 that 'for many reasons it would be better for the war to come *now* rather than later'. When in February 1912 Haldane, the Secretary of State for War, went on a mission to Berlin, a Major Viburne wrote to a friend: 'Personally, I think there must be a war between this country and Germany sooner or later, and it had better come sooner.' At the same time, the possibility that the French might take the initiative and attack Germany did not in the least embarrass the British ambassador in Paris; nor did it disturb Lloyd George, to whom Bertie confided it. Later in that year, at the time of the first Balkan War, Lloyd George was reported as having spoken 'quite complacently' about the rousing of the English national spirit for a war about the Balkans.

It is safe to conclude that, when the English-German war came there were many on the English side who welcomed it, albeit for different reasons, and many who considered it to be long overdue. These elements conditioned, to an extent, the decision that was ultimately made. That said, the decision that was ultimately made was taken not by any of the preventive warmongers mentioned above, but by the Foreign Secretary Sir Edward Grey, acting in conjunction with the Prime Minister, Asquith, and it was geared primarily to considerations of avoiding both isolation and an outright contest with Russia for supremacy in Central Asia – the possibility most feared in the Foreign Office appreciations quoted at the end of the preceding chapter. By the evening of 25 July the Russian attitude had been made clear to Grey. As the British ambassador in St Petersburg rendered the threatening language of Sazonov, the Russian Foreign Minister,

> For ourselves position is a most perilous one, and we shall have to choose between giving Russia our active support or renouncing her friendship. If we fail her now we cannot hope to maintain that friendly cooperation with her in Asia that is of such vital importance to us.

This having been made clear, on 28 July Asquith went to see King George V, whom he had discovered had told Prince Henry of Prussia two days before that Britain would remain neutral, and told him: 'Russia says to us, "If you won't say you are ready to side with us now, your friendship is valueless, and we shall act on that assumption in the future".' The same sentiments were shortly afterwards expressed by the French ambassador in London, who pointed out that if those in France who counted on British assistance were let down, 'those in favour of an alliance with Germany at the expense of Britain could feel justified' – France would look on at the ruin of the British Empire 'without a movement of sympathy'.

❖

As for the British Empire, so for the imperial powers of the continent: unless they were prepared to reverse long-standing policies and to eliminate what had developed into their *raison d'être*, war was the only alternative. Imperial considerations constituted the factor common to all the Great Powers. In 1914 the wars of the immediate and of the more distant future merged into what became known as the Great War because no Great Power, no regime, no body of ministers, was prepared to curb its imperial inclinations, tendencies or pretensions – whether these related primarily to eastern Europe, as in the cases of Austria-Hungary and Russia, or whether they related primarily to regions outside of Europe altogether, as in the cases of Germany, France, and Great Britain.

Although Austria-Hungary's policy in attacking Serbia in July 1914 was defensive in that she was attempting to reverse the recent trend of Romanian policy and to break out of what she perceived as encirclement by states sympathetic to Russia, it was also aggressive; and the longer-term the view taken of it the more aggressive it was. For not only was Austria-Hungary trying to change the status quo, she was also intending to use a new status quo, set up by her, as a springboard from which to establish her own influence and exclude that of Russia from the whole area. Whilst Russian policy was defensive, in that it was geared to maintaining the status quo, it too was aggressive in the long term, in that she too was determined exclusively to enjoy and exploit the resources of the Balkan region and beyond. The Russian Empire could not permit the establishment of a causeway of Teutonic influence from Berlin through Vienna to Constantinople and Asia Minor, which would lead to a complete domination of the peoples and potential of the Balkans by the Central Powers. Nor could she abandon the principle of 'the Balkans for the Balkan peoples'. As recently as April 1914 Nicholas II had forecast, to the British ambassador, the disintegration of Austria-Hungary as soon as Franz Josef, its ruler since 1848, died. This, he had said, was 'a mere matter of time': 'The day would come when we should see a Kingdom of Hungary, a Kingdom of Bohemia and the incorporation of the German provinces of Austria in the German Empire, while the Southern Slavs would be absorbed by Serbia and the Romanians of Transylvania by Romania.' Such a felicitous development would never transpire if the Russians stood by and allowed Austria-Hungary to do as she wished with Serbia, possibly to the extent of partitioning her. The German Empire, as already said, wished to turn back the 'Slav flood' as a precondition for a successful return to *Weltpolitik* at the expense of the British Empire. The British Empire wished above all to retain the connection with Russia, the loss of which would entail the resumption of the Great Game in Asia and the probable loss, in due course, of India.

❖

These were the wars of 1914. They overlapped. They intermingled. At least two of them – the German-Russian and the German-English – came before their time. The context in which they broke out was created by the success of Balkan nationalism in October and November 1912 and by the military incapacity of the armies of the Ottoman Empire.

18

THE WAR OF ALL AGAINST ALL:
1914–18

What follows is designed to support the following conclusions: (i) that 'war aims' expanded as the wars went on, and this not only because the number of belligerents increased; (ii) that the 'war aims' of each and every power conflicted, to a considerable extent, with those of each and every other power – not only were the aims of the Central Powers different from those of the Entente Powers, but those of Germany conflicted with those of Austria-Hungary, and those of Britain with those of France and of Russia; (iii) that the longer hostilities went on, the more clear it becomes that all the powers were concerned less with the current, and clearly indecisive, conflicts than with preparing for a future war – for the next war, against whomsoever they considered that most likely to be. In other words, what occurred between July–August 1914 and November 1918 was almost a free-for-all, a war of all against all, the international equivalent of a Hobbesian state of nature. There were, in effect, no sides. Each state was interested only in its own future and security, at the expense, fundamentally, of all the other states.

As the contests between the Central Powers have been rather more thoroughly dealt with in the secondary literature (see Further Reading section) I propose here to concentrate on Great Britain, Japan, the United States of America and France. ,

❖

Great Britain

Great Britain really went to war to protect the British Empire from the depredations which Russia and France, if abandoned at the outset, would otherwise make upon it, if they were victorious over the Central Powers; and to preserve their position in the world from Germany, France and Russia if the Central Powers defeated France and Russia and converted them into German satellites. As one senior official at the Foreign Office argued on 25 July 1914, whilst making a case for inducing Germany to apprehend 'that the war will find England by the side of France and Russia':

It is difficult not to agree with M. Sazonov that sooner or later England will be dragged into the war if it does come.... Should the war come, and England stands aside, one of two things must happen:

(a) Either Germany and Austria win, crush France and humiliate Russia. With the French fleet gone, Germany in occupation of the Channel, with the willing or unwilling co-operation of Holland and Belgium, what will be the position of a friendless England?

(b) Or France and Russia win. What would then be their attitude towards England? What about India and the Mediterranean?

Belgium, 'gallant little Belgium', did not come into the British decision for war except as an excuse, as a peg upon which to hang actions decided on for altogether different reasons, as a screen for motives too imperialistic to be disclosed.

On 30 August 1914 Britain, Russia and France offered the Ottoman Empire a guarantee of its integrity for the duration of the hostilities in return for its neutrality. This offer did not suffice to cause the Ottoman Government to waver in its loyalty to an alliance already made, on 2 August, with the German Empire. In part, this was because the Entente overture was couched in somewhat threatening terms. As Sir Edward Grey put it to the British ambassador at Constantinople:

> Were Turkey to side against us we should consider ourselves free as regards Egypt, and free to support the Arabs against Turkey and another Muslim authority for Arabia and control of the Holy Places and that the prestige of the Turkish Government in Mohammedan India would be much diminished and thus the pro-German Turks at Constantinople if allowed to pursue their present line would bring disaster to the Turkish Empire.

The Ottoman Empire declared war on Russia and Great Britain at the end of October 1914.

This declaration of war transformed the situation. It is the key to what were to become the war aims of Britain, Russia and France. It was greeted by Asquith with the words: 'It is they [the Turks] and not we who have rung the death-knell of Ottoman dominion, not only in Europe, but in Asia.... The Turkish Empire has committed suicide, and dug with its own hand its grave.' At the same time the British told the Russians, who expressed an eagerness to attack Turkey through Persia, via Azerbaijan, not to do so, or else Britain would send forces to the East at the expense of the Western Front. In return for this Russian abstention, she was assured that 'if Russia respects Persian frontiers and concentrates her forces on Germany, then if Germany is crushed, the fate of the Straits and of Constantinople cannot this time be decided in any other way than in conformity with Russian interests'. The French were not told of this assurance; they got their own back, later, by concluding an agreement with Russia by which Alsace-Lorraine, the Saar and an autonomous Rhineland state would go to France. The British learned of this arrangement only when the Bolsheviks published this, and other secret treaties, in December 1917.

In March 1915 the Russians took up the British offer, and demanded the actual possession of Constantinople by themselves. Conceding this claim on 11 March, Grey described Constantinople as 'the greatest prize of the whole war'. As far as the war aims of the British Empire were concerned, and so far as British relations, present and future, with her current allies, were concerned, some important and interesting points now began to be made by British ministers and advisers. The First Lord of the Admiralty, Churchill, stated that 'If we succeeded in shattering German naval power we ought to be able to build a Mediterranean fleet against France and Russia'. The First Sea Lord, Admiral Sir A.K. Wilson, wrote on 12 March: 'After the war Russia – being relieved for a considerable time from any danger of aggression by Germany or Austria – will be able to devote herself to internal affairs, the development of her trade, and to strengthening her position in Asia. Russia and Great Britain will be left face to face as the two dominant powers in Asia. If they are antagonistic, Russia would be in the stronger position, as, although she could not pass through the Suez Canal or the Straits of Gibraltar, she could bring her whole military forces against India, which could only be reinforced and supplied by the long sea route.' By contrast, in a memorandum of 15 March on the importance of Alexandretta, in the Gulf of Iskanderoon, as a naval base, Admiral Sir H.B. Jackson emphasised the French menace:

> Germany is not the only opponent to consider. Unless the status quo in Syria is maintained, the French are likely to occupy that region, and thus be in a position to dominate the Euphrates valley from the westward, i.e., attack our interests in Persia from a direction and along lines which our navy would be unable to command. Thus, with France established in the south of Syria, the reason for holding its most northern corner is accentuated; for Alexandretta is so situated as to be able to command the lines of communication to the Euphrates valley from the south and from the west, as well as the lines from Asia Minor to Syria, Egypt, and Arabia.

The Secretary of State for War, Lord Kitchener, produced on 16 March a memorandum entitled 'Alexandretta and Mesopotamia'. He began:

Assuming that the war is brought to a successful conclusion, a partition of a certain part of the Turkish dominions will doubtless have to be undertaken. Russia, we know, will secure Constantinople together with the control of the Dardanelles and the Bosporus. It is safe to assume that the claims of Syria, which the French have put forward for so many years, will have to be satisfied to a considerable extent. With Russia established on the Dardanelles and with France in possession of Syria, the strategical and economic situation in the Levant cannot fail to be profoundly modified, and the position of Egypt will be considerably affected. It must not be forgotten that, after the conclusion of peace, old enmities and jealousies which have been stilled by the existing crisis in Europe, may revive. We have, in fact, to assume that, at some future date, we may find ourselves at enmity with Russia, or with France, or with both in combination, and we must bear this possibility in mind in deciding how, when the time for settlement comes and the question of the partition of Turkey in Asia arises, our interests can best be safeguarded.

In his next paragraph Kitchener went on to say that the question of a British occupation of Alexandretta entirely depended on the future of Mesopotamia, and to identify Russia as 'the enemy':

To bring troops from the United Kingdom to Mesopotamia, via the Suez Canal, Red Sea, and Persian Gulf, would take nearly a fortnight longer than to move them to Alexandretta and thence by rail. Moreover, the enemy especially to be borne in mind is obviously Russia, and it so happens that any advance by Russian forces from the highlands of Armenia and Kurdistan must follow certain well – defined routes leading southwards, with their flank exposed to a British advance from about Aleppo; the possession of Alexandretta and Aleppo would, in fact, place us in a particularly favourable strategical position for countering any offensive on the part of the enemy.

Simply to retain Egypt was, in his opinion, not enough: 'if we do not take Mesopotamia, the Russians undoubtedly will sooner or later.' Their doing so would give them an outlet into the Persian Gulf, and enable them eventually to control the military situation there and the greater part of the commerce of the Gulf. He continued:

Our interests in the Persian Gulf are of very old standing, and our prestige as an Asiatic Power is inseparably bound up with our domination of those waters; but such domination would cease were Baghdad and Basra to be in the hands of Russia. So long as the Ottoman Empire controls the lower valleys of the Euphrates and Tigris, we may rest content with the situation as it is, but if the Ottoman Empire is to be wholly or partially broken up, it is imperative that Mesopotamia should become British.

For Kitchener there was yet another aspect, one adumbrated the previous autumn in Grey's clumsy bid for Turkish neutrality:

Again, should the partition of Turkey take place, it is to our interests to see an Arab kingdom established in Arabia under the auspices of England, bounded on the north by the valley of the Tigris and Euphrates, and containing within it the chief Mahommedan Holy Places, Mecca, Medina, and Kerbala. In this eventuality the possession of Mesopotamia – as we already hold the Persian Gulf, the Red Sea, and Egypt – would secure all the approaches to the Mahommedan Holy Places. This, in our position as the greatest of Muslim States, would greatly enhance our prestige amongst the many millions of our Mahommedan subjects.

To Kitchener, it was a matter of 'gaining definite control over the great line of communications to India', a line which ran from Aleppo due east to the Euphrates, along the Euphrates valley to Baghdad, and then down to the Persian Gulf. The alternative, which he rejected, was 'to leave that line permanently to another Great Power or Great Powers, which would thus dominate the Mediterranean terminus'. He hoped to avoid a frontier conterminous with that of Russia, hoped that out of the remains of the Ottoman Empire a Turkish or Armenian buffer state stretching from Anatolia to the Persian border could be created, but stated firmly that 'even a frontier conterminous with Russia, with all its grave drawbacks, would be preferable to a Franco-Russian domination of the line from the Gulf of Iskanderun to the Persian Gulf'.

Yet another memorandum was supplied by the Admiralty, on 17 March. This issued an explicit reminder of Disraeli's policy of 1878, of the Anglo-Turkish Convention, of the occupation of Cyprus as a *place d'armes* to cover the railhead of a railway across to the Euphrates which had at that time been regarded as 'the best means of checking a further movement of Russia southwards'. It also exhumed a French warning of 1879: 'Let England beware: the enterprise which she has abandoned will be taken up sooner or later by others and against her.' What this particular Admiralty memorandum concentrated on, however, and to a greater extent than had Lord Kitchener, when describing the British Empire as 'the greatest of Muslim States', was the aspect of 'prestige':

It is admitted that the power of meeting continental responsibilities in the East is mainly a question of the moral ascendancy we can develop, and here we are likely to be very weak as compared with Russia in the near future. We are putting Russia into the most famous seat of Empire in the East, allowing her to clothe herself in all the majesty of Rum, and to take possession of a throne which, in Oriental imagination, is the highest of all. The inevitable results upon the relative standing of our own Empire need no labouring.

The proposed resolution of this aspect was elaborated as follows:

Clearly it is our right and duty, if we sacrifice so much for the peace of the world, that we should see to it we have compensation, or we may defeat our own end. And where can such compensation be found in anything like so much force as in reviving the still more ancient seat of empire in the Middle East? We must play Babylon against Byzantium.

Almost exactly as Lord Salisbury had dreamt in the late 1890s, Russia at Constantinople was to be trumped by Great Britain at the site of what was then regarded as the earliest manifestation of civilisation. This could not be done 'by merely occupying and bringing to life again the old Mesopotamia'. Rather, 'The ancient empire must not only be restored to its wealth, it must be brought to the shores of the Mediterranean. The war is teaching us that the Mediterranean is still, as it always was, the centre of world politics, and it is there we must establish the gate of our new acquisition as a counterpoise to the new weight that Russia is acquiring in the dominant area'. The writer of this, clearly possessed of a classical education, as well as of an imagination more orientalist than oriental, and acting here as a witness to one of the dangers of such an education and such an imagination, went on to suggest that a counterpoise to Russian prestige was as necessary to France in Syria as to Britain, and that France and Britain might find themselves acting together against Russia as a result. He ended by combining the lessons of the classical past with what in 1915 was a very modern preoccupation:

It is obvious that the conditions which will arise out of the dissolution of the Turkish Empire must restore to the Mediterranean all its old political importance; and this will happen at a time when, as a dominant factor of sea power, coal is giving way to oil. From this point of view, Russia in possession of the Dardanelles will have all the advantage of her Black Sea supplies at her back. It is therefore vital to our position in the decisive area that we should have equally accessible a similar supply. With

Mesopotamia under our control, and with access to it at Alexandretta, we have at our feet a complete solution of the new situation; for not only should we have an inexhaustible supply in our own hands, but we should have it at a point most desirable strategically – that is, at a point most remote from our home base.

On 18 March, two days after the above was printed for the Committee of Imperial Defence, the French claimed Cilicia (which included the Gulf of Iskanderun), Syria and Palestine. The response to this of important officials at the Foreign Office complemented the views already expressed by the Service Departments. Sir George Clerk, whose reaction to the guarantee of Turkey proposed in August 1914 had been, 'Avoid for all time', immediately minuted: 'It should be pointed out that Constantinople is for Russia, and Mesopotamia for Great Britain, their main compensation for the war, while France's great reward lies outside Turkey.' Sir Arthur Nicolson agreed: 'The above minute is much to the point.'

On 18 March the British cabinet once again discussed the question of the future of Turkey in Asia. Kitchener was prompted to say, in the cause he espoused, namely that of partition:

> The Turks would always be under pressure from their strong Russian neighbour, with the result that the Khalifate might be to a great extent under Russian domination, and Russian influence might indirectly assert itself over the Mohammedan part of the population of India. If, on the other hand, the Khalifate were transferred to Arabia, it would remain to a great extent under our influence.

The Secretary of State for India, Lord Crewe, agreed. On 22 March he asked the Foreign Secretary to make it quite clear to France and Russia that Britain had a particular interest in the fate of the western half of Turkey in Asia and in that of Palestine. (So far as Palestine was concerned, since the end of January 1915 one cabinet minister, Herbert Samuel, had been pressing for the establishment of 'an autonomous Jewish State', and the annexation of Palestine by Britain for that purpose. In March the memorandum Samuel had sent to Asquith was printed and circulated to the cabinet.)

Following the discussions of March 1915, the British agreed to the Russian demand for Constantinople, 'subject to the realisation of the desiderata which they [the British] may form in other regions of the Ottoman Empire and elsewhere'. The importance of Persia, already mentioned in the context of November 1914, was re-emphasised

DIVISION OF TURKEY

ACCORDING TO SECRET AGREEMENTS 1915-17

(i) Constantinople Memorandum 18.3.1915; (ii) Treaty of London 26.4.1915
(iii) Sykes–Picot Agreement 16.5.1916; (iv) St Jean de Maurienne Agreement 17.4.1917

Scale: Miles.
0   50   100   150
━━━━ Railways.

immediately. Sir Edward Grey insisted that the neutral zone set up in the Anglo-Russian Convention of 1907 come within the British zone of influence. So far as other areas were concerned, a committee was set up to consider the desiderata of the British Empire. As Asquith put it:

> Russia intended to take a good slice of Turkey. France, Italy, and Greece each demanded a piece. If, for one reason or another, because we didn't want more territory, or because we didn't feel equal to the responsibility, we were to leave the other nations to scramble for Turkey without taking anything ourselves, we should not be doing our duty.

❖

These initial British positions in relation to war aims, positions which envisaged conflict with Russia and with France in the future – something which had to be put against the appreciation that the establishment of Russia at Constantinople would, as Kitchener put it, 'end, once and for all, the German *Drang nach Osten* to the Persian Gulf – were taken in a mood of euphoria. This mood was created by the assumption that the imminent Dardanelles operation would produce a victorious end to the war in the very near future. Although the Dardanelles operation failed, the positions already taken up and the desiderata already revealed – an enlarged sphere of influence in Persia, a dominant position in Mesopotamia, a physical connection between Mesopotamia and the Mediterranean, a 'Muslim political entity' (as Grey described it) in Arabia, the transfer of the Khalifate from Constantinople to the Muslim political entity, the securing of oil supplies from the Middle East – were largely maintained subsequently. Europe hardly came into the picture at all. Austen Chamberlain spoke for the vast majority of his cabinet colleagues when he said as Secretary of State for India in April 1917, 'The only vital British interest in Europe was the independence of Belgium. We had other obligations of honour in Europe but no vital interests'.

The Middle East, as a whole, is an excellent example of how war aims expanded. Just as Aleppo was regarded as essential if Alexandretta was taken, so Basra was essential to the maintenance of a position at the head of the Persian Gulf. And for Basra, Baghdad was essential. And for Baghdad, Mosul. And for Mosul, a military terminus on the Mediterranean for access and supply – either Haifa, or Alexandretta or both.

The interest in securing the British Empire through enlarging it necessarily surged to the fore again after the Russian collapse of 1917 and the Peace of Brest-Litovsk early in 1918. For Russia's withdrawal from the fighting opened the prospect of a German–Turkish thrust across

Persia and into Afghanistan and of a general rising of the Muslim tribes on the frontier of India. Leopold Amery, in 1918 Assistant Secretary to the War Cabinet, echoed Austen Chamberlain's sentiments of April 1917 by describing the western theatre of war as 'this little side-show'. Followed by Lord Milner, the Secretary of State for War, and Field Marshal Sir Henry Wilson, the Chief of the Imperial General Staff, Amery led the way in invoking the concept of 'the Southern British World'. This was the area, he maintained, which contained Britain's most vital interests. The western edge of this world was demarcated by the line of an arc running from South Africa, through Egypt, Cyprus, the Black Sea (with Armenia and the Caucasus to the east of the line) to the Urals or even to Lake Baikal. A slightly less ambitious 'Southern British World', which Amery put to Prime Minister Lloyd George in June 1918, ran 'from Cape Town through Cairo, Baghdad and Calcutta to Sydney and Wellington'.

❖

Japan

At the beginning of August 1914 the British hoped that they would not have to invoke the aid of their ally since 1902. The assumption within the Foreign Office was that 'Japan will in this crisis take the opportunity of assuming the role of predominant and protecting foreign power in the Far East'. There was alarm about a possible Japanese attack on Shantung, despite the German presence there, and on China generally. The British ambassador to Peking wrote: 'Japan in war would endanger the stability of the existing regime in China, to say nothing of the inevitable effect it would have upon our future political influence in this country and our prestige in Asia generally.' The Dutch, who still had some possessions in south east Asia, the Australians, the New Zealanders, and the Americans, also feared Japanese alterations to the status quo. On 8 August 1914 the United States Secretary of State, Robert Lansing, suggested the neutralisation of the whole of the Pacific for the duration of hostilities in Europe, saying: 'unless something of the kind is done, Japan would certainly take the opportunity to extract leases and other advantages from China.' On 10 August the British tried to stop the Japanese from declaring war on Germany. This failed. They then attempted to circumscribe Japanese action. This also failed. Japan declared war on Germany on 23 August 1914, and Grey was forced to recognise that Japanese compensation for her war effort, if Germany was defeated, could only be 'in the region of China'.

These initial concerns about Japanese intentions were well-founded. Between August and December 1914 the Japanese compiled a list of twenty-one demands to be made on China. These were disclosed to the British in January 1915, and presented to the Chinese three months later. The demands included the provinces of Shantung, eastern inner Mongolia, and south Manchuria; the extension of Japan's lease of Port Arthur by ninety-nine years; that no harbours or ports be leased to any foreign power other than Japan; that Japanese political, financial, and military advisers should be accepted throughout the Chinese Empire – thus producing, in effect, a Japanese protectorate over what remained of the Chinese Empire. Between them the Japanese Government, War Office, and Admiralty had decided, as they put it, that 'China is the first country to bear the brunt of our expansion policy'. Within the twenty-one demands, as another document, forwarded by the British ambassador in Peking, made clear, were demands for vital points with a view to preventing the British, Americans and Russians from interfering in the implementation of Japanese policy. This document deserves to be quoted at length:

> In the demands on China there are questions concerning the engagements of Military Advisers, the purchase of arms and ammunition, and the arsenals. These are the most vital points against the Chinese Government.... We doubt whether the Chinese Government realise the deep meaning hidden underneath the idea entertained by our army who proposed the questions. If the Chinese Government interprets these questions in the sense of ordinary engagement of advisers and purchase of arms, a speedy settlement may be expected. But on the contrary, if the Chinese suspect that these questions comprise part of the general scheme of our future national defence, then it will be very difficult to come to a settlement ... since these demands have been made, we shall have to resort to force if they were rejected.... After careful consideration we are convinced that for the sake of our national defence it is necessary for us to obtain substantial power in China.
>
> The demands connected with the Fukien province proposed by our navy are the most vital points against America. For if Japan can secure the naval control of San To Harbour and the adjacent sea coast we shall be able to reduce the value of the Philippine Islands as the American Naval Base in the Pacific and thus frustrate her policy in that direction.
>
> The three demands proposed by our army as mentioned above are also the most vital points against Russia as they would reduce the usefulness of the Siberian railway as a military weapon. The army spent more than ten years in formulating these plans, ever hoping that opportunities would arise for us to push our plans to a successful end. The settlement of these demands is a question of life and death with Japan.

So seriously was this indication of Japanese policy taken that the British Government threatened in May 1915 to abandon the alliance with Japan. It was not the British and American protests, however, which stopped a Japanese assault on China, but a major domestic crisis within Japan. Later, well aware that she had lost the confidence of Britain and the United States, Japan turned towards Russia and made an alliance with her in July 1916. As the Japanese Foreign Minister Ishii put it: 'I have established with Russia a relationship of complete co-operation for the final settlement of our policy towards Manchuria and Mongolia and have cemented our defensive policy towards China.' He expressed the rather optimistic hope of using this alliance with Russia, together with the alliance with Britain, to reinforce what he called 'our great aim of developing our power' in that region. The collapse of Russia in 1917 into revolution and civil war spared Japan the need to accommodate her, and was to provide the excuse of Bolshevism for the Japanese invasion of Siberia in 1919.

❖

United States of America

In April 1917 the United States entered the war as an 'associate' of Great Britain, France, Russia, Japan and Italy. This move looked like another step along the road indicated by her ceasing, in 1915, to lend money to the Central Powers. Appearances, however, were deceptive. The side upon which the Americans entered the war was the American side. The main American war effort was to be directed against the British Empire, and not against the Central Powers, who when deciding upon submarine warfare had rightly assessed the impact upon them of American intervention as negligible. The key to the policy of the United States is President Wilson's remark of March 1917 that he wanted to see 'neither side win', and his denunciation of both 'German militarism on land and England's militarism on sea'. Quite simply, the United States regarded the hostilities in Europe as a golden opportunity to supplant Great Britain in the markets of the world and to secure the dominance of her own commerce in the future. The Americans revelled in the fact that the British merchant marine was tied up on war work and they consistently refused to commit any of their own fast-expanding merchant fleet, which was double in 1916 what it had been in 1914, to the dangerous U-boat lanes of the Western Approaches. In November 1917, for instance, only 7 per cent of the shipping entering English and French ports was American.

In 1913 British trade with Brazil was double that of the United States; in 1916 United States trade with Brazil was double that of Britain.

Between 1915 and 1920 the United States increased its share of the Latin American market from 16% to 42%, its share of the China market from 6% to 17%, and its share of the world's export trade from 13% to 25%. In August 1917 the United States deliberately gave priority in shipbuilding to merchant vessels instead of to anti-U-boat or escort vessels. The Chief of the United States Admiralty stated that this was done 'not to sustain the war effort, but because these would get in the trade and that was the chief need'. In April 1918, at the height of the German spring offensive, the United States refused to sacrifice, even temporarily, its trade with Latin America and the Far East.

What the Americans were doing was not lost on the British. In December 1917 General Haig seriously advised the making of a compromise peace on the grounds that to continue the fighting would enable 'America to get a great pull over us'. Between August and October 1918, for most of which time it was clear only to the Germans that the Central Powers were losing the war, the British halved transport facilities for General Pershing's army. To the British Government the ships they would lose transporting United States troops were more valuable than the assistance these untrained and untried troops would provide. The British merchant marine would be better employed combating United States inroads on British trade and acquiring raw materials from overseas. In this context, it is not to be wondered at that the British intended to seize the German merchant marine as well as the German battle fleet as spoils of war and as compensation for their own losses.

In October 1918 the British had to deal with yet more United States moves of the same kind. President Wilson attempted to have control of the British fleet placed in the hands of the League of Nations, to issue peace terms guaranteeing equality of trade opportunities everywhere and to abolish economic boycotts unless imposed by the League of Nations, and to insist that German colonies go to the League of Nations in trust instead of to Great Britain – this on the grounds that the British Empire was already so large as to be generating jealousy in certain quarters. As the First Lord of the Admiralty, Geddes, remarked:

> The United States aims to employ the exercise of sea power to enforce the wishes of the League of Nations; by combining with other Powers jealous of our sea power, President Wilson aims to muster the equivalent of, or more than, the sea power of the British Empire. In other words he is pursuing the Balance of Power theory and applying it in sea power to world politics.

The War Cabinet agreed that they 'had to bear in mind, from a post-war point of view, the extensions which were being made to the American mercantile marine'.

These concerns and considerations played a part in the British acceptance of Wilson's Fourteen Points as the basis for the armistice terms. As General Smuts, a member of the War Cabinet, put it on 26 October 1918: 'If we beat Germany to nothingness, then we must beat Europe to nothingness too. As Europe went down, so America would rise. In time the United States would dictate to the world in naval, military, diplomatic, and financial matters.' In that, he said presciently, he 'could see no good'. As the British ambassador in Washington, Lord Reading, said on the same occasion: 'Every month the war continued increased the power of the United States. By continuing the war, it might become more difficult for us to hold our own.' The Fourteen Points were accepted only on condition that the clauses relating to 'freedom of the seas' and to 'no indemnities or reparations' were dropped. President Wilson agreed to this, fully intending to raise these matters again at the Peace Conference, which he duly did.

❖

France
In March 1915 the initial reaction of France to the Russian demand for the acquisition of Constantinople was that this would imply a partition of the Ottoman Empire which France had 'no good reason to desire'. The French had designs of their own on the Mediterranean and Near East, designs which cut completely across the emergence of Russia as a Mediterranean power and the development of Italy into a greater power in the Mediterranean than she already was. The importance of these French designs may be measured by the fact that, whilst much of northern France was occupied by German armies and whilst these German armies were on several occasions within striking distance of Paris, France retained an army of 350,000 men in the Balkans, at Salonika. In 1915 this army was named, symbolically, *l'Armée de l'Orient*. The French had insisted on being represented in any Balkan Expeditionary Force – otherwise, they maintained, Russia would be sole arbiter of the fate of the Balkan peoples. And Briand, who was French Foreign Minister in February 1915, wanted the peoples of the Balkans constituted as a barrier to Russian omnipotence there which the possession of Constantinople and everything that would follow from that would deliver to Russia.

Behind keeping Russia from dominating the Balkans was the intention that French influence, and economic influence in particular, should permeate this region. What the French wanted to do was to supplant the German economic preponderance in central and eastern Europe, and to use this area as a springboard for the furtherance of the post-war economic interests of France. They wished to take over, in effect, the German line of influence from Hamburg to the Persian Gulf, from the North Sea through Asia Minor to the Indian Ocean. Hence the importance to France of Salonika and of Greece. Whilst at Salonika the French forces, under General Sarrail, engaged in a great propaganda effort designed not merely to win the confidence of the local population in order to defeat the Central Powers in the current war, but to prepare the position of France in the post-war world. There could be no question of withdrawing these forces, during whose presence French exports to Greece increased by 25 per cent: to do so, as the French claimed, '*serait la fin de la France dans le bassin oriental de la Méditerranée*'. The French did not conceal from themselves, and could not conceal from their co-belligerents, that what they were doing was conducting a struggle, albeit a pacific one, '*une lutte pacifique*', against their allies.

19

PEACEMAKING, 1918–19 AND 1814–15: DIFFERENCES AND SIMILARITIES

This volume began with a consideration of one of the themes that characterised the Congress of Vienna. It concludes with a comparison between the settlement of 1814–15 with France and that of 1918–19 with Germany.

Differences

There were several significant differences between the peacemaking at the end of the Napoleonic Wars and the peacemaking at the end of the First World War. To begin with, in 1814–15 there were two peace treaties, the Treaty of Paris of May 1814 and the Treaty of Paris of November 1815, the differences between these treaties almost all accounted for by the 100 days following Napoleon's escape from Elba in March 1815 and the ensuing campaign which culminated in the battle of Waterloo in June. In 1919 separate treaties were made with the defeated belligerents – the Treaty of Versailles with Germany, the Treaty of St Germain with Austria, the Treaty of Trianon with Hungary, the Treaty of Neuilly with Bulgaria, and the Treaty of Sèvres with Turkey – but the treaty with Germany was not modified as a result of the sort of interruption that occurred in 1815.

In 1814 and 1815 peace was made at the capital of the defeated power; in 1919 peace was made at the capital of one of the victorious powers, and not at Berlin, the capital of the most formidable of the defeated powers. In 1814 Paris was occupied by the victorious Russian army which had driven Napoleon's *Grande Armée* all the way back from Moscow. In 1918–19 there was no similar pursuit of the German army into the heart of the country, or anything in the nature of a victory parade through Berlin. This failure to follow through was something drawn attention to and deplored by Ford Madox Ford in his novel *Last Post*, published in 1928. It was something which made it the less easy for the German population as a whole to admit that its armies actually had been defeated in the field, even if only on the western front. As early as December 1918 Chancellor Ebert hailed German troops at the

Brandenburger Tor with the words, 'As you return unconquered from the field of battle, I salute you'.

In 1814 there was no long wait for one of the major decision-makers to turn up, as there was for President Wilson in 1919. And in 1814 the major participants in the peacemaking were not, with the notable exception of Tsar Alexander I, heads of governments, as they were without exception in 1919. Moreover, in 1814 the discussions and deliberations on the terms to be presented to France were much less long drawn out than was the case with Germany in 1919. Nor, in 1814, was there anything in the nature of the economic blockade that was maintained on Germany, with some modification only in March 1919, from the time of the Armistice in November 1918 until the presentation of the peace terms early in May 1919.

In 1814–15 the alliance between the victorious powers of Russia, Austria, Great Britain and Prussia remained solid in the face of the renewed Napoleonic threat of March to June 1815. Formalised at Chaumont in March 1814, it was renewed in March 1815, again in November 1815, and again in November 1818. It remained, directed at France, until 1853. There was no equivalent to this in 1918–19, for one vital member of the coalition that had fought the Central Powers, namely Russia, had 'retired early' from the war, made a separate peace with Germany at Brest-Litovsk in March 1918, and was not represented at the peacemaking in Paris in 1919. There was, moreover, no post-war commitment against Germany as there had been, a century earlier, against France. An Anglo-American defensive guarantee of France was discussed at Versailles, and a Channel Tunnel mooted as a way of supplying France with reinforcements, but these prospects collapsed when the Americans disavowed the Versailles settlement as a whole, which they did in November 1919, and when the British refused to go ahead without the United States. In 1814–15 there was no such disavowal by one of the victorious powers of a settlement which its political representatives had helped to construct.

In 1919 Germany was compelled to reduce its army from over one million to a mere 100,000 men, and to adopt a voluntary, as opposed to a conscript, system of recruitment. This, and other limitations on German armaments, was supposed to last until all the other obligations imposed upon Germany had been fulfilled, 'and thereafter for as long as, and with such modifications as, the League of Nations may determine'. There was no such limitation placed upon the armed forces of France in either 1814 or 1815.

Finally, the peacemaking of 1814–15, in the shape of the Congress of Vienna, created a series of buffer states on the frontiers of France: in the north the Kingdom of the United Netherlands, in the east the German Confederation, and in the south-east an enlarged Kingdom of Piedmont-Sardinia. None of these constructions was a strong entity in itself, capable of successfully resisting French aggression, but behind each of them was a strong power: behind the United Netherlands, Prussia; behind the German Confederation, Prussia and Austria (with Russia in reserve); behind Piedmont-Sardinia, Austria. In 1919 there was no equivalent of this: the reconstituted Poland was not strong, Czechoslovakia was not strong, and the Austro-Hungarian Empire, of which Czechoslovakia had been a part, had ceased to exist. As for Russia, she could no longer be trusted. Only by bringing a Russia both strong and non-Bolshevik even further west than she had been since 1815 could a constellation equivalent to that of 1815 have been created. Why this was not attempted emerges from a consideration of the similarities between the two peacemakings.

Similarities

The principal similarity was leniency. The first Treaty of Paris, of May 1814, allowed France to retain her frontiers of 1792, namely to keep some of the gains made in the course of the first Revolutionary War. Even after Waterloo the second Treaty of Paris, of November 1815, described by Napoleon from exile on St Helena as the sort of peace only a beaten adversary, rather than victorious ones, would make, and which returned France to her frontiers of 1790, left France slightly larger and more populous than she had been in 1789. The wishes expressed by the Prussians in particular for something in the nature of a partition of France were ignored. There were several reasons for leaving France intact: British and Austrian fear of Russia, the pre-emptive removal of reasons for *revanche* and revisionism, and considerations to do with the stability of the post-Napoleonic governance of France. France had to be kept in being as a Great Power in the overall balance of Europe, lest Russia become all-powerful on the continent. The fear of Russian aggrandisement and hegemony dominated the thinking of Castlereagh, the British Foreign Secretary, as demonstrated in Chapter 1. Throughout the peacemaking he denounced the possibility of Russia's 'advance into the heart of Germany'. He insisted that Germany had to be united 'for its own preservation against Russia', that ways had to be found of keeping Russia 'within due bounds', and of preventing 'further encroachments' on the part of Russia: 'unless the Emperor of Russia can be brought to a more moderate and sound course of public conduct, the peace, which we have so dearly purchased, will be but of short duration.' At one point Castlereagh contemplated 'a union of Austria, France, and the Southern States [of Germany] against the Northern Powers [Russia and Prussia]'. As Gentz, Secretary to the Congress of Vienna, put it:

> Napoleon's downfall was a pure and unqualified advantage for Russia; for the rest of Europe, and especially the states bordering on Russia, it was largely balanced by the increased strength that Russia secured for herself at the expense of the general equilibrium.

Concern that the Bourbons should gain the support of the French people, and not lose face, or prestige, or too much in the form of possessions, at the beginning of their restoration, was responsible, amongst other things, for the rejection by the other allies in 1814 of the Prussian demand for reparations. Louis XVIII's representatives had maintained that rather than pay any such monies he would submit to be arrested and kept prisoner in his palace. In February 1815 Castlereagh remarked on the disposition of Louis XVIII's cabinet to pursue 'a conciliatory and moderate line of policy'. At the end of August 1815, when the Prussians were renewing their demands for a harsh peace, Castlereagh wrote:

> The more I reflect upon it the more I deprecate the system of scratching such a Power [as France]. We may hold her down and pare her nails so that many years shall pass away before they wound us.... But this Prussian system of being pledged to a continental war for objects which France may any day reclaim from the particular States that hold them, without pushing her demands beyond what she would contend was due to her own honour, is I am sure a bad British policy.

He appreciated and welcomed, in October 1815, what he called the Tsar of Russia's 'support of the Bourbons, and of the established order of things in France' in the first draft of what was to become the second Peace of Paris.

In 1919 leniency was not quite so pronounced as in 1814–15, but the settlement was still a lenient one, given the sort of total war that had just ended, and given what the victors refrained from doing. In the west, Eupen and Malmédy were ceded to Belgium, Alsace and Lorraine were restored to France, the coalmines of the Saar were ceded to France for fifteen years, and the Saarland to the League of Nations for the same period of time. The Rhineland was declared a demilitarised zone and was to be occupied – a northern section which included the bridgehead of Cologne was to be evacuated by the Belgian army after five years, a central section which included the bridgehead of Koblenz was to be

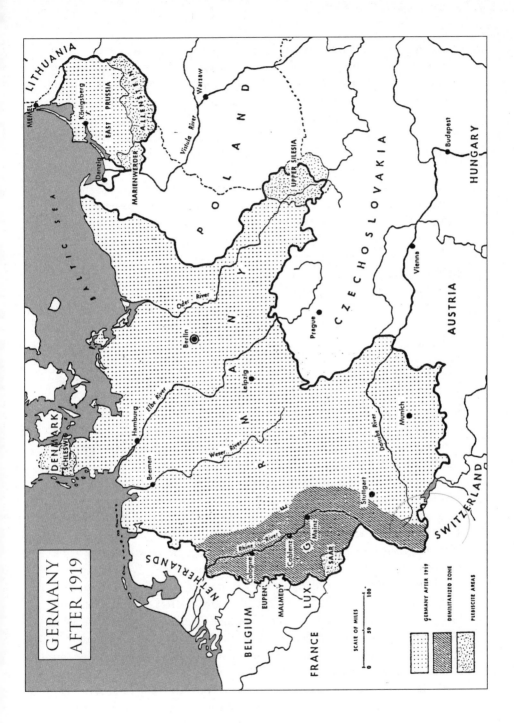

GERMANY
AFTER 1919

LITHUANIA

MEMEL

Königsberg

EAST PRUSSIA

ALLENSTEIN

Danzig

MARIENWERDER

BALTIC SEA

Warsaw

Vistula River

P   O   L   A   N   D

UPPER SILESIA

Oder   River

Berlin

Leipzig

Elbe River

Hamburg

Weser   River

Bremen

G   E   R   M   A   N   Y

Prague

CZECHOSLOVAKIA

Vienne

AUSTRIA

Budapest

HUNGARY

Munich

Danube River

Stuttgart

SWITZERLAND

Rhine   River

Cologne

Coblenz

Mainz

SAAR

LUX.

MALMEDY

EUPEN

BELGIUM

FRANCE

NETHERLANDS

DENMARK

SCHLESWIG

SCALE OF MILES

0   50   100

GERMANY AFTER 1919

DEMILITARIZED ZONE

PLEBISCITE AREAS

evacuated by the British Army after ten years, and a southern section which included the bridgehead of Mainz was to be evacuated by the French army after fifteen years. This was comparable, except as far as the time-scale was concerned, with the occupation by a 150,000 strong allied army of a military line along the frontiers of France, an occupation deemed necessary by the second Peace of Paris of November 1815, and which lasted until the end of 1818. Thus the French abandoned, in 1919, one of their main war aims, the permanent detachment of the Rhineland from Germany and its ultimate incorporation into France. Germany's greatest territorial losses were in the east, where Poland recovered an area still mainly populated by Poles that had been annexed by Prussia in the late eighteenth century. The ultimate disposition of several areas – in the east, Allenstein, Marienwerder, and Upper Silesia; in the north, Schleswig; and in the west, the Saar – was to depend upon the wishes of the populations as manifested in plebiscites.

The reasons for this leniency were much the same as for the leniency towards France in 1814–15: fear of Russia, and concern for the stabilisation of the economic, social, and political situation in Germany. As early as May 1918 General Smuts, an important member of Lloyd George's Imperial War Cabinet, had rejected the idea of the complete smashing of the German Army and the German Empire, together with a march to Berlin and the dictation of peace there. An outright victory was out of the question, he said, 'because it would mean an eternal campaign and the result might well be that the civilisation that they were out to safeguard might itself be jeopardised. It might be that in the end they would have universal bankruptcy of government and the forces of revolution would be let loose'. On the eve of the signature of the Armistice Field Marshal Sir Henry Wilson, Chief of the Imperial General Staff, detected Clemenceau's fear 'that Germany will break up and Bolshevism become rampant'. When asked by Lloyd George if he wanted this, or would rather have an armistice, Wilson replied: 'Armistice'. Wilson recorded that the Cabinet was unanimous about this. He himself wrote: 'Our real danger now is not the Boches but Bolshevism.' Both Wilson and Lord Milner, Secretary of State for War, objected to German demobilisation on the grounds that 'Germany may have to be the bulwark against Russian Bolshevism'. Colonel House, an intimate adviser of President Wilson who preceded the latter to Paris, told the President that he had pointed out to Lloyd George and Clemenceau 'the danger of bringing about a state of Bolshevism in Germany if the terms of the armistice were made too stiff, and the consequent danger to England, France, and Italy'. Article XII of the Armistice was to become Article 433 of the Treaty of Versailles. It stipulated that the German troops in the Baltic area were to stay there 'having regard to the internal situation in these territories'. These German troops were intended to carry out what Marshal Foch described as 'establishing in the Baltic Provinces a barrier against the Bolsheviks'.

Following a long weekend closeted at Fontainebleau with Lloyd George, his secretary Phillip Kerr, and the Cabinet Secretary, Hankey, Field Marshal Wilson listed in twelve 'salient' points Lloyd George's views as regards peace terms. Point 4 was: 'Refuse to put too crushing terms on Germany either in money or in cession of territory or other things'. At the same time, 23 March 1919, Lloyd George himself wrote:

> The whole of Europe is filled with the spirit of revolution.... I am told on all hands that workmen have lost their taste for toil.... [Russia's] ideas may yet triumph in Germany. There are many indications that Spartacism has not been completely overthrown, and a stern peace may make the life of any German government impossible and drive Germany into Bolshevism. This is the immediate danger. The present government is weak; it has no prestige; and its authority is challenged. I do not believe it will dare to sign an over-stern peace treaty.

This was revised by Kerr into the Fontainebleau Memorandum sent by Lloyd George to Clemenceau and President Wilson on 26 March. The relevant paragraph read:

> The greatest danger that I see in the present situation is that Germany may throw in her lot with Bolshevism and place her resources, her brains, her vast organising power at the disposal of the revolutionary fanatics whose dream it is to conquer the world for Bolshevism by force of arms.... If we are wise, we shall offer to Germany a peace which, while just, will be preferable for all sensible men to the alternative of Bolshevism.

So, *pace* D. Newton in *British Policy and the Weimar Republic 1918–1919* (Oxford, 1997) p.371, there clearly was some appreciation of the argument that moderation was required in order to bolster the credit of the existing socialist-led government in Berlin. This appreciation worked itself into the proceedings of the Council of Four (Lloyd George, Clemenceau, Wilson and Orlando) between 24 March and 28 June 1919 to such an extent that, in a review of the published proceedings, the historian A.J.P. Taylor was able to state: 'They decided every disputed point in favour of Germany. The Saar; the left bank of the Rhine; Danzig; Silesia – in all these questions they devised settlements which, they believed, would lead to reconciliation.'

Smuts, for his part, repeated at the Peace Conference his sentiments of May 1918, pointing out again the danger that only the Bolsheviks would gain should Germany be 'destroyed' by a harsh peace treaty; he concluded that German 'appeasement now may have the effect of turning her into a bulwark against the oncoming Bolshevism of eastern Europe'. His fellow South African, Botha, also supported compromise, stating on 11 April 1919 at a meeting of the British Empire Delegation that 'another reason for closing with the present agreement was that Germany must not be allowed to become Bolshevist. If Germany should join Russia, the situation would be very serious'.

❖

'Paris cannot be understood without Moscow', wrote Ray Stannard Baker, a member of the United States delegation at Paris, in *Woodrow Wilson and World Settlement*, published in 1923. 'Vienna cannot be understood without St Petersburg' seems to the present writer to be equally apt. In 1814–15 it was Russia's military might that was feared. In 1918–19 it was the ideology of Bolshevism that terrified, to such an extent that former allies of the Russian Empire, namely Great Britain and Japan, were prepared to intervene, on the side of the reactionaries, in the civil war raging there.

Other similarities can be discerned. France never fully reconciled herself to the loss in 1815 of the frontiers of 1792, any more than Germany reconciled herself to her territorial losses of 1919; but given the existence of the Quadruple Alliance France was in no position to mount the full-scale challenge to the Vienna settlement envisaged and delineated by Polignac in 1829 (see Chapter 3 part I) until the 1850s when, as has been seen in Chapter 5, a combination of French bluff and British irresolution and pusillanimity produced the required split between Great Britain and Russia, In 1918–19 Britain and France found themselves allied, in effect, with their recent enemy, Germany, against their former ally Russia, as transmogrified by Bolshevism: indeed in mid-March 1919 Field Marshal Wilson told Churchill that he would like to see 'a combination of England, France and Germany in an Alliance against Russia and Japan'. In January 1815 Britain and Austria formed an alliance with *their* former enemy, France, against their recent allies, Russia and Prussia, over the fate of Saxony. After the conclusion of the second Peace of Paris of November 1815 the ambassadors of the four victorious powers in Paris met on a weekly basis in conferences that monitored the course of French domestic politics. Following the Treaty of Versailles similar ambassadorial conferences concerned themselves with possible rectifications of the German frontiers. Finally, the way in which

Germany came to pay some of the reparations imposed on her in 1919 mirrored the idea adopted in 1815 that France should borrow abroad in order to pay off the indemnity imposed upon her by the second Treaty of Paris.

LIST OF MAPS

FURTHER READING

General

Anderson, M.S., *The Eastern Question* (London, 1966)

Bourne, K., *The Foreign Policy of Victorian England 1830–1902* (Oxford, 1970)

Bridge, F.R., *The Hapsburg Monarchy amongst the Great Powers 1814–1918* (Leamington Spa, 1990)

Fuller, W.C., *Strategy and Power in Russia 1600–1914* (New York, 1992)

Gillard, D., *The Struggle for Asia 1828–1914* (London, 1977)

Grenville, J.A.S., *Europe Reshaped 1848–1878* (London, 1976)

Hinsley, F.H., *Power and the Pursuit of Peace* (Cambridge, 1963)

Howard, C.H.D., *Great Britain and the casus belli 1822–1902* (London, 1974)

Ingram, E., *The British Empire as a World Power* (London, 2001)

Jelavich, B., *Russia's Balkan Entanglements 1806–1914* (Cambridge, 1991)

Mahajan, S., *British Foreign Policy 1874–1914: The role of India* (London, 2002)

Rich, N., *Great Power Diplomacy 1814–1914* (Boston, Mass., 1992)

Schroeder, P.W., *The Transformation of European Politics 1763–1848* (Oxford, 1994)

Taylor, A.J.P., *The Struggle for Mastery in Europe 1848–1918* (Oxford, 1954)

Yapp, M.E., *The Making of the Modern Near East 1792–1923* (London, 1987)

Chapter 1

Bartlett, C.J., *Castlereagh* (London, 1966)

Dakin, D., 'The Congress of Vienna 1814–1815 and its antecedents' in Sked, A. (ed.) *Europe's Balance of Power 1815–1848* (London, 1979)

Kissinger, H., *A World Restored: Castlereagh and the Problem of Peace 1812–1822* Boston, 1947)

Kraehe, E.E., *Metternich's German Policy* vol. 2, *The Congress of Vienna 1814–15* (Princeton, 1983)

— 'A Bi-polar Balance of Power', *American Historical Review* vol. 97 no. 3 (1992)

Mann, G., *Secretary of Europe: the life of Friedrich Gentz* (New Haven, 1946)

Schroeder, P.W., 'Did the Vienna Settlement rest on a Balance of Power?', *American Historical Review* vol. 97 no. 3 (1992)

Sweet, P.R., *Friedrich von Gentz* (Wisconsin, 1941)

Webster, C.K., 'England and the Polish-Saxon Problem at the Congress of Vienna' *Transactions of the Royal Historical Society* 1913

— *The Congress of Vienna 1814–1815* (London, 1919)

— (ed.), *British Diplomacy 1813–1815: select documents, dealing with the Reconstruction of Europe* (London, 1921)

— *The Foreign Policy of Castlereagh 1812–1815: Britain and the Reconstruction of Europe* (London, 1931)

Zawadski, W.H., 'Russia and the re – opening of the Polish Question 1801 – 1814' *International History Review* vol. 7 no. 1 (1985)

Chapter 2

Bertier de Sauvigny, G. de, *France and the European Alliance 1816 – 1821: the private correspondence between Metternich and Richelieu* (Notre Dame, 1958)

Billinger, R.D., *Metternich and the German Question 1820–1834* (Newark, 1991)

Bridge, F.R., 'Allied Diplomacy in Peacetime: the failure of the Congress "System" 1815–1823' in Sked, A., op. cit.

Bullen, R., 'The Great Powers and the Iberian Peninsula 1815–1848' in Sked, A., op. cit.

Flockerzie, L.J., 'Saxony, Austria and the German Question after the Congress of Vienna, 1815–1816' *International History Review* vol. 12 no. 4 (1990)

Grimsted, P., *The Foreign Ministers of Alexander I* (Berkeley, 1969)

Haas, A.G., *Metternich: reorganisation and nationality 1813–1818* (Knoxville, 1964)

Knapton, E.J., 'The Origins of the Treaty of Holy Alliance' *History* vol. 26 (1941)

Langhorne, R., 'Establishing International Organisations: the Concert and the League' *Diplomacy and Statecraft* vol. 1 no. 1 (1990)

Reinermann, A.J., 'Metternich, Italy and the Congress of Verona' *Historical Journal* vol. 14 no. 2 (1971)

— 'Metternich, Alexander I and the Russian challenge in Italy 1815 – 1820' *Journal of Modern History* vol. 46 no. 2 (1974)

Schenk, H.G., *The Aftermath of the Napoleonic Wars: the Concert of Europe – an experiment* (New York, 1947)

Schroeder, P.W., *Metternich's Diplomacy at its Zenith 1820–1823* (Austin, 1962)

Scott, I., 'Counter-Revolutionary Diplomacy and the demise of Anglo-Austrian Co-operation 1820–1823' *Historian* vol. 34 (1972)

Webster, C.K., *The Foreign Policy of Castlereagh 1815–1822: Britain and the European Alliance* (London, 1934)

Chapter 3

Alder, G.J., 'India and the Crimean War' *Journal of Imperial and Commonwealth History* vol. 2 (1973–74)

Avery, P.W., 'An Inquiry into the Outbreak of the second Russo-Persian War' in Boswell, C.E. (ed.), *Iran and Islam* (Edinburgh, 1971)

Bartlett, C.J., *Great Britain and Sea Power 1815–1853* (Oxford, 1963)

Baumgart, W., *The Peace of Paris, 1856* (Oxford, 1981)

Bolsover, G.H., 'Nicholas I and the Partition of Turkey' *Slavonic and East European Review* vol. 27 (1948–49)

Bourne, K., *Palmerston, the early years, 1784–1841* (London, 1982)

Conacher, J.B., *Britain and the Crimea 1855–1856: Problems of War and Peace* (London, 1987)

Cowles, L., 'The Failure to Restrain Russia: Canning, Nesselrode and the Greek Question 1825 – 1827' *International History Review* vol. xii no. 4 (1990)

Cunningham, A., *Anglo-Ottoman Encounters in the Age of Revolution* (London, 1993)

— *Eastern Questions in the Nineteenth Century* (London, 1993)

Dakin, D., *The Greek Struggle for Independence 1821–1833* (London, 1973)

Daly, J.C.K., *Russian Seapower and 'the Eastern Question' 1827–1841* (London, 1991)

Hurewitz, J.C., 'Ottoman Diplomacy and the European state system' *Middle East Journal* 1961

Ingle, H.N., *Nesselrode and the Russian Rapprochement with Great Britain 1836–1844* (Berkeley, 1976)

Ingram, E., *The Beginning of the Great Game in Asia 1828–1834* (Oxford, 1979)

— 'Great Britain's Great Game: An Introduction' *International History Review* ii no. 1 (1980)

— 'Approaches to the Great Game in Asia' *Middle Eastern Studies* vol. 18 no. 4 (1982)

— 'The Role of the Duke of Wellington in the Great Game in Asia 1826 – 1842' *Indica* vol. 25 (1988)

Kerner, R.J., 'Russia's New Policy in the Near East after the Peace of Adrianople' *Historical Journal* vol. 5 (1937)

Lincoln, W.B., *Nicholas I* (Bloomington, 1978)

Mosely. P.E., *Russian Diplomacy and the Opening of the Eastern Question in 1838 and 1839* (Cambridge, Mass., 1934)

— 'Russian Policy in Asia 1838–9' *Slavonic and East European Review* vol. 14 (1935–6)

Puryear, V.J., *International Economics and Diplomacy in the Near East: a study of British commercial policy in the Levant 1834–1853* (Stanford, 1935)

— *France and the Levant: from the Bourbon Restoration to the Peace of Kutiah* (Berkeley, 1941)

Raisonovsky, N., *Nicholas I and Official Nationality in Russia 1825–1855* (Berkeley, 1959)

Rodkey, F.S., 'Lord Palmerston and the Rejuvenation of Turkey 1830–1841' *Journal of Modern History* vol. 1 (1929), vol. 2 (1930)

— 'Anglo-Russian negotiations about a "Permanent" Quadruple Alliance, 1840–1841' *American Historical Review* vol. 36 (1931)

Schwartzberg, S., 'The Lion and the Phoenix: British policy towards the "Greek Question" 1831–2' *Middle Eastern Studies* vol. 24 (1988)

Steele, E.D., *Palmerston and Liberalism 1855–1865* (Cambridge, 1991)

Swain, J.E., *The Struggle for the Control of the Mediterranean prior to 1848: a study in Anglo-French Relations* (New York, 1933)

Verete, M., 'Palmerston and the Levant Crisis, 1832' *Journal of Modern History* vol. 24 (1952)

Webster, C.K., 'Palmerston, Metternich and the European System 1830–1841' *Proceedings of the British Academy* vol. 20 (1934)

— *The Foreign policy of Palmerston 1830–1841* (London, 1951)

Yapp, M.E., *Strategies of British India: Britain, Iran and Afghanistan 1798–1850* (Oxford, 1980)

— 'British Perceptions of the Russian threat to India' *Modern Asian Studies* vol. 21 no. 4 (1987)

Chapter 4

Austensen, R.A., 'The Making of Austria's Prussian policy 1848 – 1852' *Historical Journal* vol. 27 no.4 (1984)

— 'Metternich, Austria and the German Question 1848 – 1851' *International History Review* vol. 13 no.1 (1991)

Heydemann, G., 'The "Crazy Year" 1848: the revolution in Germany and Palmerston's Policy' in Schulze, H., (ed.), *Nation-Building in Central Europe* (Leamington Spa, 1987)

Jennings, L.C., 'Lamartine's Italian policy in 1848: a re-examination' *Journal of Modern History* vol. 42 no. 3 (1970)

— *France and Europe in 1848: a study in French Foreign Affairs in time of crisis* (Oxford, 1973)

Roberts, I.W., *Nicholas I and the Russian Intervention in Hungary* (London, 1991)

Schulze, H., *The Course of German Nationalism from Frederick the Great to Bismarck, 1763–1867* (Cambridge, 1991)

Sked, A., 'Great Britain and the Continental Revolutions of 1848' in Birke, A., Brechten, M., and Searle, A. (eds), *An Anglo-German Dialogue* (Munich, 2000)

Sondhaus, L., 'Schwartzenberg, Austria and the German Question 1848–1851' *International History Review* vol. 13 no. 1 (1991)

Sturmer, M., 'France and German Unification' in Schulze H. (ed.), op. cit.

Taylor, A.J.P., *The Italian Problem in European Diplomacy 1847–1849* (Manchester, 1934)

Weber, F.G., 'Palmerston and Prussian Liberalism, 1848' *Journal of Modern History* vol. 35 no. 2 (1963)

Chapter 5

Anderson, M.S., (ed.), *The Great Powers and the Near East 1774–1923* (London, 1970)

Conacher, J.B., *The Aberdeen Coalition 1852–1855* (Cambridge, 1968)

Echard, W., *Napoleon III and the Concert of Europe* (Baton Rouge, 1983)

Florescu, R.R., 'The Romanian Principalities and the Origins of the Crimean War' *Slavonic and East European Review* vol. 43 (1964)

Gleason, J.H., *The Genesis of Russophobia in Great Britain* (Cambridge, Mass., 1950)

Goldfrank, D.M., 'Policy Traditions and the Menshikov Mission of 1853' in Ragsdale, H., and Pnonomarev V., (eds), *Imperial Russian Foreign Policy* (Cambridge, 1993)

— *The Origins of the Crimean War* (London, 1994)

Herkless, J.L., 'Stratford, the Cabinet, and the outbreak of the Crimean war' *Historical Journal* vol. 18 no. 3 (1975)

Puryear, V.J., *England, Russia and the Straits 1844–1856* (Berkeley, 1931)

— 'New Light on the Origins of the Crimean War' *Journal of Modern History* vol. 3 no. 2 (1931)

Rich, N., *Why the Crimean War?* (London, 1985)

Rodkey, F.S., 'Ottoman Concern about Western Economic Penetration in the Levant, 1849–1856' *Journal of Modern History* vol. 30 no. 4 (1958)

Saab, A.P., *The origins of the Crimean Alliance* (Charlottesville, 1977)

Schroeder, P.W., *Austria, Great Britain and the Crimean War: the destruction of the European Concert* (Ithaca, 1972)

Temperley, H.W.V., *Great Britain and the Near East: the Crimea* (London, 1936)

Thomas, D.H., 'The reaction of the Great Powers to Louis Napoleon's rise to power in 1851' *Historical Journal* vol. 13 no. 2 (1970)

Vinogradov, V.N., 'The personal responsibility of Nicholas I for the coming of the Crimean War' in Ragsdale and Pnonomarev, op. cit.

Chapter 6

Barker, N.N., 'Austria, France and the Venetian Question 1861–1865' *Journal of Modern History* vol. 36 no. 2 (1964)

Baumgart, W., *The Peace of Paris, 1856* (Oxford, 1981)

Bernstein, P., 'Napoleon III and Bismarck: the Biarritz-Paris talks of 1865' in Brown, M., and Barker, N.N. (eds), *Diplomacy in an age of Nationalism: essays in honour of L.M. Case* (The Hague, 1971)

— 'The Economic Aspect of Napoleon III's Rhine Policy' *French Historical Studies* vol. 1 (1960)

Blumberg, A., 'Russian Policy and the Franco-Austrian War of 1859' *Journal of Modern History* vol. 26 no. 2 (1954)

Bush, J.W., *Venetia Redeemed: Franco-Italian Relations 1864–1866* (New York, 1967)

Case, L.M., *Franco-Italian Relations 1860–1865* (Philadelphia, 1932)

— *French Opinion on War and Diplomacy during the Second Empire* (Pennsylvania, 1954)

Cook, K.S., 'Russia, Austria and the Question of Italy 1859–1862' *International History Review* vol. 2 no. 4 (1980)

Echard, W., *Napoleon III and the Concert of Europe* (Baton Rouge, 1983)

Hallberg, C.W., *Franz Joseph and Napoleon III 1852–1864: a study of Austro-French relations* (New York, 1955)

Henderson, G.B., 'Some unpublished documents from the Royal Archives, Windsor' *Journal of Modern History* vol. 8 no. 4 (1936)

Mange, A.E., *The Near Eastern Policy of the Emperor Napoleon III* (Urbana, 1940)

McDonald, M.J., 'The Vicariat Proposals – a crisis in Napoleon III's Italian confederative designs' in Brown and Barker, op. cit.

Mosse, W.E., 'The Negotiations for a Franco-Russian Convention, 1856' *Cambridge Historical Journal* x (i) (1950)

— *The Rise and Fall of the Crimean System 1855–1871* (London, 1963)

Pottinger, A., *Napoleon III and the German Crisis 1865–1866* (Cambridge, Mass., 1966)

Schroeder, P.W., 'Bruck versus Buol: the dispute over Austrian Eastern policy 1853 – 1855' *Journal of Modern History* vol. 40 no. 2 (1968)

— 'Austria and the Danubian Principalities 1853–1856' *Central European History* vol. 2 no. 3 (1969)

Scott, I., *The Roman Question and the Powers 1848–1865* (The Hague, 1969)

Steele, E.D., *Palmerston and Liberalism 1855–1865* (Cambridge, 1991)

Sumner, B.H., 'The secret Franco-Russian Treaty of 3 March 1859' *English Historical Review* xlviii (1933)

Thurston, G.J., 'The Italian War of 1859 and the Reorientation of Russian Foreign Policy' *Historical Journal* vol. 20 no. 1 (1977)

Valsecchi, F., 'European Diplomacy and the Expedition of the 1000' in Gilbert, M., (ed.), *A Century of Conflict 1850–1950: essays for A.J.P. Taylor* (London, 1966)

Walker, M., (ed.), *Plombières: secret diplomacy and the rebirth of Italy* (New York, 1968)

Wellesley, F.A., (ed.), *The Paris Embassy during the Second Empire: selections from the papers of the first Earl Cowley* (London, 1928)

Wellesley, V. and Sencourt, R., (eds), *Conversations with Napoleon III* (London, 1934)

Chapter 7

Barker, N.N., *Distaff Diplomacy: the Empress Eugénie and the Foreign Policy of the Second Empire* (Austin, 1967)

— 'Napoleon III and the Hohenzollern Candidacy for the Spanish Throne' *Historian* vol. 29 (1967)

Bartlett, C.J., 'Clarendon, the Foreign Office and the Hohenzollern Candidacy
1868 – 1870' *English Historical Review* lxxv (1960)

Bohme, H., *The Foundation of the German Empire: select documents* (Oxford, 1971)

Bonnin, G., (ed.), *Bismarck and the Hohenzollern Candidature for the Spanish Throne:
the documents in the German Diplomatic Archives* (London, 1957)

Carr, W., *The Origins of the Wars of German Unification* (London, 1995)

Case, L.M., *French Opinion on War and Diplomacy during the Second Empire*
(Pennsylvania, 1954)

Clark, C.W., 'Bismarck, Russia and the Origins of the War of 1870' *Journal of
Modern History* vol. 14 no. 2 (1942)

Craig, G.A., 'A Study in the Application of Non–Intervention: Great Britain and
the Belgian Railways Dispute of 1869' *American Historical Review* vol. 50 no. 4
(1945)

Echard, W., *Napoleon III and the Concert of Europe* (Baton Rouge, 1983)

— 'Conference Diplomacy in the German policy of Napoleon III, 1868 – 9'
French Historical Studies vol. iv (1966)

Elrod, R.B., 'Realpolitik or Concert Diplomacy: the debate over Austrian Foreign
Policy in the 1860s' *Austrian History Yearbook* 1981–82

Fletcher, W.A., *The Mission of Benedetti to Berlin 1864–1870* (The Hague, 1965)

Gall, L., *Bismarck, The White Revolutionary* vol.1 (London, 1986)

Halperin, S.W., *Diplomat under Stress: Visconti-Venosta and the crisis of July 1870*
(Chicago, 1963)

— 'The Origins of the Franco-Prussian War revisited' *Journal of Modern History*
vol. 45 no. 1 (1973)

Houston, D.W., 'Emile Ollivier and the Hohenzollern Candidacy' *French Historical
Studies* iv (1966)

Medlicott, W.N. and Coveney, D.K., (eds), *Bismarck and Europe* (London, 1971)

Millman, R., *British Foreign Policy and the coming of the Franco-Prussian War* (Oxford,
1965)

Mitchell, A., *Bismarck and the French Nation 1848–1890* (New York, 1971)

Mosse, W.E., *The European Powers and the German Question 1848–1871*
(Cambridge, 1958)

Newton, Lord, *Lord Lyons: a record of British diplomacy* (London, 1913)

Pflanze, O., 'Bismarck and German Nationalism' *American Historical Review* vol. 60
no. 3 (1955)

Schmitt, H.A., 'Count Beust and Germany 1866–1870: Reconquest, Realignment
or Resignation?' *Central European History* vol. 1 (1968)

Schroeder, P.W., 'Austro-German Relations: Divergent Views of the Disjointed
Partnership' *Central European History* vol. 11 (1978)

Wellesley, V., and Sencourt, R., (eds), *Conversations with Napoleon III* (London,
1934)

Wemyss, Lady, *Memoirs and Letters of Sir Robert Morier 1826–1876* (London, 1911)

Zeldin, T., *The Political System of Napoleon III* (London, 1958)

— *Emile Ollivier and the Liberal Empire of Napoleon III* (Oxford, 1963)

Chapters 8 and 9

Bagdasarian, N.D., *The Austro-German Rapprochement, 1870–1879* (London, 1976)

Brown, M.L., 'The Monarchical Principle in Bismarckian Diplomacy after 1870' *Historian* vol. 15 (1952)

— *Heinrich von Haymerle: Austro-Hungarian career diplomat 1828 – 1881* (New York, 1973)

— 'Bismarck and Haymerle, the clashing allies' in Brown and Barker, op. cit.

Bucholz, A., *Moltke, Schlieffen and Prussian War Planning* (Oxford, 1991)

Dioszegi, I., *Hungarians in the Ballhausplatz* (Budapest, 1983)

Doerr, J., 'Germany, Russia and the Kulturkampf 1870–1875' *Canadian Journal of History* vol.10 no.1 (1975)

Fryer, W.R., 'The Republic and the Iron Chancellor: the pattern of Franco-German Relations 1871–1890' *Transactions of the Royal Historical Society* 1979

Fuller, J.V., *Bismarck's Diplomacy at its Zenith* (Cambridge, Mass., 1922)

Gauld, W.A., 'The Drei-Kaiser-Bund and the Eastern Question 1871–1876' *English Historical Review* xl (1925)

— 'The Drei-Kaiser-Bund and the Eastern Question 1877–78' *English Historical Review* xlii (1927)

Harris, D., 'Bismarck's advance to England, January 1876' *Journal of Modern History* vol. 3 no. 3 (1931)

Hildebrand, K., 'Opportunities and Limits of German Foreign Policy in the Bismarckian Era, 1871–1890: "A System of Stopgaps"?' in Schollgen, G., (ed.), *Escape into War? The Foreign Policy of imperial Germany* (Oxford, 1990)

Hinsley, F.H., 'Bismarck, Salisbury and the Mediterranean Agreements of 1887' *Historical Journal* vol. 1 no. 1 (1958)

Jelavich, B., *The Ottoman Empire, the Great Powers and the Straits Question 1870–1887* (Bloomington, 1973)

— and Jelavich, C., 'Jomini and the Revival of the Drei-Kaiser-Bund 1879–1880' *Slavonic and East European Review* vol. 35 (1956–57)

Jelavich, C., *Tsarist Russia and Balkan Nationalism: Russian influence in the internal affairs of Bulgaria and Serbia, 1879–1886* (Berkeley, 1962)

Kennan, G.F., *The Decline of Bismarck's European Order: Franco-Russian Relations 1875–1890* (Princeton, 1979)

Kiraly, B.K., and Stokes, G. (eds), *Insurrections, Wars and the Eastern Crisis in the 1870s* (Boulder, Colorado, 1985)

Kollander, P.A., 'Politics for the Defence? Bismarck, Battenburg and the origins of the Cartel of 1887' *German History* vol. 13 no. 1 (1995)

Lackey, S., 'The Habsburg Army and the Franco-Prussian War: the failure to intervene and its consequences' *War in History* vol. 2 no. 2 (1995)

Langer, W.L., *European Alliances and Alignments 1871–1890* (New York, 1950 edn)

Martel, G., 'Liberalism and Nationalism in the Middle East: Great Britain and the Balkan Crisis of 1886' *Middle Eastern Studies* vol. 21 no. 2 (1985)

Medlicott, W.N., *The Congress of Berlin and After: a diplomatic history of the Near Eastern Settlement 1878–1880* (London, 1938)

— 'The Powers and the Unification of the two Bulgarias, 1885' *English Historical Review* liv (1939)

— 'Bismarck and the Three Emperors' Alliance 1881–1887' *Transactions of the Royal Historical Society* 1945

— *Bismarck, Gladstone and the Concert of Europe* (London, 1955)

Millman, R., *Britain and the Eastern Question 1875–1878* (Oxford, 1979)

Mitchell, A., *Bismarck and the French Nation 1848–1890* (New York, 1971)

— *The German Influence in France after 1870* (Chapel Hill, 1979)

Rupp, G.H., *A Wavering Friendship: Russia and Austria 1876–1878* (Cambridge, Mass., 1941)

Schreuder, D., 'Gladstone as "Troublemaker": Liberal Foreign Policy and the German annexation of Alsace-Lorraine 1870–1871' *Journal of British Studies* vol. 17 no. 2 (1978)

Schroeder, P.W., 'The Lost Intermediaries: the impact of 1870 on the European System' *International History Review* vol. 6 no. 1 (1984)

Simpson, J.Y., *The Saburov Memoires, or Bismarck and Russia* (Cambridge, 1929)

Stojanovic, M.D., *The Great Powers and the Balkans 1875–1878* (Cambridge, 1939)

Taffs, W., 'The War Scare of 1875' *Slavonic and East European Review* vol. 9 (1930–31)

Vincent, J., (ed.), *A Selection from the Diaries of Edward Henry Stanley, 15th Earl of Derby, September 1869 to March 1878* (London, 1994)

Waller, B., *Bismarck at the Crossroads: the re-orientation of German Foreign Policy after the Congress of Berlin, 1878–1880* (London, 1974)

Zerner, R., 'Bismarck's views on the Austro-German Alliance and future European Wars: a dispatch of October 26, 1887' *Austrian History Yearbook* 1968–69

Chapter 10

Bovykin, V.I., 'The Franco-Russian Alliance' *History* vol. 64 (1979)

Kennan, G.F., *The Fateful Alliance: France, Russia and the coming of the First World War* (Manchester, 1984)

Langer, W.L., *The Franco-Russian Alliance 1890–1894* (Cambridge, Mass., 1929)

— *The Diplomacy of Imperialism* (New York, 1951 ed.)

Lieven, D., 'Pro-Germans in Russian Foreign Policy 1890–1914' *International History Review* vol. 2 no. 1 (1980)

Lowe, C.J., *Salisbury and the Mediterranean 1886–1896* (London, 1965)

Maxwell, M., 'A re-examination of the role of Giers as Russian Foreign Minister' *European Studies Review* vol. 1 no. 4 (1971)

Michon, G., *The Franco-Russian Alliance 1891–1917* (London, 1929)

Chapter 11

Cecil, Lady G., *Life of Robert, Marquis of Salisbury* (London, 1921)

Cunningham, A., 'The Wrong Horse? a study in Anglo–Turkish relations before the First World War' *St Antony's Papers* no. 17, *Middle Eastern Affairs* no. 4 (Oxford, 1965)

Douglas, R., 'Britain and the Armenian Question 1894–1897' *Historical Journal* vol. 19 no. 1 (1976)

Gillard, D., 'Salisbury' in Wilson, K.M., (ed.), *British Foreign Secretaries and Foreign Policy: from Crimean War to First World War* (London, 1987)

Jefferson, M.M., 'Lord Salisbury and the Eastern Question 1890–98' *Slavonic and East European Review* vol. 39 (1960)

Lee, D.E., *Great Britain and the Cyprus Convention Policy of 1878* (Cambridge, Mass., 1934)

Lowe, C.J., *Salisbury and the Mediterranean 1886–1896* (London, 1965)

— *The Reluctant Imperialists* (London, 1967)

Marder, A.J., *The Anatomy of British Sea Power: a history of British Naval Policy in the pre-Dreadnought era 1880–1905* (London, 1940)

Marsh, P., 'Lord Salisbury and the Ottoman Massacres' *Journal of British Studies* xi (1972)

Matson, A.T., 'A further note on the MacDonald Expedition, 1897–99' *Historical Journal* xii no. 1 (1969)

Palmer, A.W., 'Lord Salisbury's Approach to Russia, 1898' *Oxford Slavonic Papers* vi (1955)

Steele, E.D., 'Lord Salisbury at the India Office' in Blake, Lord and Cecil, H. (eds), *Salisbury: the man and his policies* (London, 1987)

— 'Lord Salisbury, the "False Religion" of Islam, and the Reconquest of the Sudan' in Spiers, E.M., (ed.), *Sudan: the Reconquest Reappraised* (London, 1998)

— *Lord Salisbury: a biography* (London, 1999)

Wilson, K.M., 'Constantinople or Cairo: Lord Salisbury and the Partition of the Ottoman Empire 1886–1897' in Wilson, K.M., (ed.), *Imperialism and Nationalism in the Middle East: the Anglo-Egyptian Experience 1882–1982* (London, 1983)

— 'Drawing the line at Constntinople: Lord Salisbury's statements of *Primat der Innenpolitik*' in Wilson, K.M., (ed.) *British Foreign Secretaries*, op.cit.

Chapter 12

Buzpinar, S.T., 'The Hijaz, Abdul Hamid II and Emir Hussain's secret dealings with the British, 1877–1880' *Middle Eastern Studies* vol. 31 no. 1 (1995)

Deringil, S., 'The Ottoman response to the Egyptian Crisis of 1881–2' *Middle Eastern Studies* vol. 24 no. 1 (1988)

Grenville, J.A.S., 'Goluchowski, Salisbury and the Mediterranean Agreements 1895–1897' *Slavonic and East European Review* vol. 36 (1957–58)

Hirsowicz, L., 'The Sultan and the Khedive, 1892–1908' *Middle Eastern Studies* vol. 8 no. 3 (1972)

Hornik, M.P., 'The Special Mission of Sir Henry Drummond-Wolff to Constantinople, 1885–7' *English Historical Review* lv (1940)

Jelavich, B., 'Great Britain and the Russian acquisition of Batoum 1878–1886' *Slavonic and East European Review* vol. 48 (1970)

— *The Ottoman Empire, the Great Powers and the Straits Question 1870–1887* (Bloomington, 1973)

— *Russia and the Formation of the Romanian National State 1821–1878* (Cambridge, 1984)

Lee, D.E., 'A Turkish Mission to Afghanistan, 1877' *Journal of Modern History* vol. 13 no. 3 (1941)

— *Great Britain and the Cyprus Convention Policy of 1878* (Cambridge, Mass., 1934)

Medlicott, W.N., 'The Gladstone Government and the Cyprus Convention, 1880–1885' *Journal of Modern History* vol. 12 no. 2 (1940)

Penson, L.M., 'Obligations by Treaty: their place in British Foreign Policy 1898–1914' in Sarkissian, A.O., (ed.), *Studies in Diplomatic History and Historiography in honour of G.P. Gooch* (London, 1961)

Sumner, B.H., *Russia and the Balkans 1870–1880* (Oxford, 1937)

Yasamee, F.A.K., *Ottoman Diplomacy: Abdul Hamid II and the Great Powers 1878–1888* (Istanbul, 1996)

— 'Abdul Hamid II and the Ottoman defence problem' *Diplomacy and Statecraft* vol. iv no. 1 (1993)

— 'The Ottoman Empire, the Sudan, and the Red Sea Coast 1883–1889' in Deringil, S. and Kuneralp, S. (eds), *Studies in Ottoman Diplomatic History V: The Ottomans and Africa* (Istanbul, 1990)

Chapter 13

Bosworth, R.J.B., *Italy, the least of the Great Powers: Italian Foreign Policy before the First World War* (Cambridge, 1979)

Gottlieb, W.W., *Studies in Secret Diplomacy during the First World War* (London, 1957)

Haines, C.G., 'Italian Irredentism during the Near Eastern Crisis, 1875–1878' *Journal of Modern History* vol. 9 no. 1 (1937)

Lee, D.E., 'The Proposed Mediterranean League of 1878' *Journal of Modern History* vol. 3 no.1 (1931)

Lowe, C.J., 'Anglo-Italian Differences over East Africa 1892–1895 and their effects upon the Mediterranean Entente' *English Historical Review* lxxxi (1966)

— 'Britain and Italian Intervention 1914–1915' *Historical Journal* vol. 12 no. 3 (1969)

— and Marzari, F., *Italian Foreign Policy 1870–1940* (London, 1975)

Marsden, A., 'Salisbury and the Italians in 1897' *Journal of Modern History* vol. 40 no. 1 (1968)

Palumbo, M., 'Italian–Austro-Hungarian Military Relations before World War I' in Williamson, S.R., and Pastor, P., (eds), *Origins and Prisoners of War* (New York, 1983)

Pribram, A.F., *The Secret Treaties of Austria-Hungary 1879–1914* (Cambridge, Mass., 1920)

Renzi, W., *In the Shadow of the Sword: Italy's Neutrality and Entrance into the Great War* (New York, 1987)

Roberts, L.E., 'Italy and the Egyptian Question 1878–1882' *Journal of Modern History* vol. 18 no. 2 (1946)

Scott, I., 'The Making of the Triple Alliance in 1882' *East European Quarterly* vol. xii (1978)

Chapter 14

Andrew, C.M., *Théophile Delcassé and the Making of the Entente Cordiale* (London, 1968)

Boyce, D.G. (ed.), *The Crisis of British Power: the Imperial and Naval Papers of the second Earl of Selborne, 1895–1910* (London, 1990)

Campbell, A.E., *Great Britain and the United States 1895–1903* (London, 1960)

Campbell, C.S., *Anglo-American Understanding 1898–1903* (Baltimore, 1957)

Cockfield, J., 'Germany and the Fashoda Crisis 1898–1899' *Central European History* vol. 16 (1983)

Darwin, J., 'The Fear of Falling: British Politics and Imperial Decline since 1900' *Transactions of the Royal Historical Society* 1986

Friedberg, A.L., *The Weary Titan: Britin and the experience of relative decline 1895–1905* (Princeton, 1988)

Galbraith, J.S., 'British Policy on Railways in Persia 1870–1900' *Middle Eastern Studies* vol. 25 no. 4 (1989)

Garvin, J.L., *Life of Joseph Chamberlain* (London, 1934)

Gillard, D., 'Salisbury and the Indian Defence Problem 1885–1902' in Bourne, K., and Watt, D.C., (eds), *Studies in International History: essays for W.N. Medlicott* (London, 1967)

Grenville, J.A.S., *Lord Salisbury and Foreign Policy: the close of the nineteenth century* (London, 1964)

Howard, C.H.D., *Splendid Isolation: a study of ideas concerning Britain's international position and foreign policy during the later years of the third Marquess of Salisbury* (London, 1967)

Kennedy, P.M., 'German World Policy and the Alliance negotiations with England 1897–1900' *Journal of Modern History* vol. 45 no. 4 (1973)

Langer, W.L., *The Diplomacy of Imperialism 1890–1902* (New York, 1951 edn)

Martel, G., *Imperial Diplomacy: Rosebery and the Failure of Foreign Policy* (London, 1986)

McDermott, W.J., 'The immediate origins of the Committee of Imperial Defence' *Canadian Journal of History* vol. 7 no. 3 (1972)

Monger, G.W., *The End of Isolation: British Foreign Policy 1900–1907* (London, 1963)

Neale, R.G., *Great Britain and United States Expansion 1898–1900* (Michigan, 1966)

Nish, I., *The Anglo-Japanese Alliance: the diplomacy of two island empires 1894–1907* (London, 1966)

Otte, T., 'Great Britain, Germany and the Far Eastern Crisis of 1897–8' *English Historical Review* cx (1995)

Platt, D.C.M., 'Economic Factors in British Policy during the "New Imperialism" ' *Past and Present* vol. 39 (1968)

Preston, A., 'Wolseley, the Khartoum Relief Expedition and the Defence of India 1889–1900' *Journal of Imperial and Commonwealth History* vol. 6 (1978)

Ronaldshay, Lord, *Life of Lord Curzon* (London, 1928)

Sanderson, G.N., *England, Europe and the Upper Nile 1882–99* (Edinburgh, 1965)

Steiner, Z.S., 'Great Britain and the creation of the Anglo-Japanese Alliance' *Journal of Modern History* vol. 31 no. 2 (1959)

Chapter 15

Anderson, P.R., *The Background of Anti-English Feeling in Germany 1890–1902* (Washington, 1939)

Andrew, C.M., 'German World Policy and the reshaping of the Dual Alliance' *Journal of Contemporary History* vol. 1 no. 3 (1966)

Berghahn, V.R., *Germany and the Approach of War in 1914* (London, 1973)

Collins, D.M., 'The Franco-Russian Alliance and Russian Railways 1891–1914' *Historical Journal* vol. 16 no. 4 (1973)

Dulffer, J., 'Limitations on Naval Warfare and Germany's future as a World Power: a German debate 1904–06' *War and Society* vol. 3 no. 2 (1985)

Earle, E.M., *Turkey, the Great powers and the Baghdad Railway* (New York, 1923)

Edwards, E.W., 'The Far Eastern Agreements of 1907' *Journal of Modern History* vol. 26 no. 4 (1954)

— 'The Japanese Alliance and the Anglo-French Agreement' *History* vol. 42 (1957)

— 'The Franco-German Agreement on Morocco, 1909' *English Historical Review* lxxviii (1963)

— 'The Prime Minister and Foreign Policy: the Balfour Government 1902–1905' in Hearder, H. and Loyn, H.R. (eds), *British Government and Administration: studies presented to S.B. Chrimes* (Cardiff, 1974)

Geiss, I., 'The German Version of Imperialism, 1898–1914: Weltpolitik' in
Schollgen, G. (ed.), *Escape into War? The Foreign Policy of Imperial Germany*
(Oxford, 1990)

Guillen, P., 'The Entente of 1904 as a Colonial Settlement' in Gifford, P. and
Louis, W.R., (eds) *France and Great Britain in Africa* (New Haven, 1971)

Hale, O.J., *Germany and the Diplomatic Revolution: a study in diplomacy and the press
1904–1906* (Pennsylvania, 1931)

Hatton, P.H.S., 'Harcourt and Solf: the search for an Anglo-German
understanding through Africa 1912–1914' *European Studies Review* vol. 1 no. 2
(1971)

Herwig, H., *Germany's vision of empire in Venezuela, 1871–1914* (Princeton, 1986)

Keiger, J.F.V., 'Jules Cambon and Franco-German detente 1907–1914' *Historical
Journal* vol. 26 no. 3 (1983)

Kennedy, P.M., *The Growth of the Anglo-German Antagonism 1860–1914* (London,
1980)

Lambi, I.J., *The Navy and German Power Politics 1862–1914* (London, 1984)

Langhorne, R.T.B., 'Anglo-German Negotiations over the Portuguese Colonies in
Africa 1911–1914' *Historical Journal* vol. 16 no. 2 (1973)

Lerman, K.A., *The Chancellor as Courtier: Bernhard von Bülow and the governance of
Germany 1900–1909* (Cambridge, 1990)

Lui, K.C., 'German fears of a Quadruple Alliance 1904–05' *Journal of Modern
History* vol. 18 no. 3 (1946)

Maell, W.H., 'Bebel's fight against the Schlachtflotte, nemesis to the primacy of
foreign policy' *Proceedings of the American Philosophical Society* vol. 121 no. 3
(1977)

Mahajan, S., 'The defence of India and the end of isolation: a study in the foreign
policy of the Conservative Government 1900–1905' *Journal of Imperial and
Commonwealth History* vol. 10 no. 2 (1982)

McLean, D., *Britain and her buffer-state: the collapse of the Persian Empire 1890–1914*
(London, 1979)

Menning, R.R., and Menning, C.B., ' "Baseless Allegations": Wilhelm II and the
Hale interview of 1908' *Central European History* vol. 16 no. 4 (1983)

Morris, A.J.A., *The Scaremongers: the advocacy of war and rearmament 1896–1914*
(London, 1984)

Nish, I., *The Origins of the Russo-Japanese War* (London, 1985)

Rich, N., and Fisher, M.H. (eds), *The Holstein Papers* vols 3, 4 (Cambridge, 1963)

— *Friedrich von Holstein: Politics and Diplomacy in the era of Bismarck and Wilhelm II*
(Cambridge, 1965)

Rohl, J.C.G., and Sombart, N. (eds), *Kaiser Wilhelm II: New Interpretations*
(Cambridge, 1982)

Rolo, P.J.V., *Entente Cordiale: the origins and negotiation of the Anglo-French Agreements
of 8 April 1904* (London, 1969)

Steinberg, J., *Tirpitz and the birth of the German Battle Fleet* (London, 1965)

Towle, P., 'The Russo-Japanese War and the defence of India' *Military Affairs* 1980

Vincent-Smith, J.D., 'The Anglo-German Negotiations over the Portuguese Colonies in Africa 1911–1914' *Historical Journal* vol. 17 no. 3 (1974)

Williams, B.J., 'The Strategic Background to the Anglo-Russian Entente of August 1907' *Historical Journal* vol. 9 no. 3 (1966)

Wilson, K.M., 'The Anglo-Japanese Alliance of August 1905 and the defending of India: the case of the worst scenario' *Journal of Imperial and Commonwealth History* vol. 21 no. 2 (1993)

Winzen, P., 'Prince Bülow's Weltmachtpolitik' *Australian Journal of Politics and History* vol. 22 no. 2 (1976)

Chapter 16

Beloff, M., *Imperial Sunset* vol.1, *Britain's Liberal Empire 1897–1921* (London, 1969)

Cohen, S., 'Mesopotamia in British Strategy 1903–1914' *International Journal of Middle Eastern Studies* vol. 9 (1978)

Crisp, O., The Russian Liberals and the 1906 Anglo-French loan to Russia' *Slavonic and East European Review* vol. 39 (1960–61)

French, D., 'The Edwardian Crisis and the origins of the First World War' *International History Review* vol. 4 no. 2 (1982)

Greaves, R., 'Some aspects of the Anglo-Russian Convention and its working in Persia, 1907–14' *Bulletin of the School of Oriental and African Studies* 21 (1968)

— 'Sistan in British Indian Frontier Policy' ibid., vol. 49 (1986)

— 'Themes in British policy towards Persia in its relation to Indian Frontier Defence 1798–1914' *Asian Affairs* 78 (1991)

Grenville, J.A.S., 'Foreign Policy and the Coming of War' in Read, D., *Edwardian England* (London, 1982)

Hamilton, K.A., 'Britain, France and the origins of the Mediterranean agreements of 16 May 1907' in McKercher, R., and Moss, D.J., (eds), *Shadow and Substance in British Foreign Policy 1895–1939: essays in honour of C.J. Lowe* (Edmonton, 1984)

Ingram, E., 'A Strategic Dilemma: the defence of India 1874–1914' *Militärgeschictliche Mitteilungen* xiv (1974)

Kazemdadeh, F., *Russia and Britain in Persia 1864–1914, a study in imperialism* (New Haven, 1968)

Klein, I., 'The Anglo-Russian Convention and the problems of Central Asia 1907–14' *Journal of British Studies* vol. 11 no. 1 (1971)

Kumar, R., 'The Records of the Government of India on the Berlin–Baghdad Railway Question' *Historical Journal* vol. 5 no. 1 (1962)

Lowe, C.J., and Dockrill, M.L., *The Mirage of Power: British Foreign Policy 1902–1922* (London, 1972)

Morris, A.J.A., *Radicalism against War 1906–1914: the advocacy of peace and retrenchment* (London, 1972)

Neilson, K., 'Watching the "Steamroller": British observers and the Russian Army before 1914' *Journal of Strategic Studies* vol. 8 no. 2 (1985)

Oppel, B.F., 'The Waning of a Traditional Alliance: Russia and Germany after the Portsmouth Peace Conference' *Central European History* vol. 5 (1972)

Spring, D.W., 'The Trans-Persian Railway Project and Anglo-Russian Relations 1909–1914' *Slavonic and East European Review* vol. 54 (1976)

Taylor, A.J.P., 'The Conference at Algeciras' in Taylor, A.J.P., *Englishmen and Others* (London, 1956)

Towle, P.A., 'The Effect of the Russo-Japanese War on British Naval Policy' *Mariner's Mirror* vol. 60 (1974)

Williamson, S.R., *The Politics of Grand Strategy: Great Britain and France prepare for war, 1904–1914* (Cambridge, Mass., 1969)

Wilson, K.M., *The Policy of the Entente: the determinants of British foreign policy 1904–1914* (Cambridge, 1985)

— *Empire and Continent: studies in British foreign policy from the 1880s to the First World War* (London, 1987)

— 'The making and putative implementation of a British foreign policy of gesture, December 1905 to August 1914: the Liberal Imperialist Entente Revisited' *Canadian Journal of History* vol. 31 no. 2 (1996)

Chapter 17

Bestuhev, I.V., 'Russian Foreign Policy, February to June 1914' *Journal of Contemporary History* vol. 1 no. 3 (1966)

Crampton, R.J., 'The Balkans as a factor in German Foreign Policy 1911–14' *Slavonic and East European Review* vol.55 (1977)

— *The Hollow Détente: Anglo-German Relations in the Balkans 1911–1914* (London, 1980)

Fischer, F., *War of Illusions: German policies from 1911 to 1914* (New York, 1975)

— 'The Foreign Policy of Imperial Germany and the outbreak of the First World War' in Schollgen, G. (ed.), *Escape into War?*, op. cit.

Geyer, D., *Russian Imperialism 1860–1914* (Leamington Spa, 1987)

Helmreich, E.C., *The Diplomacy of the Balkan Wars 1912–13* (Cambridge, Mass., 1938)

Jarausch, K., *The Enigmatic Chancellor: Bethmann Hollweg and the hubris of Imperial Germany* (New Haven, 1973)

Jelavich, B., 'Romania in the First World War: the pre-war crisis 1912–1914' *International History Review* vol. 14 no. 3 (1992)

Joll, J., 'Politicians and the freedom to choose: the case of July 1914' in Ryan, A. (ed.), *The Idea of Freedom: essays in honour of Isaiah Berlin* (Oxford, 1979)

— *The Origins of the First World War* (London, 1992)

Kaiser, D., 'Germany and the origins of the First World War' *Journal of Modern History* vol. 55 no. 3 (1983)

Keiger, J.F.V., *France and the Origins of the First World War* (London, 1983)

— *Raymond Poincaré* (Cambridge, 1997)

Leslie, J., 'The Antecedents of Austria-Hungary's War Aims: Policies and Policy-makers in Vienna and Budapest before and during 1914' *Archiv und Forschung* (Vienna, 1993)

MacDonald, D., *United Government and Foreign Policy in Russia 1900–14* (Cambridge, Mass., 1992)

Macfie, A.L., 'The Straits Question 1908–1914' *Balkan Studies* 22 (1981)

May, E.R. (ed.) *Knowing One's Enemies: Intelligence Assessment before the two World Wars* (Princeton, 1984)

Palumbo, M., 'German-Italian Military Relations on the eve of World War I' *Central European History* vol. 12 no. 4 (1979)

Remak, J., '1914 – The Third Balkan War: Origins Reconsidered' *Journal of Modern History* vol. 43 no. 3 (1971)

Rohl, J.C.G., 'Admiral von Müller and the Approach of War, 1911–1914' *Historical Journal* vol. 12 no. 4 (1969)

— *The Kaiser and his Court: Wilhelm II and the Governance of Germany* (Cambridge, 1994)

Schroeder, P.W., 'World War I as Galloping Gertie: a reply to Joachim Remak' *Journal of Modern History* vol. 44 no. 3 (1972)

— 'Romania and the Great Powers before 1914' *Romanian Studies* 3 (1976)

Seton-Watson, R.W., 'William II's Balkan Policy' *Slavonic and East European Review* vol. 7 (1928)

Shanafelt, G., 'Activism and Inertia: Czernin's mission to Romania 1913–16' *Austrian History Yearbook* vol. 19–20 (1983–84)

Stern, F., 'Bethmann Hollweg and the War: the limits of responsibility' in Stern, F., and Krieger, L., (eds), *The Limits of Responsibility, historical essays in honour of H. Holborn* (London, 1968)

Stevenson, D., *Armaments and the Coming of War in Europe 1904–1914* (Oxford, 1996)

Thaden, E.C., *Russia and the Balkan Alliance of 1912* (Pennsylvania, 1965)

Turner, L.C.F., *The Origins of the First World War* (London, 1970)

Wank, S., 'Foreign Policy and the Nationality Problem in Austria-Hungary, 1867–1914' *Austrian History Yearbook* vol. 3 part 3 (1967)

— 'Desperate Counsel in Vienna in July 1914: Berthold Molden's unpublished memorandum' *Central European History* vol. 26 no. 3 (1993)

Wedel, O.H., 'Austro-Hungarian Diplomatic Documents 1908–1914' *Journal of Modern History* vol. 3 no. 1 (1931)

Williamson, S.R., *Austria-Hungary and the Origins of the First World War* (London, 1991)

Wilson, K.M. (ed.), *Decisions for War, 1914* (London, 1995)

Wohlforth, W.C., 'The Perception of Power: Russia in the pre-1914 balance' *World Politics* vol. 39 (1987)

Zotiades, G., 'Russia and the question of Constantinople and the Turkish Straits during the Balkan Wars' *Balkan Studies* vol. 2 (1970)

Chapter 18

Andrew, C.M. and Kanya-Forstner, A.S., *France Overseas: the Great War and the climax of French imperial expansion* (London, 1981)

Brecher, F.W., 'French policy towards the Levant 1914–1918' *Middle Eastern Studies* vol. 29 no. 4 (1993)

Dutton, D., 'The Balkan Campaign and French war aims in the Great War' *English Historical Review* xciv (1979)

Fisher, J., *Curzon and British Imperialism in the Middle East 1916–19* (London, 1999)

Fitzgerald, E.P., 'France's Middle East Ambitions, the Sykes-Picot negotiations, and the oil fields of Mosul 1915–18' *Journal of Modern History* vol. 66 no. 4 (1994)

French, D., 'The Origins of the Dardanelles Campaign reconsidered' *History* 68 (1983)

— *British Strategy and War Aims 1914–1916* (London, 1986)

— 'The Dardanelles, Mecca, and Kut: prestige as a factor in British eastern strategy 1914–16' *War and Society* vol. 5 no. 1 (1987)

— 'Allies, rivals and enemies: British strategy and war aims during the First World War' in Turner, J. (ed.), *Britain and the First World War* (London, 1988)

— *The Strategy of the Lloyd George Coalition 1916–1918* (Oxford, 1995)

Galbraith, J.S., 'British war aims in World War I: a commentary on statesmanship' *Journal of Imperial and Commonwealth History* vol. 13 (1984–85)

Ikle, F.W., 'Japanese-German peace negotiations during World War I' *American Historical Review* vol. 7 no. 1 (1965–66)

Kedourie, E., *England and the Middle East: the destruction of the Ottoman Empire 1914–21* (London, 1956)

— *In the Anglo-Arab Labyrinth: the McMahon-Hussain correspondence and its interpretations 1914–1939* (Cambridge, 1976)

Kent, M.R. (ed.), *The Great Powers and the end of the Ottoman Empire* (London, 1984)

Klieman, A.S., 'Britain's war aims in the Middle East in 1915' *Journal of Contemporary History* vol. 3 no. 3 (1968)

Lowe, P., *Great Britain and Japan 1911–15: a study of British Far Eastern Policy* (London, 1969)

Macfie, A.L., 'The Straits Question in the First World War 1914–1918' *Middle Eastern Studies* vol. 19 no. 1 (1983)

— *The End of the Ottoman Empire 1908–1923* (London, 1998)

Maehl, W.H., 'Germany's aims in the East 1914–1917: status of the question' *Historian* vol. 24 (1972)

Neilson, K., 'For diplomatic, economic, strategic and telegraphic reasons: British imperial defence, the Middle East and India, 1914–18' in Kennedy, G., and Neilson, K. (eds) *Far-Flung Lines: essays on Imperial Defence in honour of D.M. Schurman* (London, 1997)

Nevakivi, J., 'Lord Kitchener and the partition of the Ottoman Empire 1915–16' in Bourne and Watt, *op.cit.*

— *Britain, France and the Arab Middle East 1914–1920* (London, 1969)

Parsons, E.B., 'Why the British reduced the flow of American troops to Europe in August to October 1918' *Canadian Journal of History* vol. 12 no. 2 (1977)

Renzi, W., 'Great Britain, Russia and the Straits 1914–15' *Journal of Modern History* vol. 42 no. 1 (1970)

— 'Who composed Sazonov's 13 Points?' *American Historical Review* vol. 88 no. 2 (1983)

Rothwell, V., 'Mesopotamia in British War Aims 1914–18' *Historical Journal* (1970)

— *British War Aims and Peace Diplomacy 1914–1918* (Oxford, 1971)

Schwarz, B., 'Divided Attention: Britain's perception of a German threat to her eastern position in 1918' *Journal of Contemporary History* vol. 28 no. 1 (1993)

Shanafelt, G., *The Secret Enemy: Austria-Hungary and the German Alliance* (New York, 1985)

Silberstein, G., *The Troubled Alliance: German-Austrian Relations 1914 to 1917* (Lexington, 1970)

Stevenson, D., *French War Aims against Germany 1914–1919* (Oxford, 1982)

— *The First World War and International Politics* (Oxford, 1988)

Trask, D.F., *The United States in the Supreme War Council: American War Aims and inter-allied strategy 1917–1918* (Middleton, 1961)

Woodward, D.R., *Trial by Friendship: Anglo-American Relations 1917–18* (Lexington, 1993)

Chapter 19

Boadle, D.G., *Winston Churchill and the German Question in British Foreign Policy 1918–1922* (The Hague, 1973)

Bradley, J., *Allied Intervention in Russia 1917–1920* (London, 1968)

Bunselmeyer, R.E., *The Cost of the War 1914–1919: British Economic War Aims and the origins of reparations* (Hampden, Conn., 1975)

Dockrill, M.L. and Fisher, J. (eds), *The Paris Peace Conference 1919: Peace without Victory?* (London, 2001)

Elcock, H., *Portrait of a Decision: the Council of Four and the Treaty of Versailles* (London, 1972)

Floto, I., *Colonel House in Paris: a study of American policy at the Paris Peace Conference 1919* (Princeton, 1973)

Gardner, L.C., *Safe for Democracy: the Anglo-American response to revolution 1913–1923* (Oxford, 1984)

Gerson, L.L., *Woodrow Wilson and the rebirth of Poland 1914–1920* (New Haven, 1953)

Jaffe, L., *The Decision to Disarm Germany* (London, 1985)

King, J.C., *Foch versus Clemenceau: France and German Dismemberment 1918–19* (Cambridge, Mass., 1960)

Kochan, L., *The Struggle for Germany 1914–1945* (Edinburgh, 1963)

McDougall, W.A., *France's Rhineland Diplomacy 1914–1924* (Princeton, 1978)

Marks, S., *The Illusion of Peace: international relations in Europe 1918–1939* (London, 1976)

Nelson, H., *Land and Power: British and Allied policy on Germany's Frontiers 1916–19* (Newton Abbot, 1971)

Nelson, K.L., *Victors Divided: America and the Allies in Germany 1918–1923* (Berkeley, 1975)

Newton, D., *British Policy and the Weimar Republic 1918–1919* (Oxford, 1997)

Orde, A., *British Policy and European Reconstruction after the First World War* (Cambridge, 1990)

Schenk, H.G., *The Aftermath of the Napoleonic Wars* (New York, 1967)

Sharpe, A., *The Versailles Settlement: peacemaking in Paris 1919* (London, 1991)

Stevenson, D., *French War Aims against Germany 1914–19* (Oxford, 1982)

Thompson, J.M., *Russia, Bolshevism and the Versailles Peace* (Princeton, 1966)

Webster, C.K., *The Congress of Vienna, 1814–1815* (London, 1919)

Wilson, K.M., 'Great War prologue' in Wilson, K.M., and Pronay, N. (eds), *The Political Re-education of Germany and her allies after World War II* (London, 1985)

— *Channel Tunnel Visions 1850–1945: dreams and nightmares* (London, 1994)

INDEX